LOOKING GOOD
AND
DOING GOOD

PHILANTHROPIC STUDIES

ROBERT L. PAYTON and
DWIGHT F. BURLINGAME,
general editors

KAREN J. BLAIR
*The Torchbearers: Women and Their Amateur Arts
Associations in America*

DWIGHT F. BURLINGAME, editor
The Responsibilities of Wealth

DWIGHT F. BURLINGAME and DENNIS YOUNG, editors
Corporate Philanthropy at the Crossroads

MARCOS CUETO, editor
*Missionaries of Science: The Rockefeller Foundation
and Latin America*

GREGORY EISELEIN
Literature and Humanitarian Reform in the Civil War Era

THOMAS H. JEAVONS
*When the Bottom Line Is Faithfulness:
Management of Christian Service Organizations*

MIKE W. MARTIN
Virtuous Giving: Philanthropy, Voluntary Service, and Caring

MARY J. OATES
The Catholic Philanthropic Tradition in America

J. B. SCHNEEWIND, editor
Giving: Western Ideas of Philanthropy

LOOKING GOOD

AND

DOING GOOD

Corporate Philanthropy and
Corporate Power

JEROME L. HIMMELSTEIN

Indiana University Press
Bloomington and Indianapolis

The paper used in this publication meets the minimum requirements of American National Standard for Information Sciences— Permanence of Paper for Printed Library Materials, ANSI Z39.48-1984.

Manufactured in the United States of America

Library of Congress Cataloging-in-Publication Data

Himmelstein, Jerome L.
Looking good and doing good : corporate philanthropy and corporate power / Jerome L. Himmelstein.
p.   cm. — (Philanthropic studies)
Includes bibliographical references and index.
ISBN 0-253-33237-0 (cl. : alk. paper). — ISBN 0-253-21103-4 (pbk. : alk. paper)
1. Corporations—Charitable contributions—United States.
2. Social responsibility of business—United States.   I. Title.
II. Series.
HG4028.C6H56   1997
361.7′65′0973—dc20   96-34217

1 2 3 4 5   02 01 00 99 98 97

To My Mother, Bertha Himmelstein
In Honor of Her 90th Birthday

CONTENTS

ACKNOWLEDGMENTS

Looking Good and Doing Good is a logical, if indirect, extension of my 1990 book, *To the Right: The Transformation of American Conservatism.* Chapter 5 of that book puzzled over the relationship between big business and the Right. Large corporations played a big role in the overall rise of the Right in the late 1970s and 1980s; yet over the longer historical haul, corporate politics has not always been aggressively conservative. It has often operated in a pragmatic, moderate, seemingly acquiescent mode. In other words, there seem to be "two faces of business power," as I argued in a 1992 article in *Business and the Contemporary World.*

With this basic idea in mind, I decided to explore corporate politics further and to do so, I decided to move off the beaten track a bit. Sociologists and political scientists have spent ample time studying corporate funding of political candidates and corporate lobbying of Congress and government agencies. They have also paid considerable attention to the more subtle ways in which corporate leaders and corporate-supported think tanks have helped frame debates over public policy. But these things are only part of corporate efforts to manage their relationships with the rest of society. Business school courses often talk about corporate "public affairs," a term that embraces not only supporting political candidates and lobbying government but also public relations, community relations, consumer relations, philanthropy, and many other activities.

I set out to look at corporate public affairs activities as a whole, with the idea of getting into a corporation and examining these activities up close. Robert Jackall's *Moral Mazes* was an early inspiring model. When I discussed my initial ideas with people who knew the corporate world better than I, however, I was quickly brought up short. Ken Bacon, then at the *Wall Street Journal,* complained that the whole project sounded a bit vague. Joan Spero, who as an executive vice president at American Express presumably knew what she was talking about, was more pointed: There is no such thing as "corporate public affairs," she told me. The term is simply a rubric for a set of diverse activities that often bear little day-to-day relation to each other. Choose a specific activity, she urged.

◆

The drive for specificity led me to corporate philanthropy, as did my ongoing preoccupation with the complicated relationship between big business and the Right. I knew that anti-abortion groups had organized a boycott of corporations that supported Planned Parenthood. Digging a little deeper, I found that this was but one of a series of controversies that pitted conservative groups against corporate philanthropy programs. I decided to study these controversies and the politics of corporate philanthropy generally by talking to the men and women who run corporate philanthropy programs.

I found an admirable model for this kind of research in *Money Talks: Corporate PACs and Political Influence* by Dan Clawson, Alan Neustadtl, and Denise Scott. I had known Dan, a sociologist at the University of Massachusetts, since the early 1980s, when our paths first crossed at a faculty seminar on the Right. My ideas on corporate politics and on the relationship between big business and the Right owe a lot to our conversations over the years. Reading the manuscript of *Money Talks* not only helped clarify my ideas further but also provided an exemplary model of doing sociology through in-depth interviews.

Before I could do any interviewing, of course, I had to gain access to the managers who run corporate philanthropy programs. Initially I figured that I needed intermediaries who would ease my entry into that world. Phillip Blumberg, professor of law at the University of Connecticut, helped facilitate one of my first interviews (and also shared his expertise in the laws governing corporate philanthropy). Axel Schupf, an Amherst College alumnus (and now a trustee), got me another. Despite their efforts, however, setting up interviews moved along rather slowly. Enter Dan Clawson, again. You don't need contacts to reach these corporate managers, he told me. Just write them and they will come. He was right.

Another thing I had to do before I could intelligently talk to corporate philanthropists about the controversies they faced was learn more about those controversies myself. Several people facilitated my education by providing collections of press clippings: Anne Bailey of the *Chronicle of Philanthropy,* Lori Vacek of the Council on Foundations, and Beth Daley and Bob Bothwell of the National Committee for Responsive Philanthropy.

As my research and writing unfolded, a number of others provided ideas and feedback. I learned a great deal from the writings and comments of Michael Useem and Joseph Galaskiewicz, who have done the most systematic sociological research on corporate philanthropy. Working with Denise Scott on her Ph.D. research on corporate government relations managers provided me with a useful perspective on my own work. Others

◈

who helped include Donna Bird, Bill Domhoff, Bill Gamson, Bob Gross, Craig Jenkins, Bert Knauft, Leslie Laurie, Jerry Marx, Carl Milofsky, Vic Murray, Susan Ostrander, Mike Rion, Paul Schervish, and Mayer Zald.

I also benefited greatly from opportunities to present preliminary reports on my research at the American Politics Workshop at the University of Chicago and the Program on Non-Profit Organizations at Yale University, as well as at annual meetings of the American Sociological Association and the Association for Research on Nonprofit Organization and Voluntary Action (ARNOVA).

Amherst College provided me a year of sabbatical leave in 1992–93 as well as ample research support. The Indiana University Center on Philanthropy funded that part of my year's salary that Amherst did not. My thanks to Dwight Burlingame, Director for Academic Programs and Research at the Center.

Thanks also to my colleagues in anthropology-sociology at Amherst College for always providing a stimulating intellectual environment; to Susan Urquhart for producing the manuscript; to Jane Pemberton and Skills for transcribing the interviews; to my editors at Indiana University Press; and, of course, to the corporate giving officers I interviewed for providing me insight into corporate philanthropy.

Finally, my love to Evelyn Bogen, my wife, and to Daniel and Joel, my sons, who as always are the best part of my life.

LOOKING GOOD
AND
DOING GOOD

1

Introduction

Hanging Up on Planned Parenthood

"CAVING INTO EXTREMISTS, AT&T HANGS UP ON PLANNED PARENT-HOOD" read the angry full-page ads in newspapers across the country in April 1990. This certainly was not the kind of attention AT&T hoped to get from the tens of millions of dollars it gives away to philanthropic causes every year. Being hailed as a "corporate Medici" for its unequalled support for nonprofit theater was more what it liked.[1]

Corporations donate about $7 billion a year to universities, art museums, symphony orchestras, human service agencies, and many other kinds of nonprofit organizations.[2] They hope to reap numerous benefits from this—among them, a better public image, higher sales, greater consumer loyalty, higher employee morale, a greater ability to attract top job candidates, and improved community relations. The last thing they want to do is get people angry by being beneficent.

Much to its dismay, AT&T had gotten just about everybody angry by first supporting Planned Parenthood consistently for over two decades, which by the late 1980s upset the Christian Action Council and other anti-abortion groups, and then by abruptly terminating support in early 1990, which angered Planned Parenthood and its supporters (the source of the full-page ads). Without quite meaning to, AT&T had gotten caught up in the battle over abortion, as had at least twenty more of the hundred largest corporate philanthropy programs.[3]

The Planned Parenthood controversy is not the only instance in which corporate philanthropy has caught flak in recent years, most of it coming from the Right. Every year since the mid-1980s, the conservative Capital Research Center has published a volume criticizing corporations for supporting liberal and radical groups eager to undermine the capitalist system. The 1994 volume caught the attention of new House Majority Leader Dick Armey who angrily accused "big business" of being "firmly behind the welfare state."[4] Other right-wing groups have attacked corporations for funding artists whose work they deemed pornographic or

◆

sacrilegious, for supporting Hispanic groups resistant to crackdowns on illegal immigration, or for refusing to fund the Boy Scouts directly because of their anti-gay policies. Corporate philanthropy has its progressive critics as well, but they are less visible and disruptive.

Of course, most corporate philanthropy hardly raises an eyebrow. It is hard for anyone to get worked up about grants to the local university, hospital, museum, or United Way. That corporate giving becomes controversial at all, however, reminds us that it is more than a simple act of either open-hearted generosity or calculated self-interest. Corporate giving sometimes becomes politicized because it is always inherently a complex social and political act.

Looking Good and Doing Good asks why corporations manage to get in trouble by giving money away and why in particular so much of the protest and criticism comes from the Right. These questions are interesting not only in themselves but also because studying how corporate managers think and act under fire sheds light on how corporate philanthropy operates in normal times as well. Accordingly these questions fit with more general questions about how profit-oriented corporations came to give away money, about how exactly philanthropy programs fit into these corporations, and about their relationship to the corporate world as a whole. To what extent do corporations and philanthropy go together "naturally," to what extent are they a contradiction in terms?

Corporate philanthropy, in turn, is interesting not only in itself but also for what it may tell us about how corporations organize their relationships to society—in other words, about the politics of big business in the broadest sense. Although corporate philanthropy presents itself as nonideological and apolitical, it presumes a political vision, a tacit understanding about the nature of American society and the role of large corporations within it. What is this understanding and what is its broader political significance?

To deal with these issues, I draw on in-depth interviews I conducted with representatives of fifty-five of the largest corporate philanthropy programs between June 1992 and June 1993. With a handful of exceptions, my subjects are the ones with everyday authority over those programs. They are women and men in roughly equal numbers and mostly white with occasional minorities. Most reside near the top of middle management in their companies. Although they are not themselves part of top management nor on the fast track to it, nearly all report to committees made up of an array of senior and executive vice presidents and sometimes directly to CEOs, presidents, and chairmen. I shall call them "corporate philanthropists" or "corporate giving officers (CGOs)."

◆

The Ideas

Because of the issues it addresses, *Looking Good and Doing Good* of necessity differs from nearly all other writing about corporate philanthropy. Most of those works offer practical advice for corporate philanthropists on organizing giving programs, deciding where to donate the money, positioning the program within the corporation, and (sometimes) dealing with controversy. They include numerous volumes from the Council on Foundations, as well as articles in periodicals such as *Corporate Philanthropy Report, Foundation News and Commentary,* and the *Chronicle of Philanthropy.*[5] Rather than contributing to this practical literature, I incorporate it into my study by asking how it helps create a culture of corporate philanthropy.

Other writing has openly addressed the broader, especially the political, meaning of corporate philanthropy, but in a way quite different from what I have in mind. The right-wing Capital Research Center, mentioned earlier, has routinely criticized corporate giving programs for contributing to liberal, anti-business political advocacy groups. From the Left and with less notoriety, the National Center for Responsive Philanthropy has argued that corporate giving, like philanthropy in general, is too conservative, supporting established nonprofit organizations while ignoring fledgling ones that address the needs of women, minorities, and the poor. I have more sympathy for the latter critique than the former, but neither "liberal" nor "conservative" fully captures the politics I see in corporate philanthropy.

More important, my purpose is neither practical advice nor a simple political critique but a sociological understanding of corporate philanthropy. Accordingly, my work draws on a relatively small sociological literature on corporate philanthropy, notably the work of Michael Useem and Joseph Galaskiewicz, and a broader literature in political sociology.

My argument centers on a simple yet important claim: Corporate philanthropy is first of all an economic act, but it has social and political dimensions as well. The first part of this assertion can be developed in a paragraph, the latter takes up most of the book.

Corporate philanthropy is an economic act in the sense that it is oriented to corporate interests and corporate profit, much as is corporate advertising or finance, engineering or marketing. To be sure, its connection to the bottom line may be less direct and harder to document, but it is not a mere managerial frivolity. That is, it is not primarily a way that top managers direct more money to their favorite charities, regardless of corporate interests. Patterns of corporate giving in fact reflect patterns of corporate interest. For one thing, the level of corporate giving varies with the level of spending on related activities that are clearly profit-oriented. Corporations that spend a lot on advertising, for example, also tend to spend a lot on corporate philanthropy, suggesting that giving is but another way of creating markets for products and maintaining a positive public image. For another, how much a corporation gives away and to whom reflect the specific strategic interests of a company. Companies that are relatively labor intensive give more than those that are less so, because giving to local human services or cultural activities helps attract and keep a workforce. Companies who sell most of their products to consumers tend to give at a higher rate than those who sell primarily to other businesses, because they have a greater need to maintain a favorable public image. High-tech companies and industrial products companies tend to give disproportionately to higher education, because such donations help train and recruit scientific and engineering talent. Consumer product companies, in contrast, tend to favor human services spending, because that has a more visible, direct impact on the consuming public. Companies with regional markets are more likely to concentrate donations in their regions, while nationwide companies have a broader geographic range. Finally, companies in industries that have especially difficult public-image problems (e.g., oil companies) often tend to support especially visible projects in the arts. In short, the specific needs of the corporate donor tend to determine both the level and the distribution of giving.[6]

At the same time, corporate philanthropy is not simply an economic act. It is geared toward corporate interests, but it is not the product of a simple, abstract calculation of economic costs and benefits. The calculation is never simple, and it certainly does not occur in a vacuum: Corporate philanthropy, like all business behavior, "is not an immutable product of a company's market position or economic calculus," as sociologist Michael Useem puts it; it is "embedded" in social relationships.[7]

More specifically, how corporate philanthropy is done is a function both of its complex relationship to the individual corporation and of a broader culture that spans the corporate world. Corporate philanthropy, first of all, is shaped by its complicated, contradictory relationship to the corporation. There may be nothing inherently paradoxical about giving away money in an institution dedicated to making it, or about doing well for the corporation while doing some bit of innocuous good for society. Still, the place of corporate philanthropy is hardly simple or smooth. Corporate giving certainly seeks to serve corporate interests, but often it can claim to do so only indirectly and in the long term. Indeed, what makes it distinctive is precisely this claim. This may not sit well in a corporation focused resolutely on the short-term bottom line, especially given pressures from international competition, a sluggish domestic economy, or the specter of hostile takeovers. Corporate philanthropists often find themselves under pressure to demonstrate immediate payoffs from their donations, especially in terms of improved public relations for the corporation. One prominent corporate giving officer calls this dilemma "the struggle between looking good and doing good."

At the same time, corporate giving programs have to negotiate a complex relationship with top management. On the one hand, they need the support and involvement of the CEO and other top managers. Every advice manual tells corporate philanthropists how to go about getting this. On the other hand, corporate philanthropy needs to maintain a degree of distance from the top, to avoid being reduced to a mere vehicle through which top managers support their favorite nonprofit organizations. Corporate philanthropy, in other words, faces the dilemma of being close to the CEO, but not too close. The complex relationship that corporate philanthropy bears to the corporation lies at the core of what corporate philanthropy is about, and efforts to negotiate this relationship are integral to what corporate philanthropists do.

Corporate philanthropy is also embedded in a network of relationships between corporations; it has a strong collective dimension. No corporate giving program is an island; no corporate giving officer thinks in a social vacuum. As sociologists Useem and Galaskiewicz have shown, the ties that the CEO of a corporation may have to the corporate and philanthropic elite or the ties that corporate philanthropists have with each other can shape how much and to whom corporations give.[8]

More to the point, these ties sustain a culture of corporate philanthropy, a shared set of understandings about how philanthropy serves corporate interests, to whom donations should be made, and how giving programs should be organized. Individual corporate philanthropists participate in this culture through their reading and their conversations with their peers, and it frames their everyday thinking. They are aware of what other corporations are doing, and they know which giving programs are widely regarded as exemplary. They do not have to develop their rationales and repertoires of giving from scratch. Individual corporate philanthropists do not independently arrive at the idea that supporting universities might serve their corporation by increasing the supply of engineering talent, or that funding the arts might garner good publicity, or that contributing to

◆

local human service agencies might reduce the costs of recruiting labor. Ideas like these are part of the culture of corporate philanthropy.

Furthermore, beyond whatever ways a corporate philanthropy program serves its own company, corporate philanthropy in the aggregate has a broader political significance as well. It is part of what I shall call corporate politics in the broad sense, the way that large corporations manage their relationship not only to government but also to other major social institutions. Implicit in it (though rarely articulated) is a broad understanding of the place of large corporations in American society and a strategy for securing that place, which corporate philanthropy shares with other corporate political activities as well.

Sociologists have discussed at some length whether (and under what conditions) corporations act collectively in politics. Taking issue with the once common argument that large corporations lack the unity to apply their immense resources effectively to the political process, many sociologists argue that a network of ties between corporations (such as interlocking or shared directors) and the existence of an "inner circle" of corporate leaders capable of articulating general business interests provide the structural basis for corporate political unity. This unity, it is argued, is manifest not only in the activities of policy-planning organizations and other groups that speak for big business as a whole but also in the way that individual corporate political activities such as contributions to political candidates fall into coherent patterns.[9]

One result of this unity is that large corporations develop a shared understanding of how to serve the general interests of big business (what some call a "classwide rationality"), as well as pursuing their individual interests (and following a "company rationality").[10] *Looking Good and Doing Good* explores the way both kinds of rationality play out in corporate philanthropy.

Chapter 2 examines the development of corporate philanthropy. Although giving by individuals is as old as the republic itself, corporate philanthropy in the United States has flourished only since World War II. Its creation has been very much a collective act on the part of corporations. Important corporate leaders and organizations have played an important role in encouraging the expansion of corporate philanthropy and articulating a broad, classwide rationale for it. As corporate giving has grown and diversified so has the transcorporate network of ties among corporate philanthropists, especially in the form of organizations that speak for and to corporate givers. Corporate elites and transcorporate networks in turn have facilitated the development of a culture of corporate philanthropy.

◆

Chapter 2 looks in some detail at the central themes of this culture, paying particular attention to how it has justified corporate giving in terms of the interests of both the individual corporation and big business generally—in other words, how it has combined company and classwide rationales for philanthropy.

Chapters 3 and 4 look at how individual corporate philanthropists use their shared culture to understand what they do. Together they portray the paradoxical way in which corporate philanthropists understand the relationship between philanthropy and the corporation. On the one hand, these men and women portray what they do as a "seamless web," in which doing good for society and doing well for the corporation just "naturally" go together. They do this through the particular way they understand both what philanthropy is and what the interests of their individual corporations are. On the other hand, many corporate giving officers readily acknowledge important tensions in their relationship with their corporations, articulating the very contradictions to which I have already alluded.

Whichever way corporate philanthropists describe what they do, we shall see that they modify their shared culture in significant ways even as they draw upon it. On one level, they rarely voice the broad, classwide themes of this culture. On another level, they have a more nuanced appreciation of the complexities of what they do than their collective culture allows for.

Chapter 5 looks at how corporate philanthropists responded to boycott threats and letter-writing campaigns from anti-abortion groups aimed at getting them to stop funding Planned Parenthood. It attempts to explain an apparent paradox: Those corporations most subject to public pressure from the Right rarely decided to stop their support, while nearly all those who stopped were not in the spotlight. Why this is so can be understood partly in terms of the complexities or dilemmas inherent in the relationship of a philanthropy program to the corporation. The need to balance looking good and doing good and to maintain the integrity of the giving program shaped corporate responses to the controversy.

The Planned Parenthood controversy also allows us to examine further the role of the culture of corporate philanthropy in the everyday work of corporate philanthropists. How did corporate giving officers draw upon their ties to their peers in crafting a response to outside pressure? Did those in the heart of the controversy receive generalized sympathy and support from their peers or were they marginalized? Did corporate philanthropists develop a collective response to a collective problem or did they craft more individualized solutions? As in chapters 3 and 4, we shall identify not

◆

only how the thoughts and actions of corporate philanthropists reflect the shared culture but also how they diverge from it.

Chapter 6 looks at the clash between corporate philanthropists and the right-wing Capital Research Center, examining in particular how large corporations and the Right could possibly come into conflict. The answer to this question lies in a conflict of political visions, of broad understandings of how to pursue the general interests of big business in American society. Almost despite themselves, corporate philanthropists articulate one such vision as they attempt to explain why the Capital Research Center's claims are not just wrong, but ludicrous. I call this the Pragmatic Vision or Corporate Pragmatism. It pictures corporations as situated in a society in which they face other social actors with interests different from theirs, but few real enemies. Securing corporate interests in this situation requires establishing relationships with and gaining access to these interests. Philanthropy is one way of doing this with the nonprofit sector. The Capital Research Center, in contrast, articulates a Conservative Vision or Corporate Conservatism. From this perspective, large corporations face not just competing interests but enemies bent on destroying them. Securing corporate interests, in effect, requires fighting back.

The ultimate point of *Looking Good and Doing Good* is that Corporate Pragmatism is not limited to philanthropy but constitutes an important dimension of corporate politics in general. Chapter 7 develops this point, arguing that corporate politics is a changing mix of pragmatic and conservative strategies. The two together give large corporations a distinctive kind of influence in American society. Corporate Pragmatism in particular, whether in philanthropy or campaign contributions to congressional incumbents, embodies a subtle but important kind of power.

The Interviews

I began my research with two related but distinct interests: how the largest corporate philanthropy programs in the United States go about their work in general, and how they deal with political controversy in particular. Accordingly, I set out to interview corporate philanthropists who work for the largest giving programs and/or who had recently faced political controversy.

Drawing on the Taft Group's 1991 ranking of corporate giving programs (using contribution figures from 1989 for the most part), I identified the fifty largest programs and contacted all of them for interviews, except for Kraft General Foods, whose giving program had been combined with that of its

◆

parent company, Philip Morris. Because less than a third of these had faced significant political controversy, I also sought interviews with thirteen programs among the second fifty largest whom the media had identified as foci of controversy. By doing this, I hoped to have both a representative sample of the largest corporate giving programs (those from the top fifty) on the basis of which to discuss large-scale corporate giving generally and a reasonably large sample of programs that had faced controversy on the basis of which to examine the Planned Parenthood controversy, among others.[11]

In each case, I sought to interview the person with day-to-day authority over corporate philanthropy. This was not always the person formally in charge of the program, who sometimes was a high-ranking executive with many other responsibilities. The person with whom I wanted to talk was more likely to be manager of corporation contributions than vice president of public affairs or vice president of the corporate foundation rather than its president.

Of the sixty-three corporate giving programs I approached, fifty-five (or 87 percent) consented to interviews, including forty-three of the top fifty and twelve of the thirteen others. Together these corporations provide a reasonable cross section of corporate America. They include IBM, Digital, and Hewlett-Packard; General Motors, Ford, and Chrysler; Sears, J. C. Penney, and Dayton Hudson; ARCO, Mobil, Exxon, and Chevron; Du Pont, Kodak, Dow, and Monsanto; Merck, Lilly, Bristol-Myers Squibb, and Johnson & Johnson; AT&T, US West, Bell Atlantic, and Southwestern Bell; American Express, Prudential, and Citicorp; Honeywell, 3M, and General Electric—in short, representatives of most major industries and regions in the United States.

I conducted twenty-three (or 42 percent) of the interviews in person, the rest by phone. The interviews ranged from twenty-five minutes in length to 105 minutes, averaging 61.5 minutes. In-person interviews (seventy-eight minutes on average) tended to be longer than phone interviews (fifty minutes). This was partly due to the kind of interview, but it was also because I devoted in-person interviews to those managers who had faced the most political controversy and hence had the most to say. Some of my longest interviews were with AT&T, Citicorp, General Mills, Philip Morris, American Express, and Chase Bank.

Gaining access to these corporate managers was relatively easy, confounding my early misgivings. I began thinking that these "near elites" would be hard to reach. They would be protected by layers of receptionists and assistants; they would be reluctant to talk, especially about political controversy, for fear of generating more controversy; above all, they would be too busy.

Accordingly, I initially approached these corporate philanthropists by painstakingly cultivating access. I tried to reach them one by one through contacts—a law professor at a nearby university in one case, an alumnus of Amherst College in another. This worked, but very slowly. After nearly four months, I had managed to set up but two interviews this way. Out of frustration, more than anything else, I simply began mailing out (and later faxing) requests for interviews en masse. I followed up the letters with phone calls and surprisingly found it quite easy to reach the corporate giving officers themselves, or often more fruitfully, the persons who kept their appointment books. Appointments for interviews followed with minimal prodding. As my confidence grew, I stopped asking *whether* we could schedule time to talk and started asking *when.*

And they were *eager* to talk. Both phone and in-person interviews usually ran over the allotted time. Nearly all (86 percent) of those whom I asked to tape consented. Many expressed great interest in my research and were eager to get copies of anything I wrote. A number went out of their way to get me additional information or to help set up other interviews. In one case, a corporate giving officer, who had already talked with me well beyond the scheduled time and who had announced emphatically that she simply had to stop, spent additional time contacting a colleague at another company when she discovered I had been unable to get past his assistant (the "dragon who guards his gate," as she put it).

More important, these corporate philanthropists responded at length and usually energetically to my questions both about corporate giving generally and political controversy in particular. Those who had been most mired in controversy, usually over support for Planned Parenthood, were especially eager to talk about what had been a difficult and sometimes emotionally wrenching interruption of their normal work lives. One told me that our conversation was the first opportunity that she had had to sit back and reflect on what had happened. Our conversations in many cases, moreover, did not end with the formal interview. I sent all my subjects summaries of my interview notes as a way of eliciting additional informa-tion. About one-third responded, usually with substantive comments.

So, why did they talk to me so readily? They did so for at least three related reasons. First, talking to people, after all, is what they do for a living. Like managers who run corporate political action committees (PACs) or do public relations work, corporate philanthropists live at and manage the boundaries between their corporations and the rest of society. (Indeed, this is central to the broad political significance of corporate philanthropy discussed later in the book.) They are the corporation's voices and also its "eyes and ears," as one of them put it. They offer and receive information. Talking to me was simply part of that. Generally speaking, researchers who have studied heads of corporate PACs or government relations specialists have found them equally accessible.[12]

At least one subject explicitly said that she consented to the interview because she hoped to learn from it something about what her peers were doing. Several others questioned me about how their experiences compared to those of their peers, and a number seemed eager to use my work to put their own experience in perspective.

Second, I presented myself as someone acceptable and worthwhile to talk to. In addition to explaining my research, my initial letter of inquiry prominently identified me as a professor at Amherst College whose work was supported partly by the Indiana University Center on Philanthropy. It also assured them of confidentiality and emphasized that I planned to present the results of my research in a scholarly format. My subjects thus identified me as a "serious researcher," an expert with substantial knowledge of corporate philanthropy already, not a "journalist" eager to dig up more controversy out of which to make new headlines or perhaps an uninformed, potentially unsympathetic academic. One subject, half jokingly, half nervously expressed concern that what he said not appear in the *New York Times* the next Sunday. Others pointedly noted my connections to Amherst and the Center on Philanthropy. The latter tie may have been especially important. Several corporate philanthropists knew that the Center had been founded by a former colleague, Robert Payton, one-time head of the Exxon Education Foundation. Even some who did not seem to know this still took my connection to the Center as a mark of legitimacy.

Third, in retrospect, the willingness of corporate giving officers to talk to me was the first palpable indication I had of the influence of the culture of corporate philanthropy, of the ties among corporate philanthropists, and of the shared understandings sustained by these ties. Although the overall response rate was high to begin with, it was virtually unanimous among those corporate giving officers whose ties to peers I was able to tap or who are centrally located in the philanthropic culture.

I asked each subject to suggest colleagues for further interviews and then used these subjects as references in subsequent requests for interviews. In all, I approached twenty-one of my potential subjects this way; all agreed to talk (compared to 81 percent of those I approached cold). Several in fact noted that they had actually spoken to the colleague who had

◨

referred me to them; one explicitly said that knowing that his friend X at corporation Y wasn't too "busy" to talk with me encouraged him to do so as well. In short, having peers vouch for me increased the willingness of corporate philanthropists to talk.

While peer influence was important so was something a bit more elusive. Forty of the sixty-three corporations I approached are members of the Contributions Council of the Conference Board, one of two main organizations representing corporate philanthropy programs. All but one of these agreed to talk; in contrast, only about half of the nonmembers agreed. I also asked all my subjects to name those corporate giving programs they found "exemplary." Fifteen of the sixteen programs that received three or more mentions were among those I contacted; all of these high-status programs agreed to interviews (though 84 percent of lower-status programs also agreed). In short, the more deeply involved a corporate philanthropy program was in the transcorporate world and the higher its status therein, the more willing the manager was to talk with me. This suggests a set of cultural assumptions at work, a shared understanding that however busy one is with pressing daily tasks, discussing corporate philanthropy with a researcher is still an important thing to do.

In short, the vast majority of corporations that I approached agreed to talk. These corporate philanthropists spoke at some length (or at least longer than they had planned). They usually spoke with considerable energy and passion about their work and its occasional controversies. They saw me as a highly credible interviewer and the interview and its written results as a way of learning more about themselves and their peers.

Some Questions

We can re-frame the ideas underlying *Looking Good and Doing Good* as a set of questions:

1. What is the relationship between philanthropy and the individual corporation? How do corporate philanthropists understand the relationship between doing good for society and doing well for the corporation? In what ways is combining the two problematic in everyday practice?

2. To what extent is there a culture of corporate philanthropy, a shared understanding of how and why corporate philanthropy is done and a network of relationships connecting corporate philanthropy programs? What mix of company and classwide rationalities does it embody? What does it assume about the relationship between large corporations and the rest of society, especially the nonprofit sector? How does the everyday

thinking of corporate philanthropists both draw upon and differ from this culture?

3. How is corporate philanthropy part of corporate politics? What keys does it hold for understanding the nature of corporate power in general? What is distinctive about this power?

Implicit in all these questions is the assumption that corporate philanthropy is both a collective and a political activity. That is, it is quite different from what it appears to be at first. Certainly, the corporate philanthropists whom I interviewed would strongly object to this characterization. They see themselves as serving their own company, not some collective entity called big business. They also maintain strongly that what they do is apolitical and nonideological. They see little connection between corporate philanthropy and, say, political action committees. In the face of political challenges to their grantmaking, they insist that they do not apply "ideological litmus tests." And, in a sense, they are right, but so am I. How this can be is part of what this book is all about.

2

The Making of Corporate Philanthropy

Philanthropy has always been a part of American life. Corporate philanthropy, however, is a new arrival relatively speaking, coming of age only
since the 1950s. When F. Emerson Andrews of the Russell Sage Foundation
wrote his classic *Corporation Giving* in 1952, he had trouble finding
anything there.

At that time, U.S. corporations gave away only a few hundred million
dollars a year, mostly in response to community fundraising drives. To talk
of anything as structured as corporate giving *programs* would have been
grossly misleading. "Corporate giving is not at present a carefully considered, integrated program in most companies," Andrews wrote.[1] Only one-
third of the major corporations he studied even had a distinct line for
corporate contributions in their budgets. Only a handful had any written
guidelines whatsoever or a contributions committee to oversee the activity.
Corporate giving, such as it was, was stuck in a rut of tradition, "each new
year largely duplicating the past year," with change coming only "by bits
and pieces" in reaction to "new pressures."[2] It lacked any hint of either
professionalism or creativity, Andrews complained. It was little more than
a hobby of top corporate executives.

Much has changed since Andrews wrote. Today, corporations give
away about $7 billion a year, and they do so to a wide range of nonprofit
organizations in education, the arts, social services, and public policy.
Corporate philanthropy programs have budgets, guidelines, and serious
managers to run them. Observers may differ on how professional or
creative they are, but the institutional basics are undeniably there.

Philanthropy by individual corporations increased, diversified, and
became institutionalized partly because philanthropy became a collective
corporate activity. The key to why and how corporate philanthropy came
of age, in other words, lies in transcorporate relationships.

The "collectivization" of corporate philanthropy has had three related
elements—elite influence, a common culture, and transcorporate networks: (1) Recurrently since the early 1950s, *important corporate leaders
and central corporate organizations* have played major roles in shaping the

◈

rationale and direction of corporate giving. They have argued for the importance of philanthropy to the corporate world as a whole, urged corporations to expand their giving programs, facilitated the diffusion of information and know-how, and sponsored whole new areas of corporate giving. (2) A *common culture* has developed that provides general rationales for corporate philanthropy as well as practical advice about how much corporations should give, to whom, and through what kind of procedures. (3) *Transcorporate networks* of relationships among both top executives and corporate giving officers have become a conduit for the norms and practical advice of this culture.

As a result no corporate giving program is an island; and while each corporate giving officer undoubtedly thinks his or her own thoughts, they do so in a common language. Indeed having a shared culture upon which to draw makes individual giving programs of any coherence and organization possible to begin with. This chapter traces the collectivization of corporate philanthropy and its relation to other important changes in corporate giving.

The Prehistory of Corporate Philanthropy

Philanthropy by rich individuals is as old as the republic and as American as apple pie. Historian Peter Dobkin Hall has argued in rich detail and grand historical sweep that from the late eighteenth century right up to the eve of the New Deal, economic and social elites sought to build up nonprofit educational and cultural institutions as a way of pursuing "public goals through private action" and thus providing a bulwark against a state they deemed too democratic and unpredictable. By the early twentieth century, this practice had matured into a broad vision of a "private-sector alternative to socialism," in which a network of nonprofit organizations, closely tied to for-profit organizations, would provide the human services delivered elsewhere by emerging welfare states.[3]

Industrialists, Hall also notes, sometimes used their own money to provide their workers with housing, health care, education, and other benefits, especially when labor markets were tight or when state-controlled social welfare programs seemed poised to expand.[4]

Corporate philanthropy, in contrast, arose later and took longer to legitimate itself than the private largesse of the wealthy. While it was broadly acceptable for rich individuals to dispose of their wealth as they saw fit (despite the misgivings that many Americans had about great wealth and the uses to which it was put), corporate giving raised the distinct issue

◙

of whether or not the managers of corporations may donate money belonging not to them personally but to shareholders. The earliest recorded instances of corporate philanthropy thus date only from the late nineteenth century and its history was dogged by legal controversy that did not fully abate until the 1950s.

Corporate giving (or what in retrospect has been called such) trod a narrow path in the late nineteenth and early twentieth centuries.[5] Corporations gave money either to provide benefits directly to their workers or for clear commercial gain, but for little else. Corporations might support housing projects, schools, libraries, benefit associations, or churches primarily or exclusively for the use of their workers. In addition, they might underwrite projects by others that promised a fairly direct economic benefit for themselves. Hotel companies might support a reunion or exposition that would attract additional guests; railroads might use contributions to attract businesses to areas they served; or a development company might underwrite the cost of a bridge or road providing access to its land. Clearly these are cases where charity, if such it was, began at home and largely stayed there.

The most noteworthy example of this early corporate philanthropy was the support railroad companies gave to YMCA facilities at divisional and terminal points on their routes to house their workers. By 1911, there were 230 such railroad associations getting about 40 percent of their support from the railroad companies themselves. This support was especially important for the future of corporate philanthropy, because it provided the YMCA connections to the corporate world that it drew upon in the early 1900s to pioneer the community fundraising drive, the systematic solicitation of corporations and individuals for charitable causes.

Such drives became vastly more important when America entered World War I: The YMCA, the Red Cross, and later the United War Work Campaign systematically solicited funds from individuals and businesses for war-related social welfare work. Corporations gave at least $18 million to the Red Cross drive in 1917, and a pattern of giving to annual fundraising campaigns was set. For example, the Computing-Tabulating-Recording Company recorded its first donations, totalling $8,000, in 1918, including $3,700 to the American Red Cross War Fund, $2,000 to the United War Fund Campaign, $876 to Liberty Loan Advertising, $250 each to the Community War Chest and the Patriotic Fund, and $182 to the YMCA—an inauspicious beginning in philanthropy for a corporation, which under its later name of IBM would become the largest corporate giver in the United States.[6]

◆

After the war, corporations continued their preference for annual campaigns by supporting the first federated community fundraising efforts initiated by what came to be known as the Community Chests and Councils of America. By 1929, corporations were contributing about $13 million a year, or about one quarter of all money raised by these campaigns.

These fundraising drives dominated corporate philanthropy right up to 1950 (and to a lesser degree beyond). In his 1950 survey of 326 corporations, Andrews found that contributions to Community Chests alone still made up 36 percent of all corporate giving and that more than 90 percent of all corporations gave at least half of their contributions to annual drives of one kind or another (and half did nearly all their giving in this way).

The cramped nature of corporate giving through midcentury reflected in part the cultural and legal vacuum in which it found itself. The corporate world had yet to develop a strong culture that sanctioned broad corporate responsibilities to society. There were few studies of actual corporate giving practices and virtually no treatises on why and how it should be done. Such work dates largely from the 1950s. More important, although case and statute law progressively gave more leeway to corporate giving, a significant degree of ambiguity remained until 1953.

The very earliest cases, decided at a time when many corporations still had very narrowly defined charters, ruled against any donations not directly related to the purposes for which the corporation had been organized.[7] Thus the Supreme Judicial Court of Massachusetts ruled in 1881 that neither a railroad nor a musical instrument company could legally underwrite the expenses of a music festival along the railroad's lines, even though both clearly stood to benefit from attendance at the festival. Nothing in the charter of either company authorized them to participate in music festivals.

As corporate charters became broader, the criteria applied by the courts changed. Typically, courts upheld only those donations that were intended to increase revenues and actually did provide a direct benefit to the corporation. Prior to 1936, the Board of Tax Appeals and the Tax Court used a similar standard to determine whether a donation qualified as a legitimate business expense. While employee-benefit donations consistently passed muster, donations to higher education, community funds, and commercial projects faced a less predictable response. For example, in a 1934 case, *Old Mission Portland Cement Co. v. Helvering,* the United States Supreme Court upheld a Bureau of Tax Appeal ruling that a contribution by the cement company to the San Francisco Community Chest was

◆

not a legitimate business expense. Although the company acted on the belief that the donation would increase public goodwill and hence business, there was no finding of "direct benefit" to employees or to the business.

Changes in legal statutes gradually clarified the status of corporate philanthropy, but only to a point. Beginning with Texas in 1917, several states (numbering twenty-six by the early 1950s) passed laws allowing corporate donations for a range of charitable and related purposes. The Revenue Act of 1935 allowed corporations to deduct donations of up to 5 percent of pretax profit for federal tax purposes. In 1949 the American Bar Association's Committee on Business Corporations for the first time provided standard language for state laws empowering corporations "to make donations for the public welfare or for charitable, scientific, or educational purposes."[8] Still, how directly donations had to be tied to corporate interests and whether the state laws applied to corporations chartered prior to the enactment of those laws remained ambiguous.

The only point on which the courts were perfectly clear was that corporate giving could not be wholly philanthropic. In 1916, Henry Ford abruptly announced that the Ford Motor Company was cutting its dividends to stockholders dramatically and using the money instead to produce more cars at lower prices. He stated purely philanthropic motives for this move: "My ambition is to employ still more men; to spread the benefits of this industrial system to the greatest possible number, to help them build up their lives and their homes."[9] The Dodge brothers, minority stockowners in Ford and planning to start their own car company, sued to compel payment of dividends at their customary level. In *Dodge v. Ford,* a Michigan court ruled against Ford, saying in part that there was a difference

> between an incidental humanitarian expenditure of corporate funds for the benefit of employees, like the building of a hospital for their use, and the employment of agencies for the betterment of their condition, and a general purpose to benefit mankind at the expense of others.

The Court added that

> [a] business corporation is organized and carried on primarily for the profit of shareholders. The powers of the directors are to be employed for that end. The discretion of the directors is to be exercised in the choice of the means to attain that end, and does not extend to a change in the end itself. . . .[10]

The right of corporations to donate money to a broad range of causes

◆

was established definitively only in 1952 in a New Jersey case, *A. P. Smith Manufacturing Company v. Barlow.* To grasp its significance, however, we need to look at changing attitudes toward philanthropy in the corporate world.

Transforming Corporate Philanthropy

In the years after World War II, important organizations and leaders in the corporate world called upon corporations to make their giving programs serious enterprises. Both the Conference Board and the National Planning Association addressed the matter in the early 1950s, but the most important contribution came from a group of corporate executives concerned about the fate of America's private universities.[11]

Corporate leaders had much on their minds at the time. The Great Depression had destroyed whatever positive regard Americans had for large corporations. The New Deal had initiated a substantial expansion of government intervention in the economy, which the war had reinforced. Coming out of the war, large corporations faced both a loss of public support and the specter of ever-expanding government.

Supporting higher education seemed a likely way of restoring the reputation of big business and a good place to stem the growth of big government. After all, what was more reputable in American culture than education? And where was the need to restore faith in big business greater than among intellectuals and academic leaders? Furthermore, higher education had been a major area of government expansion in the 1940s: As college enrollments expanded dramatically in the postwar years, government support at all levels increased from less than 40 percent of all funds for higher education to about 60 percent. Furthermore, America's private colleges were in financial trouble as tuition and other private forms of income failed to keep up with expenses: In the early 1950s, the *New York Times* reported, half of all private colleges operated on a deficit.

Corporations, however, hardly seemed poised to shower money on the beleaguered institutions of private higher education. Support for higher education made up only about 15 percent of all corporate giving in the late 1940s and early 1950s according to data from both the Conference Board and Andrews's sample.[12] These limited funds were concentrated almost exclusively on scholarships and fellowships for company employees and research in areas directly relevant to a company's business. Only a few corporations at the time had undertaken more general support for higher education, and there were substantial barriers to others doing so: The

◆

tradition-bound nature of corporate giving made innovation unlikely. The law remained ambiguous about how directly donations had to benefit the donor corporation. Finally, any corporation willing to buck tradition and weather legal ambiguity faced the daunting task of figuring out which of the nation's several thousand private colleges to support.

Several corporate leaders set out to increase broad corporate support for higher education. Among the most important were Frank Abrams, Alfred P. Sloan, Irving S. Olds, and Arthur W. Page, all of whom played important roles in both the corporate and the nonprofit worlds. Abrams was chairman of Standard Oil of New Jersey and a trustee of the Ford and Sloan foundations as well as of Syracuse University. Sloan had been chairman of General Motors, founder of the Sloan Foundation, and a trustee of M.I.T. Olds had been chairman of U.S. Steel, a fellow of the Yale Corporation, and an original incorporator of the College Retirement Equity Fund. Page was a vice president at AT&T as well as a trustee of the Carnegie Corporation.

These men were central to founding the Committee for Financial Aid to Education, which became a clearinghouse for information for corporations contemplating greater support for private colleges. They also provided a powerful rationale for such support. Olds stated their position well when he argued in a speech at Yale, his alma mater:

> Capitalism and free enterprise owe their survival in no small degree to the existence of our private, independent universities. Both are not only important to each other—they are dependent upon each other. . . . I want to say emphatically that . . . every American business has a direct obligation to support the free, independent, privately-endowed colleges and universities of this country to the limit of its financial ability and legal authority.
>
> If the day ever comes when our tax-supported competitors can offer the youth of America a better education than we can—and at a lower price—we are through.[13]

Abrams added to this a concern over the possible alienation of intellectuals from American capitalism: "Our teachers must be strengthened in their belief in the American system of democratic capitalism by a more equitable participation in the rewards of the system."[14]

Beyond providing both organizational framework and rationale for expanded corporate support for higher education, corporate leaders probably initiated the challenge that led to clarifying the legality of such donations. In 1950, New Jersey amended its laws to allow corporations chartered in the state to contribute to educational institutions, but it remained unclear whether or not the law applied retroactively to corporations chartered before its passage. The next year, the A. P. Smith Company, a manufacturer of valves, fire hydrants, and equipment for water and gas industries, abruptly decided to give $1,500 to Princeton University. A group of stockholders challenged the gift, which historians Merle Curti and Roderick Nash argue "may have been a maneuver planned by New Jersey corporations themselves to provoke a test case."[15]

The resulting case, *A. P. Smith Manufacturing Company v. Barlow* became the "American landmark case in the field of corporate philanthropy," according to legal scholar Phillip I. Blumberg.[16] The New Jersey court not only ruled that the amendment to state law applied retroactively but also articulated a justification for corporate philanthropy broad enough to encompass all corporate support of higher education, no matter how remote from the specific interests of the individual donor. Emphasizing concerns similar to those of Olds and Abrams, the opinion argued,

> there is now widespread belief throughout the nation that free and vigorous non-governmental institutions of learning are vital to our democracy and the system of free enterprise and that withdrawal of corporate authority to make such contributions within reasonable limits would seriously threaten their continuance. Corporations have come to recognize this and with their enlightenment have sought in varying measures . . . to insure and strengthen the society which gives them existence. . . .

A few years later, Richard Eels, a consultant on public policy for General Electric, generalized this broad-gauged rationale to cover all kinds of corporate giving, even as he provided corporate givers with a set of practical guidelines. The first step in a serious corporate giving program, he wrote in *Corporation Giving in a Free Society,* is recognizing that it should be based on long-term "enlightened self-interest," not immediate corporate gain. Corporate giving should aim at more than promoting short-term "good will for the donor":

> Corporation giving is not a branch of advertising, nor properly chargeable to advertising costs. Philanthropy is justifiable—and indeed necessary—whether or not the donor-company takes steps to garner the fruits of publicity attending its good works. The aim is to protect and preserve the donor's autonomy by protecting and preserving the conditions within the greater society which ensure the continuity of a system of free, competitive enterprise.[17]

The key to preserving free, competitive enterprise lay in protecting the

◆

principle of "voluntary association" and the various "private sectors" of society. That is, corporations had to protect not only the private for-profit sector but also the private nonprofit sector from state encroachments, because the fate of the two were closely tied:

> Business enterprise has a direct interest in promoting the strength of private sectors because it is itself a private sector. For this reason, business must maintain the barriers against the progressive absorption of these sectors into State-controlled areas.[18]

The efforts of corporate leaders such as Olds and Abrams and well-placed consultants such as Andrews and Eels helped transform corporate philanthropy from an ad hoc response to occasional fundraising appeals to a more systematic effort to support nonprofit organizations generally.

Where the legal status of corporate philanthropy had once been ambiguous, now court cases consistently ratified the right of corporations to donate money to a wide range of nonprofit organizations. Although the courts never formally gave up the requirement of "direct benefit," legal scholar Blumberg argues, the Smith case and several following it extended that requirement to "cases where a contribution, not resulting in immediate economic results, was made as a matter of business judgment to fulfill business objectives."[19] In 1958, for example, a Utah court upheld a donation by the Union Pacific Railroad Company to its own corporate foundation, arguing that the goodwill engendered by the donation constituted the benefit for the corporation. The donation, the court argued, was like sponsoring a concert or a baseball team, giving to the local Community Chest, or advertising on radio or in the newspaper. "Such actions seldom produce any immediate and direct corporate benefits," but they still make good business sense.[20] In 1969, a Delaware court upheld a similar corporate gift to a charitable foundation, arguing in part that the small loss of immediate income to stockholders was more than offset by

> the overall benefits flowing from the place of such gift in channels where it serves to benefit those in need of philanthropic or educational support, thus providing the justification for large private holdings, thereby benefitting plaintiff in the long run.[21]

In short, while corporate philanthropy still required a business justification, that justification became very broad, and the courts largely left executives free to exercise their "business judgment" as they saw fit.

Corporate philanthropy overall expanded dramatically from $252 million in 1950 to $482 million in 1960, about $1 billion a year in the early 1970s, hitting about $6 billion per year in the late 1980s. These figures are

◆

in current dollars; in constant dollars, the corporate giving levels of the late 1980s were about twice as great as those of the early 1970s. Corporate giving also rose from about 0.5 percent of corporate pretax profits in the 1950s to about 2 percent in the late 1980s.[22]

Corporations also greatly diversified the kinds of activities they supported. The share of the pie devoted to health and human services (much of it through Community Chests and later United Ways) fell from an overwhelming 66 percent in 1947 to less than 30 percent in the late 1980s and the 1990s. Support for education (primarily higher education) increased in particular, from about 15 percent of all corporate giving in the late 1940s to about 35 to 40 percent in the late 1980s and the 1990s.[23] What had once seemed a risky or innovative donation had become the staple of even the most conservative giving programs. Furthermore, the arts and civic/community activities each built up a 10- to 15-percent share.

At least among the very largest corporations, corporate giving also became professionalized or at least aspired to become so. More and more companies devoted a specific budget line to contributions, appointed a contributions committee or established a corporate foundation, assigned day-to-day administration of the function to an executive deemed to have special skills in the area, and developed written guidelines and formal objectives for their giving program.[24]

Most important, corporate philanthropy came to have a *collective shape.* Central corporate leaders and organizations continued to play an important role in initiating or at least articulating trends in giving; a common culture developed; and transcorporate networks became an important influence on the giving of individual corporations.

Corporate Elites and Corporate Philanthropy

Irving Olds, Frank Abrams, and their colleagues did not conjure corporate support of higher education out of nothing in the early 1950s; they had no authority to command the corporate world to follow their dictates. They did, however, wield considerable influence by giving legitimacy and direction to an inchoate concern among big business generally about its sagging reputation and the growth of government. Certainly, support for higher education expanded dramatically in the wake of their actions and became a staple of corporate giving.

This established an ongoing pattern of corporate leaders playing a formative role in corporate giving. Recurrently important corporate leaders or central corporate organizations have either opened up new directions in

◆

philanthropy or encouraged trends already under way by giving these changes legitimacy, providing concrete models for how to do it, or by creating an organizational framework to facilitate change.

In 1966, for example, David Rockefeller, head of Chase Manhattan Bank and effectively business spokesperson for his family, founded the Business Committee for the Arts to encourage support for a range of cultural activities to which corporations had given virtually no money previously. In his founding address, Rockefeller talked broadly about the arts as a "vital part of human experience" and as the defining element of a civilized society. Although Americans were showing increasing interest in the arts, too many outside the largest cities simply did not have sufficient access to them. Increasing income and leisure time, rather than being devoted to "artistic and intellectual pursuits," were being given to "unproductive and often aimless activities."[25]

Rockefeller, however, did not make his case for corporate support of the arts solely by appealing to broad values like civilization and quality of life. The genius of his address was that it gave corporations a broad range of self-interested reasons for funding the arts. On the most general level, supporting the arts contributed to the very viability of "our way of life":

> The ultimate dedication to our way of life will be won, I am convinced, not on the basis of economic achievements alone but on the basis of those precious yet intangible elements which enable the individual to live a fuller, wiser, more satisfying existence.[26]

Granted that the arts are important for a way of life upon which business as a whole depends, what is in it for the individual corporation? To begin with, Rockefeller argued, in recent years the modern corporation has "developed ideals and responsibilities going far beyond the profit motive. It has become, in effect, a full-fledged citizen." Furthermore, "the public has come to expect organizations such as yours and mine to live up to certain standards of good citizenship." Finally, on the most mundane level, supporting the arts can provide tangible economic benefits to the corporation:

> From an economic standpoint, such involvement can mean direct and tangible benefits. It can provide a company with extensive publicity and advertising, a brighter public reputation, and an improved corporate image. It can build better customer relations, a readier acceptance of company products, and superior appraisal of their quality. Promotion of the arts can improve the morale of employees and help attract qualified personnel.[27]

◆

Rockefeller thus provided both rationale and organizational framework for increasing business support for the arts. The Business Committee for the Arts continues to track and encourage this support by gathering information on existing giving patterns, surveying the attitudes of corporations toward support for the arts, offering detailed reports by CEOs about how arts programs are organized and serve corporate interests, giving awards to exemplary corporate programs. Support for the arts has consistently been over 10 percent of corporate giving in recent years, and such individual corporations as Philip Morris, AT&T, and Dayton Hudson have become extremely important sources of funding for the arts.[28]

The protest movements of the late 1960s and early 1970s put corporations on the defensive. Whether the issue was civil rights or women's rights, the Vietnam War or the environment, large corporations were often identified as part of the problem. This led many corporate leaders to worry about how they might secure a legitimate place for big business in American society and ward off social criticism and state control. In 1971, the Committee on Economic Development issued a report on "The Social Responsibility of Business Corporations," which concluded:

> Today it is clear that the terms of the contract between society and business are, in fact, changing in substantial and important ways. Business is being asked to assume broader social responsibilities to society than ever before and to serve a wider range of human values. Business enterprises, in effect, are being asked to contribute more to the quality of American life than just supplying quantities of goods and services.[29]

The Council on Trends and Perspectives of the U.S. Chambers of Commerce tersely noted the likely consequences of failing to meet these new public expectations: "Unless sizeable business firms initiate 'social responsibility' policies now, government will force such action later."[30]

The broader implication here is that corporations get their right to exist from society, and they can maintain that right only if they live up to general societal expectations about how they ought to behave. These expectations had expanded in the late 1960s and early 1970s, so corporations had to adjust their behavior accordingly. As Louis Lundborg, then head of the Bank of America, the nation's largest bank at the time, put it:

> Those in corporate life are going to be expected to do things for the good of society, just to earn their franchise, their corporate right to exist. That is why I am both amused and amazed that there should even be a question about the propriety of corporate social involve-

◧

ment, when it is to me so clearly an obligation. The corporation has to earn its right to exist and to function. . . . It is not a fixed, vested property; it is not a guaranteed right. It is a privilege that can be given—has been given—and can be taken away.[31]

Oil companies at the time were a particular target of public criticism both for polluting the environment and setting high gas prices, so Lundborg's point had special meaning for them. Thomas Bradshaw, a former CEO of ARCO, noted in retrospect that in the 1970s, "whether society would grant [oil companies] the right to operate" had become problematic: "It did not take a lot of leadership . . . to recognize that the problem during the '70s was not one of making money for shareholders. It was simply staying in business."[32] Not surprisingly, major oil companies increased their donations even faster than their rates of profit. By 1980 five of the twelve largest corporate donors were in oil.[33]

Walter A. Haas, Jr., of Levi Strauss, argued in a similar vein that "government regulation of the private sector and curbs on business's independence of action" tend to occur in response to public perceptions of "widespread abuses on the part of business." To maintain its "present level of independence," therefore, big business needs to maintain its legitimacy among the public by acting in socially responsible ways.[34]

Much of the corporate talk about social responsibility had a defensive, reactive tone to it: Important elements of the public seemed increasingly critical of corporations, and corporations had to prove themselves worthy in their eyes, or else. Beginning in the late 1970s and reaching fruition in the early 1980s, however, corporate leaders took a different tack, one that was more aggressive, proactive, and conservative. Increasingly, corporate leaders were convinced that American society was out of (their) control: Unions were too strong, regulatory agencies too restrictive, government in general too big, and the overall culture too critical of big business. Corporations responded by mobilizing individually and collectively. They opened public affairs offices in Washington, D.C. and invested in overtly political advocacy advertising. They directed more of their money to conservative Republican candidates for Congress and to aggressively conservative think tanks. They formed new organizations, such as the Business Roundtable, to represent more effectively the common interests of large corporations. In the early 1980s, corporate leaders strongly supported Ronald Reagan's tax and spending cuts and the reorientation of American government that these implied.[35]

The rise of Corporate Conservatism, however, did not diminish support for corporate philanthropy; indeed it provided new reasons for it. Corporate executives were quick to take up the call by the President's Task Force on Private Sector Initiatives, chaired by C. William Verity, Jr., former head of Armco, Inc., for corporations to compensate for some of the Reagan budget cuts by increasing their giving from 1 percent to 2 percent of pretax profits. The alternative to big government in their eyes was not simply the marketplace but the marketplace supplemented by the nonprofit sector. Furthermore, they argued, if corporations did not step in, they risked increased public hostility and they would lose an opportunity to shape the social agenda.[36]

In early 1981, the Business Roundtable, which had become the premier political representative of big business, issued a position paper on corporate philanthropy subsequently endorsed by the National Association of Manufacturers and the U.S. Chambers of Commerce.[37] The paper presented corporate philanthropy as both a responsibility and a matter of considerable self-interest:

> The Business Roundtable believes that corporate philanthropy . . . is an integral part of corporate social responsibility both as good business and as an obligation if they are to be considered responsible corporate citizens of the national and local communities in which they operate.[38]

The Roundtable did not elaborate on the notion of social responsibility, but it spent several paragraphs explaining how giving money away was good business. To begin, its statement argued, businesses have "a self-interest in philanthropic activities which serve to strengthen the fabric of society," because "business cannot survive and prosper unless society continues to improve and develop." Moreover, if big business didn't support the activities of the nonprofit sector, then government would inevitably step in. If big business was serious "in seeking to stem over-dependence on government" through the Reagan budget cuts, it simply had to "increase its level of commitment" to the private nonprofit sector:

> The principal alternative to private philanthropy is government funding, which is . . . inherently less efficient in the distribution and control of funds for these purposes. . . . Accordingly, if the business community is serious in seeking to stem over-dependence on government and still allow the private not-for-profit sector to make the same contribution to society that it has in the past, business must itself increase its level of commitment.[39]

The strong support of the Business Roundtable and corporate leaders for corporate giving reflected and reinforced a broader sentiment among

◈

corporations: In the decade from 1978 through 1987, corporate giving nearly doubled, even after taking inflation into account.[40]

In the late 1980s, large corporations took up the broader public concern with the state of public elementary and secondary education, what executives came to call "K–12" or "precollege" education. In 1989, the Business Roundtable announced a ten-year commitment to "education reform" and in 1992 published a detailed brochure for its corporate members entitled "Agents of Change: Exemplary Corporate Policies and Practices to Improve Education." This brochure detailed what exemplary corporations were doing in the area and laid out an action plan for others who wanted to follow in their footsteps. Noting the limited range of traditional corporation support for precollege education, the Roundtable announced:

> What are needed to meet today's immense challenges are long-term, corporate-wide commitments with more ambitious goals: to change the way that students learn, teachers teach, and school systems function.[41]

As in the previous cases, the Roundtable's efforts seem both symptomatic and influential. The percentage of corporate donations going to precollege education nearly doubled in the late 1980s and early 1990s.[42] When I spoke with corporate philanthropists in late 1992 and early 1993, one of the positive developments in corporate philanthropy they mentioned most frequently was the recent corporate foray into precollege education.

The Culture of Corporate Philanthropy

In the last half century major corporate leaders and their advisers have encouraged the expansion of corporate philanthropy and helped articulate broad rationales for giving. In doing so, they have in effect helped create a *culture of corporate philanthropy,* which now has taken on a life of its own. This culture is sustained by a network of contacts among corporate giving officers, especially through the Contributions Council of the Conference Board (for the very largest corporate giving programs) and the Corporate Grantmakers Committee of the Council on Foundations (for those corporations who channel their donations through company foundations rather than giving directly). It is embodied in the speeches of countless CEOs and giving officers and in numerous publications, especially those of the Council on Foundations. Certainly in the 1990s, no corporate giving program operates in a void, and no corporate giving officer need start from scratch in thinking about her firm's giving program.

This culture cuts in two directions. On the one hand, as quotes from important corporate leaders and organizations have made clear, it urges corporate philanthropists to think broadly and in the long term about maintaining societal conditions that will insure the continued viability not only of the corporation itself but of corporate capitalism in general. The corporate culture calls this "enlightened self-interest," a term that dates back at least to Eells. I shall also call this "classwide rationality," a term introduced by sociologist Michael Useem, to underscore the emphasis on securing a climate favorable to big business generally.

On the other hand, the culture also encourages corporate philanthropy to tie itself closely to the immediate interests of its company, to become part of that company's strategic plan, and to make itself more businesslike. In the contemporary culture, these themes fall under the rubrics of "strategic (or focused) giving" and "professionalism." I shall call them collectively "company rationality," again a Useem term, to flag the emphasis on the immediate role of philanthropy in its home corporation.[43]

Although these two sets of themes in the abstract appear diametrically opposed to each other, the one situating corporate philanthropy in a broader understanding of business and society, the other tying it resolutely to the needs of its corporation, in practice the two have developed together. The connections between the two go back at least to Eells's work. Eells, like others in the 1950s, found much to dislike about corporate philanthropy. It was "an undeveloped area of managerial thinking"; it lacked a "systematic base"; and above all, "it has too often been run-of-the-mill charity— drives, pet projects, and ephemeral undertakings—moved by opportunism and restricted by inertia."[44] His solution to these problems, in effect, was two-pronged: First, corporate giving needed to be rooted in long-term "enlightened self-interest," which, as we have already seen, meant to Eells preserving the nonprofit sector and the principle of voluntary association. Second, corporate giving had to "become an important element of business strategy, complementing other strategic moves to increase productivity, profitability, and services of the donor over the long run," and it had to become subject to the same "principles of scientific management" as all other corporate functions.[45] In this context, going beyond the immediate interests of the corporation and becoming integrated more closely to them were simply two different ways that corporate giving could become thoughtful, systematic, and something more than "run-of-the-mill charity."

◈

Classwide Themes

Broad rationales abound in the culture of corporate philanthropy. We have already seen them in Olds's call for corporate support for higher education to stave off further growth of big government, in Rockefeller's argument for supporting the arts to protect "our way of life," and in the Business Roundtable's claim that corporate philanthropy improves the business climate generally by helping society "improve and develop." What these arguments have in common is that they either explicitly justify corporate giving as helping big business or free enterprise per se or simply urge corporations to make donations for the general benefit of society, benefits that will clearly be reaped by other businesses as well.

These classwide rationales take three basic forms. The first and most general is simply that no individual corporation or big business can prosper if society as a whole does not prosper. This was the Business Roundtable's point in the 1980s, and many corporate representatives have echoed it in the early 1990s. Stanley Karson, head of the Center for Corporate Public Involvement, which represents the philanthropy programs of the insurance industry, writes:

> A business and its community are closely interrelated, and . . . festering social and economic problems will eventually—sooner than some think—have a negative impact on the bottom line.
>
> Education, housing, health, jobs, violence, drugs, transportation, and the quality of life affect business, its workforce, its market, its costs and profitability. That is why so much of corporate America is involved with these vital community and social issues.[46]

Jack MacAllister, CEO of US West, notes that "a business cannot succeed if society fails. We cannot market successfully if the marketplace does not prosper. We cannot compete if graduates of our schools cannot read, write, and reason."[47] Finally, Walter V. Shipley, Chair and CEO of Chemical Bank, acknowledging his corporation's receiving the Lawrence A. Wien Prize in Corporate Social Responsibility, emphasizes that "we have a stake in ensuring and improving the vitality of the markets we operate in, because if they thrive, we thrive. It's really that simple."[48]

A second theme, enunciated first by Olds and Eells in the early 1950s and echoed in the 1980s by the Business Roundtable is that big business has a general interest in supporting nonprofit organizations both to reinforce the general principle of voluntary association and to provide alternatives to government programs.

◆

In the early 1990s, Brian O'Connell, head of Independent Sector, an organization representing major nonprofit organizations, foundations, and corporate donors, reinforced this theme, using words reminiscent of Eels's: The for-profit and nonprofit sectors share a commitment to "the freedom of individuals to pursue their own ideas" and thus are equally threatened by the growth of the state:

> Both the for-profit and the nonprofit sides of private enterprise are faced with growing domination by government. . . . If this so-called third sector becomes further dominated by government, we will in fact have only two sectors and, inevitably, one sector."[49]

The final variant of the classwide rationale is that corporate philanthropy maintains or improves the legitimacy of business by fulfilling public expectations that business behave in a "socially responsible" way by addressing pressing societal problems as well as producing useful products, providing jobs, and paying taxes. These expectations, in effect, are part of an implicit social contract, part of what corporations have to do to maintain their right to do business. Failure to meet these expectations may lead to increased government regulation. We have seen this theme already in Rockefeller's case for increased corporate support for the arts, and throughout the writings of business organizations and CEOs in the 1970s. In the late 1980s, John H. Bryan, Jr., Chair and CEO of Sara Lee Corporation, reiterated this idea. If corporations are not involved in the community, he argued, they run the risk that "our franchise to conduct our business will not be renewed by the society we serve. Or that the role of the private sector in providing goods and services to society will be reduced."[50]

Company Rationality

Classwide rationales for giving, however, do not stand alone in the culture of corporate philanthropy. From its very beginnings in the 1950s, it has provided individual corporations with a rich set of more narrowly self-interested rationales for giving away money. Indeed, given the relatively unreflective and limited nature of corporate giving prior to the 1950s, this common culture created the company rationale for giving quite as much as the classwide rationale.

While company rationales are present everywhere in the culture of corporate philanthropy, they are most striking with regard to the arts, an area of support that at first glance seems totally removed from any kind of direct corporate self-interest. Recall that Rockefeller couched his original case for supporting the arts not only in terms of validating "our way of life" or meeting public expectations but also in more mundane, economic terms as well.

Ever since, the Business Committee for the Arts has made a similar point. Supporting the arts certainly benefits big business generally, because it can "spark economic development, revitalize urban areas and improve the business climate," argues a recent BCA pamphlet. Every dollar spent on the arts, the Committee claims, yields an additional three to the economy. But supporting the arts reaps copious advantages as well for the donor corporation itself by (1) developing the artistic talent the corporation will need for "advertising, packing, marketing and promotion" (Business Committee for the Arts, 1992); (2) helping the corporation "reach special markets" through "joint advertising, marketing, and public relations ventures"; (3) improving "the image" of the corporation "with employees, shareholders, customers, clients, and government representatives."[51]

Beyond providing a rich array of self-interested reasons for giving money away, the culture of corporate philanthropy encourages a company rationality through the notions of *strategic giving* and *professionalism.*

Strategic giving combines a general idea with a specific one. The general idea is that a corporate giving program cannot support everything; to have any impact, it must set priorities and focus. "A company should clearly focus its grantmaking," writes Sanford Cloud, Jr., one-time head of the Aetna Foundation. "An organization's effectiveness is limited if its grantmaking is scattered."[52] "Do not try to support every worthwhile cause," says MacAllister, CEO of US West. "Throwing money at problems does not work and, moreover, there is never enough money to go around."[53] Similarly Shipley of Chemical Bank says, "As a bank, I know that we can't successfully be all things to all people—we have to focus and choose. In our corporate responsibility efforts, we've learned the same."[54]

The specific idea is that corporate giving should focus particularly on areas especially close to corporate interests and expertise. Cloud notes that corporations generally have concluded that "their best opportunities to effect meaningful social change lie in areas where they have a legitimate business-related interest and expertise to add to the equation."[55]

Peter Hutchinson, former head of the Dayton Hudson Foundation, puts it this way:

> A company should work on issues or concerns that are of direct and important strategic value to the company itself: for a publishing company that might mean literacy, for a drug manufacturer that might mean health care concerns, for employers of entry-level workers it may mean K–12 education reform, for a national company it may

mean issues that have a national scope, and for an individual business proprietor it may mean concern for things in the immediate neighborhood.[56]

Mary Hall, former head of the Weyerhauser Foundation, gives more examples: a maker of pacemakers that focuses on aid to the elderly; an airplane manufacturer that emphasizes support for technical education; a producer of school rings and diplomas that gives grants to education.[57]

Beyond this, the notion of strategic giving implies both that philanthropy should be enlisted to serve other corporate goals and that the full range of corporate resources should be applied to philanthropic goals. On the one hand, corporate giving can be systematically enlisted to sell products (as in "cause-related marketing"), to maintain the goodwill of important communities, or to strengthen ties with universities where a company does major recruiting or has large research contracts. On the other hand, philanthropic dollars can be "leveraged" or augmented by other corporate resources. "Do more than write checks," urges MacAllister of US West.[58] "The corporation should be sure that it can bring something special to the table," says Cloud.[59] Corporations can share equipment, space, facilities, and technology with programs they support. They can loan executives and encourage employee volunteering. They can provide training and expertise.[60]

Phrases like "doing more than write checks" and "bringing something special to the table" echo throughout the culture of corporate philanthropy. They embody not only an ideal of how a corporation should do philanthropy but also practical advice for how the philanthropy program can "position" itself within the corporation. The linkages they imply provide the basis for a survival strategy centered on building close ties both to top management and to the rest of the corporation. There is broad consensus that an isolated corporate giving program is a weak one. The program must maintain CEO interest and commitment and promote a sense of ownership among employees. In his "Profiles of Effective Giving Programs," based on interviews with the heads of major corporate giving programs as well as his own experience at Aetna, E. B. Knauft emphasizes both these things:

> Managers in many staff functions tend to stress the importance of personal support from the CEO and the need for a reasonably close reporting relationship to him. However . . . the contributions function especially benefits from senior management's thoughtful affirmation. Several contributions managers noted that board level support for the contributions function is especially dependent on the CEO.[61]

◈

He also notes the importance of "a process to involve company personnel in the program, thus encouraging feelings of ownership of and involvement with the program across the company."[62] Frank Koch, former head of giving at Syntex Corporation, likewise urges, "Get your employees involved in corporate contributions; get your contributions program involved in things that interest and affect your employees."[63]

While the notion of strategic giving emphasizes the importance of tying corporate contributions to the business, the closely related notion of *professionalism* emphasizes making corporate giving itself businesslike. Koch, among others, details what this means:

> There is no way to develop and initiate successful [giving] programs and projects without having competent people to direct these activities, without support from top management, without coordination and communication throughout the company, without an adequate budget, without sound policies and procedures, and without a sense of mission.[64]

Professional, businesslike giving programs have explicit goals and priorities; formal, objective procedures for grantmaking; and reasonably steady, ample budgets. Above all they are run by a professional staff with special grantmaking skills and knowledge of the nonprofit sector and its interface with the corporation. "The person handling the contribution's function should be selected carefully," cautions Koch. "This is not a place to semiretire an executive 'who likes people.'"[65] And David Stanley, CEO of Payless Cashways, Inc., warns:

> The philanthropic program . . . should not be run by—how to say this politely?—well-intentioned individuals without the training to make them peers of the other leaders in the corporation. A philanthropic program should be run by professionals trained in the business of philanthropy who know what is needed and who can solicit proposals, evaluate grant applications, oversee grants, evaluate results, and who know when to sustain programs and when to drop them.[66]

Being professional or businesslike is ultimately the key trait of an "effective" corporate philanthropy program, and the quickest criticism of a giving program is that it lacks some elements thereof. James Shannon, former head of the General Mills Foundation and editor of *The Corporate Contributions Handbook,* complains that "in many corporations the office charged with overseeing contributions is still poorly staffed, poorly funded, and poorly managed."[67] Knauft bemoans the number of philanthropy programs that are "reactive" rather than "proactive," responding case by case to requests for support rather than systematically adhering to "well-developed priorities."[68]

Transcorporate Networks and Classwide Rationality

For individual corporations, philanthropy is part of doing business, like marketing or advertising, finance or research and development. At the same time, corporate philanthropy is something more than simply the province of the individual corporation. It has developed as a collective business activity. Important corporate leaders and central business organizations have played major roles in shaping the rationale and directions of corporate giving. A culture of corporate philanthropy has developed which provides a common language for discussing why corporations should give money away, to what, and how.

Examining these elements of the history of corporate philanthropy helps us understand an important contemporary fact: Corporate giving is "embedded" in social relationships. That is, how much a corporation gives and to what are shaped not only by the interests of the individual corporation but also by relationships among corporations, by transcorporate networks. As a result, corporate giving officers, though certainly very much creatures of their corporations, are not atomized actors. Grantmaking decisions, though done very much in the corporate interest, are not abstract economic calculations.

Sociologist Joseph Galaskiewicz, for example, studied corporate giving in the Minneapolis/St. Paul area in the early and again in the late 1980s. He found, not surprisingly, that "strategic factors" certainly affect the giving of Twin Cities firms. Those that are especially labor intensive and those that sell primarily to consumers are especially generous, more so if their employees or their sales tend to be concentrated in the Twin Cities area.

However, Galaskiewicz also found that the more ties that a CEO has to the local philanthropic elite, the more money his corporation gives away. Philanthropic generosity enhances not only the status of the CEO but also the reputation of the corporation as a successful, reliable enterprise and hence its ability to do business.[69] In related work, Galaskiewicz also discovered important ties at a lower level, among corporate giving officers themselves. They consult their peers in other corporations when they are uncertain about a particular grant, and peer opinion influences their evaluations of nonprofit organizations.[70]

In a similar vein, sociologist Michael Useem, using both a national sample of corporations and a sample from Massachusetts, concluded that

◆

intercorporate ties tend to create a degree of uniformity in corporate giving.[71] Large corporations, for example, tend to be more like each other in level and type of giving to the arts than are smaller corporations, in part because they are more likely to share information with each other. In addition, the more professionalized a corporation's giving program the closer its allocation of funds to major nonprofit areas (education, health, the arts) lies to the average for all companies. This is presumably because professional corporate giving officers frequently interact with their peers in other corporations through professional associations. Finally, those corporations most influenced by other corporations in their giving decisions and headquartered in areas with a higher overall rate of corporate giving to the arts are more likely themselves to support the arts.

Galaskiewicz concludes from this evidence that "network ties" and "sociocultural" factors are as important as "structural variables" in explaining corporate giving. Useem argues that intercorporate ties promote the application of "generalized business norms and procedures" to corporate giving. These ties, he adds, also encourage corporations to view philanthropy in terms of "classwide business considerations" rather than just "narrow company self-interest."[72]

> Professional and managerial networks typically stretch across many corporations, and they distill and communicate aggregated business outreach strategies that are distinct from individual business strategies. . . . Corporate contributions to nonprofit organizations (and to political candidates) . . . are shaped and embedded in networks that build upon—but at the same time transcend—the firm.[73]

Our discussion of the history of corporate philanthropy suggests that network ties influence corporate giving patterns because they are conduits for elite influence and for the culture of corporate philanthropy. As we have seen, however, this culture is not a simple vehicle for a "classwide rationality" or for "aggregated business outreach strategies." Although it encourages corporate giving officers to think in terms of the general interests of big business, it also urges them to focus all the more closely on their corporation's needs and goals and to tie their giving programs tightly to these. From its earliest days in the 1950s, it has cultivated *both* company *and* classwide rationales for giving and included a complex mix of themes.

As a result, the culture of corporate philanthropy sanctions a range of giving strategies. General Electric, for example, takes a classwide approach to supporting higher education by underwriting the graduate careers and early professional development of young science and engineering professors. It may well reap the long-term benefits of strong

◈

university programs in these areas, but so will all corporations that rely on science and engineering talent. In contrast, Chevron and many other corporations have limited their grants to higher education to those universities from which they recruit a substantial number of employees or with whom they have major research contracts, thus pursuing a company-oriented strategy from which each hopes to reap much of the benefits. Within the culture of corporate philanthropy each approach is equally legitimate and laudable, and corporate giving officers are about equally likely to hold out the one or the other as an exemplar of how corporate giving should be done.

Apparently contradictory classwide and company impulses developed together in the culture in joint opposition to an old style of corporate philanthropy that was nearly universal half a century ago and has given way only slowly. In contrast to the old practice of giving money to a narrow and predictable set of causes, Community Chests, Red Cross drives, and the like, the notion of enlightened self-interest has held out a wide range of causes to which corporations may legitimately give. In contrast to the old style in which corporate giving was seen as charity carried out at the whim of top managers, the notion of strategic giving has insisted that giving is and should be treated as integral to corporate strategy.

That broader and narrower rationales for corporate philanthropy developed together historically is important to keep in mind, because many observers too easily pull them apart. They do so by arguing that while enlightened self-interest guided corporate giving in the 1960s, 1970s, and early 1980s, a more strategic, company-oriented approach has taken over since the later 1980s. There is some truth to this, as we shall see in chapter 4. Certainly corporate philanthropists have been under great pressure in recent years to demonstrate the immediate benefits they offer the corporation. At the same time, however, the starkness of the change is overstated; both rationales have always been from the beginning of organized corporate philanthropy.[74]

The culture of corporate philanthropy mixes together classwide and corporate rationalities and does not unambiguously favor either. It simultaneously pulls philanthropy beyond the corporation to consider the broader relationship between big business and society and urges it to stick closely to its parent corporation. The salience of this culture and of the network ties that sustain it for individual corporate giving officers will become clear in chapters 3 and 4 as we look at the complicated relationship between corporate philanthropy and the corporation.

3

"A Wonderful Job"

The Workaday Worldview of Corporate Philanthropists

> I think that I probably have one of the best jobs in corporate America
> and sometimes I get together with my peers from other corporations
> and we all agree. What a wonderful job to be able to work for a great
> company and at the same time be able to address real social ills and
> needs!

This enthusiastic statement from the corporate giving officer of a major oil
company speaks as well for her peers in large corporations generally. What
is noteworthy here is not simply that they like their jobs, which comes
across in the excitement even the most dour of them convey in talking
about what they support and why, but what they like about them. It is the
combination of working for "a great company" and addressing "real social
ills and needs," a combination that strikes them as at once natural and
unique.

Outsiders may wonder how one can possibly do philanthropy for a
corporation, how one goes about giving away money for an institution
dedicated to making it. For the men and women who run the philanthropy
programs of the country's largest corporations, this in itself is not a
problem. Far from it: The working assumption of most corporate philanthropists is that doing good for society (as they see it) and doing well for the
corporation are not at all contradictory. They see themselves as serious
philanthropists and as serious corporate managers. Their talk moves easily
from corporate strategic interests to the needs of the homeless, battered
women, or teen mothers and back again. Corporate philanthropy, which
may appear to outsiders as a contradiction in terms, to them is simply a
seamless web.

Corporate philanthropists also see what they do as *sui generis,* as
different from both other kinds of philanthropy and other corporate
functions. They do not give money away quite the way that private
foundations with independent endowments do, they insist. They never
forget that they are corporate managers and that there is a "difference

◈

between a private foundation and a private enterprise" (as one put it). Their work contributes to the corporate bottom line, they maintain, but hopefully not in quite the same way as marketing or engineering, finance or advertising.

The emphasis on the naturalness and uniqueness of corporate philanthropy lies at the heart of an everyday understanding that nearly all corporate philanthropists share. Their *workaday worldview* can be understood partly by examining how they develop these themes. It can be clarified further by looking also at what corporate philanthropists do *not* say, or at least what only a few of them say. Although they are corporate managers, who emphasize the contribution of their work to corporate profit, hardly any of them take a purely utilitarian approach to philanthropy. Only a few, the "corporate animals," talk about grantmaking solely in bottom-line terms. Similarly, although most talk eagerly about the good their philanthropy does, even fewer, the "visionaries," situate their work in a broader vision of social change.

The relationship of philanthropy to the corporation, however, is more complicated than images of naturalness and uniqueness suggest. Despite the belief of corporate philanthropists that doing well for the corporation and doing good for society flow smoothly together, the place of corporate philanthropy in the corporation *is* problematic. Many corporate philanthropists acknowledge this, though in a way that puts their worries subsidiary to their fundamental optimism.

The most obvious problem is that overall spending for corporate philanthropy has been flat since the late 1980s and the budgets of many of the largest programs have declined. In times of corporate restructuring and downsizing, philanthropy programs are inviting targets for the cost-cutting corporate ax. The immediate fiscal squeeze, as well as the ways corporate philanthropists attempt to deal with it, moreover, exacerbate less obvious and more general contradictions inherent in corporate philanthropy itself. To survive in general, corporate giving programs need to involve top management and align themselves with the strategic interests of the corporation. Yet too close a relationship in each case threatens the autonomy of the giving program and the kinds of philanthropy that corporate philanthropists themselves value the most.

Chapters 3 and 4 look closely at the relationship between philanthropy and the corporation, as seen through the eyes of corporate philanthropists themselves. This chapter examines how corporate philanthropists conceive of their work as an unproblematic and distinctive activity, as a seamless web. The next chapter looks at the inherent contradictions of their enterprise, as they themselves portray it.

◈

At the same time, we shall look at how transcorporate networks and the culture of corporate philanthropy, which chapter 2 examined in the aggregate, figure in the lives of individual corporate giving officers. Among other things, we shall see how the workaday worldviews of corporate philanthropists, while drawing heavily on their common culture, also diverge from it in significant ways.

Men and Women of the Corporate Giving Program

Who are the men and women who run America's largest corporate giving programs? As we noted in chapter 1, they are mostly white and about evenly divided between men and women. Information provided by corporate giving officers from the forty-three of the fifty largest programs who consented to interviews points as well to four characteristics that will be important to our discussion.[1]

First, these corporate philanthropists are largely insiders to the corporate world. The charge by some right-wing critics that they are outsiders from the nonprofit sector (who smuggle into the corporation an ideology alien to it) is simply inaccurate.[2] In fact, about three-quarters have had careers solely in the corporate world and several other outsiders have mixed backgrounds. The few who have worked primarily in the nonprofit sector, furthermore, are often outsiders only in a formal sense. One, for example, had been a professor of nuclear engineering who had taken a number of leaves from academia to do business consulting. Several other outsiders have been in the corporate world for so long that they seem indistinguishable from their insider colleagues.

Second, within their companies, these corporate philanthropists rarely are members of top management. About 85 percent hold corporate ranks of "director," "manager," or lower. The rest are vice presidents; only one is a senior or executive vice president. One corporate giving officer described himself as "upper middle management" (and as "one step away from executive pay grade"), and that seems to fit his peers as well. Only about 15 percent report directly to the CEO, president, or other of the highest officers of the corporation, though an additional 43 percent report to senior or executive vice presidents. In addition, hardly any of these corporate philanthropists expect to climb much higher up the corporate ladder. Many expect to hold the same or a similar job five years hence; some of the older ones expect to be retired. Corporate philanthropists are very much company insiders, but they are not among those who run it.[3]

Third, most corporate giving officers have spent relatively few years

◈

actually doing philanthropy. The term "professionalism" may accurately capture the degree of organization and seriousness of what they do, but not the extent of their experience with it. Fewer than half had spent five or more years as corporate giving officers at the time of the interview, and only about one in four had had experience in philanthropy prior to their current job.

Finally, and most important, most corporate philanthropists have substantial contact with their peers at other companies and share a common sense of the world of corporate giving. The transcorporate network and the culture described in chapter 2 are not mere abstractions, but are a palpable part of their lives.

Asked with whom they discuss philanthropy outside their corporation, corporate giving officers not surprisingly name other grantmakers in their geographical area or industry as well as potential grant recipients. In addition, however, over two-thirds also mention national organizations for corporate giving, especially the Contributions Council of the Conference Board and the Corporate Grantmakers Committee of the Council on Foundations. (In contrast, only about one in four mentions major national private foundations or nonprofit organizations.) One corporate philanthropist, after ticking off several contacts in his industry and region, remarks:

> And then we have the Conference Board's Contributions Council which I'd almost say is indispensable to my work. That's about 55 of my counterparts. We get together about three times a year and devote a meeting to a particular subject whether it be health care, education, inner city—whatever it happens to be so that we'd have an in-depth discussion on all these various things.

Another says he is "frequently on the phone to one or another of my peers" on the Contributions Council "to size up what's been going on in other companies."

Partly as a result of these contacts, most corporate philanthropists talk with confidence and at some length about the world of corporate philanthropy generally, its positive developments and problems. They also share a sense of what programs are especially good and why.

Asked to name "exemplary" corporate giving programs (other than their own), 80 percent did so readily, often with supporting detail. Several of those who could not were new to their jobs. Another, who had been on the job several years, readily acknowledged that he *should* be more involved with his peers:

> We don't spend a whole lot of time going out to conferences and this is a failing. I'm not suggesting this is a strength, but . . . we just don't

give ourselves the luxury of a lot of time to see what a lot of other companies are doing and why.

More typical was the following response:

> There really are a number [of exemplary programs]! I believe Cliff Smith at General Electric does a fine job. I believe that they have developed a program that has two sides that I think are good. One is education and community development around the places where they have plants. Another one is at the college level: programs to help minorities succeed in science and engineering majors. . . . If I take an oil company . . . [there's] Skip Rhodes at Chevron. One of the things I think that he's done well is on a selective basis get his senior management involved in some demonstration projects. It increases the effectiveness of the program in a number of important ways. I think that Gene Wilson at ARCO has done some marvelous stuff in minority engineering programs and community development in Los Angeles and other aspects of education. I think the RJR Nabisco Foundation, Roger Semerad, has done some fine things in elementary and secondary education. I think that Mary Stewart Hall who is at Weyerhauser (she's on a leave of absence right now) has been a very thoughtful grantmaker as well. I could go on . . .

This response is fairly representative in its enthusiasm as well as the sense it conveys of personal contact with peers and more than cursory knowledge of their programs.

All but one of those who did name exemplary corporations included at least one from outside their industry and headquarter city. The response of one corporate philanthropist is particularly interesting in this regard:

> Let's see. There're so many. I've just returned last week from a meeting of both the Council on Foundations and the Conference Board's Contributions Council and you hear about various programs that people do. Boeing has done some superb work in the Seattle area on K-12 [primary education]. Monsanto has done some good things. General Mills, AT&T, Aetna in Hartford, Southwestern Bell in education, Honeywell has done some fine things. And again I can go on— General Electric. It goes on.

Clearly, he is not at a loss for "exemplars"; they pour from his mouth. They range across the country from Hartford to Seattle and across the economy from packaged food and insurance companies to chemical and telecommunications firms. He knows about all this not through happenstance but from having recently attended national meetings of corporate philanthropists.

Corporate philanthropists, moreover, generally agree on what corpo-

◈

rate giving programs are the best. Although together they name forty-two different companies a total of 138 times, just four get about 40 percent of these mentions: ARCO, IBM, AT&T, and General Electric. Another four get about another fifth: Chevron, Merck, Honeywell, and Johnson & Johnson.

In short, despite the fact that they work for diverse companies, from banks to cereal makers, department stores to oil companies, corporate philanthropists share a broad set of relationships with each other and a common sense of what their enterprise is about.

The Seamless Web

The central assumption that corporate philanthropists make is that doing well for the corporation and doing good for society fit smoothly together. This is expressed most clearly in the way they easily slip from the utilitarian rhetoric of corporate profit to the moral rhetoric of philanthropy and back again. It is also expressed in the way they distinguish corporate philanthropy as a distinctive activity from both other kinds of philanthropy and other corporate functions.

The Mixed Rhetoric

Ron Starks has managed corporate contributions for an oil company for a little more than six years.[4] Before coming to his current job, he spent nearly thirty years in various positions both in operating units and at corporate headquarters. Like most of his peers, he had had little experience doing philanthropy before landing his current job, a position he seemed to fall into during a corporate reorganization:

> I came over to see the Manager of Community Affairs when we were going through the reorganization of 1986. And he said to me, "Have you ever thought about going into corporate contributions?" And I said, "Quite frankly I don't know much about it, I know we have it but—why don't you tell me about it." So he did and after he got through he said, "Would you be interested?" And I said, "Sure." And two days later they offered me the job and here I am.

Not surprisingly given his vast background in the business end of the corporation and sparse one in philanthropy, Starks emphasizes the importance of "aligning your contributions program with the business" and sees a healthy trend among corporate giving programs toward emphasizing these ties when dealing with nonprofit organizations:

> Some of the greatest positives that we've had is that we're more focused on what we want to do and in what areas. We're also . . .

◆

indicating to the nonprofits, "Not only do you have needs, but we
have needs too. So recognize that, plus the fact that we want some
results." We're more and more results oriented, and so therefore it isn't
just giving you a grant and that's the last of it. We want to hear back.

Yet for Starks, corporate philanthropy is not simply one more contributor to the corporate bottom line. Although accountability of nonprofit
organizations to his philanthropy program and of his program to the
corporation preoccupy him, he is also deeply involved in doing philanthropy and seems genuinely enthusiastic about it. Indeed, Starks has
become a central figure on both the Corporate Grantmakers Committee
and the Contributions Council. He talks frequently about his "wonderful
job," one "you could savor for the end of your career." He highlights
especially contacts with the "community":

But believe me, if you're doing your job, you're out there in the
community, you're aware of what's going on, you meet a whole host
of people in all walks of life.

He cannot seem to say enough, moreover, about the various grants his
program has made. More important, like many of his peers, he talks at
length about ones that seem remote from the immediate interests of his
company. He dwells not on his program's extensive grants to universities
from which his company recruits scientists and engineers, but on "entre-
preneurial" grants to "fledgling" human service agencies. Asked about the
grants of which he is most proud, Starks replies:

There are a whole bunch. There's one here in [headquarters city] that we
did four years ago, which was to make a $125,000 grant to a fledgling
organization that was operating in the basement of a church. . . . We
gave them $125,000 as a down payment for the building they're in now,
and this is a group that turns out three or four thousand meals a day to
patients with AIDS.

He talks at length as well about support for battered women's shelters, low-
cost housing, and a program to help school dropouts.

Like most of his peers, in short, Starks doesn't want simply to align his
program with corporate interests; he also wants to "make a difference" in
society both by providing direct help to people palpably in need and by
helping new organizations or new ways of addressing old problems get
started. He moves easily between the two sets of concerns with no hint of
tension, for the most part.

Hannah James, who has run her company's giving program for four
years and worked in it for a number of years before that, emphasizes a
similar mix of themes. Assessing the positive developments in corporate

◆

philanthropy in recent years, James, like Starks, emphasizes the growing integration of giving programs into their companies:

> I see more companies integrated into their business, so there's not this nice thing that they do off to the side. . . . We want it to be integrated and to work with our people and not be a nice activity but much more part of our business. So I think there's a trend toward better integration.

Her giving program is indeed very integrated with her company: Primarily, it donates the company's high-tech products to universities where students who will be making future decisions about purchasing these products can become familiar with them. Yet asked to identify the grants of which she is personally most proud, James focuses instead on support for a homeless shelter and a program to help missing children.

James also mixes corporate and philanthropic themes in a second way common among her peers. To explain why her corporation has a philanthropy program, she initially invokes the language of social responsibility. Her corporation, she says, "has a responsibility to be part of [its] community and part of the bigger picture." This seems to imply a rationale for giving that transcends immediate corporate interest; yet, asked to elaborate, James slips without noticing into the language of day-to-day public relations. She mentions support for an AIDS program, which increased the "visibility" of the company and identified it as "one concerned for true quality of life issues," and for a popular concert series on public radio, which established a "commitment to the arts," an important part of the company's image. James continues,

> Investing in education and culture . . . raised our visibility through the years. Our CEO still gets letters today from other CEOs and customers about [the company's] commitment to the arts and the enjoyment that's brought into every American living room.

Another corporate philanthropist paints a similarly broad rationale for corporate giving; yet when asked what would happen if corporate giving disappeared, she focuses only on the immediate public relations disaster for the corporation: "There would be a lot of community groups, the government agencies with whom we deal, our own employees at all levels, all would be unhappy [with us]."

In short, Starks, James, and their peers move easily between two different ways of thinking and talking, an ease which reflects that for them corporate philanthropy is indeed a seamless web. Nearly all value closer alignment to the corporation as a positive development. As one corporate giving officer puts it:

◆

> I think corporate giving has become more focused. We've become a
> part of the business plan. . . . And we're held accountable. . . . You're
> not out there giving money away. You're not just wining and dining.
> You've got to have some justification as to why you're doing it and how
> it impacts the business.

But they also value doing discrete bits of good in creative ways. One corporate
philanthropist describes his favorite grants as "enabling grants, visionary
grants," ones that started new programs whether in early science education or
teen drug abuse prevention that later became models in their field.

Private Foundation vs. Private Enterprise

Serving the corporation and doing philanthropy flow together easily in
the minds of corporate philanthropists partly because they understand
each activity in a distinctive way. On the one hand they distinguish their
philanthropy programs favorably from private foundations. On the other
hand, they believe that they serve the corporation in a way different from
many other corporate functions.

A number of corporate philanthropists readily distinguish their giving
programs from those of private foundations. The distinction may seem
confusing at first, because some corporations also organize their giving
programs as corporate foundations. Yet, the Ford Foundation (private) is
quite different from the Ford Motor Company Fund (corporate). A private
foundation is endowed with sometimes substantial amounts of money
from an individual or family fortune. It has no legal connection to any
corporation. A corporate foundation is established by a corporation as one
way of running its philanthropy program. Compared to a simple "contributions program," a foundation allows a corporation to put aside more
money than it donates in good times and donate more than it puts aside in
bad times. It is usually responsible to trustees who include the top officers
of the corporation and rarely has any appreciable endowment.

Barbara Connors has worked in contributions for over a decade,
heading her company's foundation for the last three years. Before that she
worked in the nonprofit sector. After lamenting the tight budgets of the
early 1990s, she tried to explain how the fiscal constraint is nonetheless
positive. Corporate giving programs are going to have to act more like part
of the corporation and less like private foundations, she says. For one thing,
they will have to do with less staff:

> We won't have the private foundation look that we had in the 1970s
> and 1980s. A lot of [corporate] foundations really looked like private
> foundations. I mean, we had a staff of seventeen when I arrived here

◈

in 1981. We got down to one and we're back up to four. We will never
be at seventeen again.

For another, they will have to build "coalitions" within the corporation to
gain support and to gather the expertise that a staff would otherwise
provide. Corporate philanthropies will have to "network" within the
corporation, "create synergy and consensus" to survive. They can no
longer stand aloof (if they ever could). "There's going to be less hubristic
largesse and a little more strategic, focused contributions and investment,"
she concludes.

Connors here makes a virtue of necessity. Corporate giving programs
do not have the large budgets and staffs of private foundations; but that is
all right, she implies, because much of this is mere padding and leads to
"hubristic largesse." Furthermore, once pared back, corporate giving
programs have to spend more time doing precisely what makes them
unique and important, perfecting their strategic ties to the corporation,
drawing on the corporation's many resources and serving its many needs.

Other corporate philanthropists draw a contrast with private foundations
as a way of explaining the particular constraints under which they work
when dealing with a politically controversial grant. Corporations, unlike
private foundations, they note, have to be sensitive to consumer opinion;
they cannot just give money to anyone they choose. As one puts it:

> Well, you know, we are not a private foundation. We're a private
> enterprise. That is quite a difference. . . . I think if our customers rose
> up in large numbers [in opposition to a particular donation], that very
> definitely could influence our plans.

In short, corporate giving officers implicitly define philanthropy in a way
that makes it inherently part of the corporation, separating it from more
independent kinds of organized giving.

Philanthropy Isn't Marketing

More often, corporate philanthropists try to distinguish what they do
from marketing or public relations. To be sure, corporate philanthropy
serves the corporate bottom line, but in a different way, they maintain. This
sentiment is particularly striking when it comes from managers who have
made careers in engineering, finance, or some other more "businesslike"
part of the corporation. They speak frequently about how corporate
philanthropy serves the corporation only indirectly by improving the
quality of life in the community in the long run or about how it is simply
different from other corporate functions.

◈

Ron Starks, for example, despite his emphasis on "aligning" philanthropy with the corporation, remarks that while it is certainly reasonable for senior management to expect a "return" for its philanthropic "investment," this is "not like the return on a tanker or a pipeline or a service station." That is, it is not that direct or that easily measured.

Mark Peters elaborates on this point. He worked in corporate finance at a chemical company for over two decades before becoming manager of corporate contributions eight years ago. Like Starks, he has become a major figure in the world of corporate philanthropy, playing a leading role in the Contributions Council. Although he also acknowledges that his philanthropy program must serve corporate interests, he stresses the "indirect" nature of this relationship:

> We spend a lot of time and effort in identifying what the needs are in our various communities. They range from substance abuse problems to environmental problems, education problems, and we will try and focus our programs to make a difference in those areas that the community feels are important. And obviously, the indirect business relationship is there, that's where you're doing business and that's where your people are hired from, and to the extent that the community feels good about [us], we're in a better position to operate in those areas. But [the key is to] address the community needs and to make a difference in what it is that we're doing.

Wilma Carter has run her bank's giving program for three years after eight in branch banking and before that another ten in the public sector. Like Peters, she emphasizes that corporate giving is supposed to serve corporate interests indirectly and in the long run, and she contrasts this with the sponsorship of highly visible events like marathons or concerts in the park:

> I think we feel and I think most [corporations] feel that by trying to improve the quality of life . . . either across-the-board or in certain focused areas, [we] will ultimately improve the overall economic health and well-being, the societal well-being in the areas where our employees and customers live and work, which will in turn positively affect the bottom line down the road without there being a direct connection.
>
> I would separate to some degree corporate contributions and sponsorships. Clearly where you give sponsorships there's more of a PR focus. There is definitely more self-interest. But most corporations are not trying to make every single last one of their contributions visible.

In a similar vein Harriet Paulson, who has directed her company's

◆

giving program for six years and worked in public affairs there for a total of fifteen, spends some time distinguishing appropriate and inappropriate notions of corporate giving. Corporate philanthropy should not be driven by marketing considerations, she says, giving to organizations seen as good bets for buying the energy conservation equipment her company produces. "We're not going to do it, if the reason people want to do it is because it's going to bring them business directly." Instead, corporate philanthropy should have distinct focus areas independently determined by assessing community problems. If as a result of these donations, people perceive her company as "a good corporate citizen" and this helps business, she says, "I'm not opposed to that." After all, "we can't be sitting here not having any connection to the company."

In short, corporate philanthropists typically believe that ideally corporate philanthropy serves the corporation, but not necessarily by directly affecting the bottom line. It thus distinguishes itself from other corporate functions, or at least ought to do so. We shall see in chapter 4 that matters are not always this simple.

Exceptions That Prove the Rule

The understanding that corporate philanthropists share about their work comes across in what they do not say as well as what they do. Few of them express fundamental skepticism about the place of philanthropy in the corporation and emphasize the need to overhaul it systematically to make it more businesslike. Fewer still paint grand visions of social change in which corporate giving programs become part of a broader alliance of private foundations and nonprofit organizations and hence are pulled away—at least conceptually—from the corporation.

The Corporate Animal

Winona Kenan is one of the very few skeptics. President of her company's foundation, she is also an executive vice president in the corporation, which makes her the highest ranked manager in my sample. Her office is located in a suite housing those of other top executives of the company. She has worked in philanthropy for three years, coming to it after nine years running various operating areas in the company and additional experience at other firms in the same industry. She describes herself as a "corporate animal," someone who goes wherever her company needs a job done. She came to the foundation because top management felt it needed "a little stewardship."

◆

Throughout our conversation, she consistently suggests that corporate philanthropy and the nonprofits they support are not sufficiently business-like. A few years before our interview, her foundation had inadvertently placed itself in a controversial political position by explicitly stating it would not fund organizations that discriminate against gays, including the Boy Scouts. This statement led to a firestorm of protest from right-wing groups throughout the country. While Kenan (and other top executives) stood by their position, they decided in the aftermath to cut back philan-thropic donations drastically and were contemplating ending their giving program altogether. What interests us here is the way she explains this decision. "We have no obligation to be philanthropic in our activities," she reminds me.

> Every corporation has a million things to worry about and this is money that could be going back to shareholders. We could use it for employee benefits. It's not that much money, but it's the principle. . . . We have no obligation.

Talking more generally about why her corporation gives away money, Kenan at first invokes a norm of reciprocity: "We make money in those communities and we like to give back." However, asked about the argument that corporations have no responsibility to the community beyond providing jobs and paying taxes (a paraphrase of Milton Friedman that I often threw at CGOs) she disarmingly says, "I don't disagree with that. The way we're going, we may end up right there."

Discussing the most important positive developments in corporate philanthropy in recent years, Kenan unhesitatingly says that the most important thing that corporations give nonprofit organizations is not money, but business discipline:

> I think the positives are the more businesslike scrutiny of the nonprofits and the discipline we've seen in the nonprofits. . . . Without it I think that many of those nonprofits just would cease to function in this very difficult environment, so I think corporations are doing them a favor by being hard taskmasters.

> Corporations are beginning to force nonprofits to run more like businesses and be really accountable.

Two or three other corporate giving officers sound similar themes. One complains that too many nonprofit organizations are either misdirected or inefficient and hopes that corporations could make them more account-able. "But it's like turning the Nimitz around," he says with an air of helplessness. Another speaks frequently of "accountability" and injecting a "businesslike perspective" into corporate giving, concluding, "I want to

◧

see these organizations that we're giving money to really doing what they say that they're doing and looking for some measurable goals."

Few of Kenan's peers talk this way, however. Although most emphasize the importance of accountability (of giving program to corporation and of nonprofit organization to giving program), few do so single-mindedly. Although many have faced substantial political controversies about grant-making, none has seriously considered terminating a whole giving program as a result. All others confronted with the Milton Friedman line about the limits of corporate social responsibility wave it away as old-fashioned or unrealistic. Asked about positive developments in corporate philanthropy, few focus solely on making nonprofits more businesslike (though few see anything wrong with this either). Instead they speak about exciting new areas of funding or the growing sophistication of their work.

In general, most corporate philanthropists do not share Kenan's thinly veiled suspicion of corporate giving and the nonprofit sector, a sense that unless carefully supervised they are not likely to be either sufficiently businesslike or of use to the corporation. They do not see the relationship between corporation, philanthropy, and the nonprofit sector as problematic.

Strikingly Kenan and her fellow corporate animals differ from their peers in another important way: They are marginal to transcorporate networks and the culture of corporate philanthropy. They de-emphasize their ties to national organizations like the Conference Board and the Council on Foundations and seem to have little sense of the national scene. Kenan, for example, mentioned no contacts outside her corporation except with other local grantmakers, and named only other corporations in her company's headquarter city on her list of exemplary programs.

The Visionary

Steve Clinton has been president of his company's foundation for three years. Before that he had been a university professor and adminis-trator, a career dotted with occasional leaves to consult for corporations. He sees his being hired by his current company as part of its effort to "professionalize" its giving program, a term he uses in a way different from most of his peers:

> They [top management] were concerned with higher education . . .
> [and] decided to get someone who understood that area very care-
> fully. They also wanted to bring more focus to it. They wanted to
> professionalize the foundation a little bit in the sense that one of my
> charges was to bring people in who were not necessarily inside [the
> corporation] but people who by their very achievements knew the
> area they were giving to.

◈

Unlike most of his peers, Clinton understands professionalism not in terms of business savvy or discipline but experience in the area being funded. He contrasts the mixed bag of people he finds in corporate philanthropy unfavorably with private foundations, run "by a staff with people who are professionals in their discipline." He thus at the same time reverses the contrast most of his peers draw between the two kinds of giving.

This is not to say that he dislikes doing philanthropy for the corporation. To the contrary, as an educator, he finds working on his foundation's large program of education grants "a real pleasure." Indeed, he quips, "I spend more time on education than I ever did as chancellor of a university." Unlike in his former job, he now has the time to "think about curriculum, new ways of educating kids for the twenty-first century in engineering or business or science."

Still, Clinton holds himself separate from the world of his peers in other ways. Like only a few others, he markedly prefers contacts with the nonprofit sector to those with other corporate giving officers. Asked about with whom he discusses philanthropy outside his company, he ticks off Independent Sector, the National Science Foundation, the Institute for International Education, and similar organizations. Asked explicitly about the Contributions Council and the Corporate Grantmakers Committee, which most of his peers put central to their outside contacts, he replies,

> Well, I have to be honest with you. That's not where my interests lie. My interest is with what the National Science Foundation is doing, with what the Institute for International Education is doing. It's with what the universities that I'm involved with are doing. That's where I get my kicks. That's what turns me on. The Contributions Council bores the hell out of me and I don't even go to the Council on Foundations meetings. I don't know how many ways you can talk about the act of making grants. It's just, to me, a lot of it is repetitious and on a nonstimulating level.

It makes sense that Clinton's corporation hired an outsider with a broad interest in education, because it has committed itself to a broad program of support. While many other companies focus grants on universities from which they recruit large numbers of employees or with whom they have substantial research contracts, this company has undertaken to help train and support a new generation of university professors in science and engineering. As Clinton explains it,

> One of the major concerns has been [that] in order to continue to have good people from a lot of the universities adequately educated, you've

got to have cracker-jack faculty. And there have been enough reports out indicating that we're going to have a lot of professors retiring in the next ten to twenty years. And in engineering, it's even going to be more critical. The other thing that we have noticed is a much smaller number of American youngsters going on to get Ph.D.s in the sciences. . . . The picture is even worse when you think of women and minorities.

Clinton's company is not simply using grants to colleges and universities to serve its interests in a simple, direct way by targeting "those institutions from whom we recruit." It is investing in the long-term viability of its enterprise by helping underwrite the careers of those who will educate its future employees. To be sure, the corporation will benefit from this, but the benefit is long-run and will inevitably be shared with other corporations (and perhaps society in general).

This is not to lionize Clinton's company. It has committed more than its share of depredations on American society, as any social activist would tell you. Nor is it clear that corporate philanthropy is better when it casts its net broadly rather than narrowly. If one is wary of corporate power to begin with, the closer it stays to home the better. Finally, as Clinton himself acknowledges, not all of his company's education grants are so broadly conceived; many are conventionally targeted to "those institutions from whom we recruit."

The point is that Steve Clinton articulates something that most of his peers do not. He expresses what we have called "classwide rationality," an approach to corporate philanthropy that focuses on the benefits it offers not just to the individual corporation but to corporate America as a whole. This broad vision is a rarity in the workaday worldview of corporate philanthropists, and the few who articulate it have strong ongoing ties outside the corporate world.

Workaday Worldview and Official Culture

Corporate philanthropists picture their work as both natural and unique. These themes are central to their workaday worldview. They also resonate with the official culture of corporate philanthropy, the body of written practical advice and philosophical ruminations whose development we traced in chapter 2. In its broadest arguments for corporate philanthropy, the official culture also pictures doing good for society and doing well for the corporation as naturally in harmony. The idea of enlightened self-interest, a concept central to the official culture and often used as well by corporate philanthropists, encapsulates the idea that philanthropy serves the corporation in a unique, perhaps indirect way that may well distinguish its role from that of marketing or public relations. The notion of strategic giving, again central to the official culture and important as well in the workaday worldview of corporate philanthropists, stresses that its connection to the company makes corporate philanthropy different from other kinds of organized giving.

The congruence between official culture and workaday worldview is not surprising given what we have learned about the relationships of corporate philanthropists to each other. Most of them not only interact with peers in their own industries and regions but also participate in national organizations like the Contributions Council and Corporate Grantmakers Committee. Nearly all share a clearly articulated sense of the field in which they work, right down to a high degree of agreement on which programs are paragons of what they do.

The differences between the official culture of corporate philanthropy and the workaday worldview of corporate philanthropists are also striking, however. In particular, while a classwide rationality—a broad vision of how philanthropy may serve not just the individual corporation but corporate America as a whole—is frequently presented in the official culture, it is rarely articulated by corporate philanthropists. They may have powerful notions of doing good, but it is usually piecemeal good, not broad, long-term projects.

Corporate philanthropists rarely articulate classwide themes despite the fact that most of them are tied into national networks of corporate philanthropists, the kinds of ties that sociologists have argued should encourage a broader vision of corporate giving.[5] The irony is that this vision is articulated not by those whose ties outside the corporation are primarily to the national organizations of corporate philanthropy (and thus who are most exposed to the official culture) but those like Steve Clinton, who have strong ties to organizations in the nonprofit sector instead of or in addition to their intercorporate connections.

The irony, however, dissolves on closer inspection. To begin, although the official culture articulates a classwide rationality, it gives at least as much, indeed more, attention to a company rationality that encourages corporate philanthropists to fit their programs tightly to their corporations. More important, the broad vision essential to classwide rationality fits poorly with the workaday worldview of most corporate giving officers for two reasons. First, the everyday pressures of their work require them to focus on the more immediate interests of their individual companies, as we shall see in more detail in the next chapter. Second, a broad vision inevitably implies identifying large-scale problems, the solutions to which require long-term ties between corporate giving programs and a variety of nonprofit and public organizations. It thus tends to pull corporate philanthropy away from the corporation, at least conceptually. This makes even the most adventuresome corporate philanthropist a bit edgy.

Walter George provides a good example of this edginess. Head of his company's foundation for more than a decade and highly respected among his peers, George nonetheless talks differently from many of them. When he speaks of "strategic giving," for example, he means not primarily aligning corporate giving closely to the corporation, but rather a serious, systematic effort to address the causes, not merely the symptoms, of societal problems. When he talks of corporate self-interest, he emphasizes self-interest "rightly understood" (invoking Alexis de Tocqueville, which none of his peers do). Most important, he paints a grand vision of democracy rooted in strong local communities to be implemented by large-scale programs of development and empowerment for minority communities, including low-cost housing, better social service delivery, job and literacy training, and leadership training. The specific programs are certainly ones his peers applaud, but few paint the big picture so boldly. He talks of his corporate foundation as but one small part of this larger effort which should combine the efforts of nonprofit sector and government as well. In short, like Steve Clinton, he is a visionary.

After listening to George for over an hour, I commented that he seemed to describe himself almost "as part of the nonprofit sector," rather than the corporation. He seemed to agree, but in later correspondence, he was eager to clear up any misconception that "we do not align our priorities with the self-interest of the company."

Put another way, the official culture of corporate philanthropy is ideological, in the sense of having a broad understanding of American society and how large corporations should best position themselves in it. Corporate philanthropists, in contrast, seem to be of a much more practical bent. We shall see in later chapters that underlying this practical bent is in fact a broader social vision and a political strategy, but they lie largely hidden and unarticulated. They emerge only when certain kinds of political controversy interrupt corporate philanthropy, as we shall see in chapter 6.

4

"The Struggle between Looking Good and Doing Good"

The Dilemmas of Corporate Philanthropy

◆

Philanthropy programs are certainly part of the corporation and serve its interests, but their place in it is problematic and contradictory, more so than the images of a "wonderful job" explored in the last chapter convey. This is reflected in the ambiguous way that the official culture talks about corporate philanthropy. On the one hand, writings by CEOs, professional observers, and corporate philanthropists themselves, as collected in the publications of the Council on Foundations and other organizations, confidently assert that philanthropy is an integral part of the overall strategy of the corporation; it has become an accepted, grown-up function. On the other hand, this same literature pictures philanthropy programs as perennially insecure in the face of less-than-sympathetic senior managers under strong pressure to cut costs. It provides copious advice to corporate philanthropists on how better to "position" their programs in treacherous terrain.

In their conversations with me, corporate philanthropists betrayed some of the same ambiguities. As we saw in chapter 3, they usually picture their work as an unproblematic combination of doing well for the corporation and doing good for society, a "wonderful job." At the same time, significant concerns crept into our talks about budget cuts as well as deeper dilemmas.

One reason for concern is quite clear. After growing significantly for several decades, corporate spending on philanthropy has remained flat since the late 1980s. At some companies, budgets and staff have been dramatically slashed. Increasing international competition, a sluggish domestic economy, the possibility (or the reality) of mergers and takeovers all have created pressures for top corporate managers to restructure and downsize their operations. In this climate, corporate philanthropy programs are prime targets for cuts. Corporate philanthropists may regard what they do as integral to corporate well-being; senior executives are not always so sure.

The official culture articulates a clear, if not always easily implemented, solution to the fiscal squeeze on corporate philanthropy. Work all the harder to maintain the support and involvement of top management, tie the giving program all the more closely to corporate goals, and if possible, provide hard evidence that the giving program really affects the corporate bottom line.

Corporate philanthropy, however, faces problems that are deeper and longer term than the immediate fiscal squeeze. The position of philanthropy in the corporation is inherently contradictory, but not primarily because of a generic incompatibility between doing well for the corporation and doing good for society or the general incongruity of giving money away in a corporation dedicated to making it. Instead, the contradiction involves two more specific, subtle conflicts.

First, corporate philanthropy programs need to be close to top management, but not too close. On the one hand, like all functions in the corporation, but especially like those regarded as soft (i.e., as not having a clear, direct impact on the bottom line), a philanthropy program needs the understanding, support, and involvement of the CEO. On the other hand, philanthropy programs need to maintain their autonomy to avoid reverting to being (in the words of one corporate philanthropist) "playthings of the CEO." If an apathetic, unappreciative CEO is a bad thing, one eager to impose a personal charitable agenda is hardly better, especially given the historical roots of corporate philanthropy reviewed in chapter 2.

Second, corporations may be too impatient to wait for the more indirect, long-term ways in which their philanthropy programs may serve corporate interests by making society a better place to live. They may insist on palpable benefits in the short term, especially in the form of a clear boost to the corporate public image. Once doing well for the corporation is defined in this way, it may well come in conflict with doing many kinds of good for society, including those that corporate philanthropists most like. One corporate philanthropist has called this "the struggle between looking good and doing good," a theme echoed in other words by several of her peers.

Both these problems underline that corporate philanthropy programs and those who run them have contradictory needs for close ties to the corporation and a degree of autonomy from it. The fiscal squeeze and the strategies adopted to deal with it often exacerbate this contradiction, but they do not create it.

◆

The Fiscal Squeeze

Corporate spending on philanthropy increased dramatically from midcentury until the mid-1980s. From 1975 through 1987 alone, spending doubled in real terms from $3.7 billion to $7.3 billion (expressed in 1995 dollars). From 1987 on, however, corporate philanthropy stagnated, amounting to only $7.4 billion in 1995 (again, expressed in 1995 dollars). As a percentage of corporate profits, giving fell by half from 1.91 percent to 1.17 percent between 1987 and 1994, according to one estimate.[1] At some major corporate giving programs, things have been worse than that, with budgets and staff cut significantly. The most dramatic case occurred in the summer of 1994. As part of a broader corporate cost-cutting plan, the ARCO Foundation dismissed its president, Eugene R. Wilson, and most of his staff and announced plans to reduce its giving by 40 percent. The planned cuts, moreover, came on top of already draconian budget reductions. In 1991, the Foundation had given away $29.8 million, by 1994 just $12.5 million.[2] The ARCO Foundation, moreover, was not just any corporate giving program; it was one of the most prominent: In my interviews, corporate philanthropists named it more often than any other as an exemplary program.

Kodak, long a paragon of corporate civic duty, cut its donations 35 percent nationally from $20 million in 1988 to $13 million in 1994. Pressed by growing international competition, it also began rethinking its extensive and increasingly expensive commitment to affordable health care in the Rochester, New York, area, its headquarters.[3]

Not surprisingly, the fiscal squeeze preoccupies corporate giving officers at major corporations. Asked about the major problems facing corporate philanthropy in the early 1990s, they emphasize tight budgets above all else. Ron Starks, whom we met in chapter 3, puts it this way:

> The number one problem is as a result of the economy that we find ourselves in. There are certainly many more needs out there with fewer corporate resources. . . . We reduced our corporate giving program from 23 million last year to 19 million this year simply because we have to cut back in all areas.

"There are more needs than we have money," Starks continues.

> We are getting more and more requests from people and organizations that we have never heard from in the past: police departments, fire departments, all sorts of government agencies that—I mean schools, my gosh schools, I mean we could dump our whole worldwide contributions project into one district here in [our headquarters city] . . . and probably not make a dent.

◈

The same concern came out vividly at a 1994 conference on corporate philanthropy sponsored by the Mandel Center for Nonprofit Organizations and the Indiana University Center on Philanthropy. The corporate philanthropists attending emphasized repeatedly the importance of generating research that might document that what they do is a "hard" part of the corporation, that it, in other words, contributes directly to the "bottom line."[4]

The official culture of corporate philanthropy has been quick to diagnose the sources of the fiscal squeeze and to suggest remedies. Reports from the Council on Foundations have been especially attentive to the problem. A 1991 publication titled *How to Position the Corporate Grantmaking Program* notes that

> even the most successful company giving programs are not immune to the effects of such financial adversities as mergers and acquisitions, budget cuts, global competition, and the nation's changing economy.[5]

Competition, the specter of hostile takeovers, and a sluggish economy put pressure on top management to make their companies leaner and meaner, and this pressure is transmitted downward to the corporate philanthropy program as well as other functions. The persons running American corporations, moreover, have changed in recent years, argues another Council report, *Corporation Giving in the 1990s—The Next Generation.* CEOs have come to their current jobs after fewer years with the corporation (and more experience in other corporations). More important, their backgrounds have changed: They come to the executive suite more frequently from finance, sales, and marketing and less often from production, engineering, or general management than a generation before. The implications are that the new generation of CEOs has less time to get to appreciate the company's philanthropic agenda and has corporate experience that encourages a relatively short-term mentality.[6]

The official culture remains optimistic in the face of these pressures. "There are methods to strengthen the giving program to lessen its vulnerability," the Council on Foundations announces hopefully. One "key" is the time-honored one of cultivating "the support of the company's chief executive officer, his or her successor, top management, and employees in general."[7]

Another remedy, equally time-honored, is to tighten the ties between the focus of corporate philanthropy and the strategy of the corporation. In the late 1980s and early 1990s this advice has often meant tying corporate giving closer to or making it more like marketing, sales, or personnel functions.

◈

For example, in a 1987 *California Management Review* article, Timothy S. Mescon and Donn J. Tilson hail the emergence of "a more market-driven strategic management, bottom-line approach to philanthropy" with corporations using it much "like sales forces or advertising, to advance their business objectives." They present as exemplars of this "new" kind of corporate philanthropy a variety of sponsorships of highly visible athletic and cultural events as well as "cause-related marketing," which advertises that a company will donate to a popular cause every time someone buys its products or services. The overall implication is that corporate philanthropy works best when it contributes visibly and immediately to the corporation's public image.[8]

Corporate Philanthropy Report, a monthly newsletter popular among corporate giving officers, heralds in its November 1991 issue the "destruction of the wall that had separated corporate philanthropy from corporate communications," including public relations, advertising, sales promotion, and internal communications. The newsletter views this not as "just a matter of grantmakers kowtowing to the marketeers," pointing out that corporate philanthropists can use the corporation's public relations, promotional, and marketing capacities to further their philanthropic goals.[9] Still, they emphasize donations that have a direct impact on public image or recruitment. The *Report* urges corporations, for example, to direct donations for higher education carefully to colleges and universities from which they recruit heavily.[10] It also warns that corporate giving programs face perilous financial times unless they "can think of ways to heighten 'visibility' (a euphemism for good press) of their own companies as a result of their donations."[11]

Yet another recommended way of dealing with the fiscal squeeze is somehow to provide clear evidence that corporate philanthropy directly enhances the corporate bottom line. Corporate donations are now seen as "social investments" that "aim to add value for the company as well as for the recipient," concludes a 1995 Conference Board survey of grantmakers.[12] "Measuring impact. Adding value to a corporation. These are important concerns of corporate grantmakers and community affairs players in the 1990s," reports *Foundation News.*[13]

At the 1994 conference on corporate philanthropy, Craig Smith, editor of *Corporate Philanthropy Report* and keynote speaker, elaborated on this idea:

> Corporate philanthropy now is required to demonstrate how it can "add value" to business strategies while still advancing social causes.

◆

But to do this corporate philanthropy practitioners need the results of good research.

Smith holds out as exemplars other corporate functions that have used "research" to show their usefulness for the corporation—to show, in other words, that they are "hard," not "soft" functions: sponsorships, government affairs, human resources management, and research and development. Once corporate giving officers "gain the research tools they need," Smith continues, "the field itself is sure to change."[14]

> Undoubtedly corporate philanthropy initiatives will emerge from the bargaining between the in-house foundation executive and the managers who control marketing, human resources, and other functions. Increasingly, we will see hybrid projects simultaneously funded from business units and philanthropy. And more companies will find their own version of, say, Ronald McDonald House—projects that serve as an overall rallying point for all semi-autonomous members of a disparate corporate family.[15]

Cultivate the CEO ever more assiduously, tie corporate philanthropy ever more closely to other corporate functions, show more clearly how corporate philanthropy contributes to the bottom line—these are all variations on the time-honored theme of strategic giving. They are also the voice of realism in the world of corporate philanthropy today.[16] They offer a way of surviving the fiscal squeeze. As we shall see, however, they also threaten to intensify the underlying dilemmas of corporate philanthropy, its problematic relationships with both the CEO and the corporation in general.

Close to the CEO, but Not Too Close

The importance of having the support of top management when a company is undergoing general cutbacks and restructuring is certainly not lost on corporate philanthropists themselves. Mark Peters, already encountered in chapter 3, puts it this way:

> An awful lot of companies have been faced with cutbacks . . . , and the economic reality in the business world is putting severe pressures on the level of funding . . . and on staff in this profession [i.e., corporate philanthropy]. . . . I'm sure you can imagine that when you are laying people off and going through very severe cost reductions, it is difficult for many to say their corporate giving program is critical to the business success of your enterprise. A lot of people, I think, are facing

◆

that issue. We have . . . escaped many severe implications for our
program to date. That's, I think, because of the strong involvement of
our chairman and the senior management people in the whole
process [and their] understanding of the importance of it.

Of course, support from top management may be important for any corporate function, but note that Peters is quite candid why it is especially crucial
for philanthropy. Despite all the talk about the many ways that giving
money away helps a corporation make money, when the fat is in the fire,
it is hard to argue seriously that "the corporate giving program is critical to
the business success of your enterprise." In other words, the philanthropy
program needs special support from top management because of its
perceived softness.

Peters, however, also emphasizes the dangers of too much CEO
involvement:

When I first came into the profession [in the early 1980s], it was a lot
more of the CEO-directed type of giving. They just gave wherever the
CEO wanted it to go, or senior management wanted it to go. . . . It's my
belief that the profession is working away from that now, and is
becoming more professionalized in its approach.

Asked to clarify the appropriate role for the CEO, Peters replied by in
effect distinguishing CEO "involvement" from CEO "direction," thus suc-
cinctly stating a central dilemma of corporate philanthropy. On the one
hand, corporate philanthropy programs really need "senior management
involvement and support," so that they "have an understanding of what it's
all about and the benefits that are generated from it." On the other hand,
giving programs need to avoid a situation in which CEOs "have their own
individual charities that they want to see the money go to."

Other corporate philanthropists in effect outline the same dilemma by
discussing both the importance of CEO involvement and the dangers of
CEO direction. That corporate giving programs need to cultivate CEO
support reflects the common sense of corporate giving officers as well as
the conventional wisdom of the official culture. Nearly all corporate
philanthropists claim that their relationships with top management are
quite good or talk about the importance of cultivating such relationships.

At the same time, several note pointedly why maintaining CEO involvement may be difficult (at other corporations, they usually say, not
their own). Drawing upon the official culture, they emphasize both the
background of new CEOs and the nature of economic conditions. The
problem is complicated, some argue, by the high rate of turnover at the top
and by the rise of a new generation of senior managers who have not

cultivated a sense of civic responsibility, perhaps because their track to the top has simply been too fast. As one corporate philanthropist put it in a matter-of-fact way:

> I think that everyone knows that there's this new generation of corporate leaders that didn't grow up necessarily with the tradition of civic involvement. They got to where they are because they worked fourteen hours a day, six days a week on sales or marketing, or engineering or one of the functional areas of the company. They're going into corporate leadership at fairly young ages. . . . Frankly, they have never been involved in a civic and community world the way their predecessors have who grew up in a slightly slower time and I think had a little bit more time on issues beyond the bottom line.

The problem, then, is "to educate . . . the next generation of leadership on the value of this function [i.e., philanthropy] and not have it just sort of a red flag for cost containment."

To others, the difficulty of establishing relationships with CEOs stems from the fact that they are too busy dealing with adverse economic conditions to bother with other matters:

> Over the last couple of years by virtue of the economic environment in which we've operated, the CEO has not typically been oriented to being involved in a lot of outside activities and therefore having a real grasp of what the issues are that people in my field deal with day in and day out. There isn't the level of interest in contributions that there was let's say in the 1970s and early 1980s on the part of senior management.

The problems of maintaining CEO involvement in corporate philanthropy aside, several corporate giving officers make the opposite point as well, that corporate giving programs need a degree of autonomy from top management. More important, this idea is implicit in the common sense of corporate philanthropists, in their notion of professionalism and in the way they define their job and their identity.

While most corporate giving officers boasted about how frequently and easily they interacted with the CEO or Chairman (over the phone and by memo, if not in person), one brought me up short by forthrightly acknowledging that he rarely sees his current Chairman, who was, he figured, too busy dealing with record losses to concern himself with philanthropy. Then he added:

> My own feeling is that the less contact you have the more professionalized the function becomes because it is delegated the full responsibility for managing this particular activity. Because if you go

◨

back to how corporate contributions were started, it was often the handmaiden of the CEO or his spouse.

What gives this comment considerable authority is not only the source, who is one of the most senior corporate philanthropists with ten years of experience running two major philanthropy programs, but also the way he ties distance from the CEO to the very professional identity of the corporate giving officer, as this emerged historically.

Other corporate philanthropists similarly define themselves and their work in a way that implies the need for a degree of autonomy from top management. One way they do so is to draw pointed and invidious contrasts between the "professional" corporate philanthropy they do and an older regime of corporate giving. Fran Lunt, a career corporate manager who has worked for eleven years in the philanthropy program of a major manufacturing company, devoted considerable time to drawing out the difference between contemporary corporate giving and the old regime that was just ending (she said) during her first years on the job in the early 1980s. "I think there's been an overall trend of corporations taking a greater interest in what the philanthropy programs are doing," she says.

> I think until not too many years ago [corporate philanthropy] was sort of a backwater place where you sent someone and they just sort of handed out money. . . .
>
> When I first came into this particular position, I think I was coming in at the very end of what I would perceive as the old boys' network really. You know, the CEO telling the senior person who is about to retire that "the next year or so, Charlie, you handle our charitable giving."

Back in those days not long past, she adds later, corporate philanthropy was "just somebody doing good at the behest of the CEO."

This picture of the old regime is interesting. Corporate philanthropy was then a "backwater place," not taken very seriously because not very serious. In what ways was it not very serious? First of all, it was a place "where you sent someone," presumably anyone, regardless of background or expertise, an over-the-hill executive, nearing retirement and apparently not very useful anywhere. Connections, "the old boys' network," got one the job, not any special aptitude or promise. And no wonder: All you did was "just sort of hand out money," and writing checks requires no special expertise. Moreover, it was little more than charity, "doing good at the behest of the CEO," nothing significant.

This description captures the perceptions of many other corporate

◆

giving officers, for whom this old regime is not yet comfortably in the distant past. One described an old style of philanthropy "that was just sort of what the CEO had in mind at any given time, you know, . . . the old boys' network . . . if you do my charity, I'll do your charity." Another referred to a time when philanthropy "was run by senior executives who the company didn't want around any more, but they didn't know what to do with them, and they put them as the vice president of the foundation." Another noted that before he took over the helm of his program five years before, it had been run by a "writer in public relations," to whom the CEO had offered the job several years before retirement.

These images of what corporate philanthropy once was inform the sense corporate philanthropists have of what it should not now be. It should not be an activity for over-the-hill executives ("dysfunctional white males," as one relatively new female corporate philanthropist from outside the corporate world pithily put it); it should not be just giving money thoughtlessly away; it should not be just charity; and above all, it should not be the mere whim of the CEO. Pejorative phrases like "old boys' network," "just giving money away," and "charity" all are tightly connected to a negative image of CEO-directed giving.

Instead, to return to Fran Lunt, corporate philanthropy should be "integrated with the whole business goals of the company"; it should do "the right thing as far as the company is concerned and not just only the right thing for the community." It should "invest money wisely rather than just giving it away." This in turn requires an "overall professionalization of the field, a general upgrading . . . in terms of the awareness and in terms of the professional technical expertise of the participants."

These themes of strategic giving and professionalism, of course, are familiar ones in our analysis so far. They are central to both the official culture of corporate philanthropy and the workaday worldview of its practitioners. The important point here is how corporate philanthropists use them to justify a degree of autonomy from top management that they see as central to what they do and who they are, even as they otherwise emphasize the importance of close ties to the CEO.

Their ambivalent feelings are captured by the contradictory way they view the late 1970s and early 1980s. It was a time, some remember, when CEOs were more familiar with corporate philanthropy and had a higher "level of interest" in it than today's harried corporate chiefs. It was also a time when corporate philanthropy was more of a "backwater," merely "doing good at the behest of the CEO."

Corporate philanthropy, in short, needs to be close to the CEO, but not

◈

too close. The dilemma remains a sticky one because in fact the profession-alization and autonomy of corporate philanthropy have developed unevenly and continue to be tenuous.

As we saw in chapter 2, corporate philanthropy for a long time indeed was little more than "doing good at the behest of the CEO." Experienced observers of the field, moreover, disagree over how professionalized corporate giving has really become. Some have emphasized the great strides corporations have made: Sociologist Michael Useem has noted the proliferation of formal policy statements on giving, corporate foundations, and professional giving staffs. Hayden Smith, former head of the Council for Financial Aid to Education, speaks glowingly of corporate philanthropy attaining a "maturity of a very high order." In contrast, E. B. Knauft, former head of the Aetna Foundation, concludes from his close study of a number of major corporate giving programs that professional forms often belie unprofessional content. In many corporations, he concludes, decisions about contributions still tend to be "reactive" or "grant driven" rather than "reflecting established priorities." Historian Peter Dobkin Hall concludes that up to the 1980s, corporate philanthropy remained "underdeveloped and poorly understood." While he finds recent developments "encourag-ing," he reserves final judgment.[17]

Certainly, there are enough instances of disorganized giving among the very largest corporate philanthropy programs to justify the more cynical observers and to underline the extent to which professionalization even at the top of the corporate philanthropy world remains only partly achieved. At one of the largest corporate philanthropies, responsible for nearly $30 million in grants annually, the new head stressed in our conversation the previously ad hoc nature of his program and the control that top executives exercised over it:

> It's been more or less of a reactionary [sic] and sort of random decision on the part of our executives, [who] get together three times a year and say, you know, "Show me some requests. Let's pick a few." [laughs] And they've been well attended, and I think they've done some good, but we've never done it in a planned process.

The head of another, even larger philanthropy program said that her corporation "did not have an organized philanthropic program until I took over the program in January [1993]." Rather corporate giving was just "check processing." At still another, the giving officer reported that she was the lone professional manager running a program that gives away close to

$25 million a year. Finally, another corporate philanthropist, whose program disburses only a little over $10 million, described how until three years ago or so, corporate giving was pretty much a "random walk," with money given away to whatever requests came "over the transom" with little direction.

Not only is professionalization unevenly achieved but it may also be tenuous. For one thing, far from being totally oblivious to their philanthropy programs, top corporate managers have powerful incentives to direct corporate giving to organizations strongly favored by themselves and their peers—to become involved in the "wrong" way. Based on his study of the Minneapolis–St. Paul area, sociologist Joseph Galaskiewicz concludes that corporate giving is a kind of "social currency," a means by which the CEO wins and maintains status among the local business elite.[18] A study by the *Chronicle of Philanthropy* suggests that this happens in many cities, especially those with strong cultures of philanthropy (and hence high levels of giving relative to per capita income). As the head of the local grantmakers forum in one such city noted, "Charitable giving is kind of how you get ahead here. You give and you get involved in organizations. That raises your social capital."[19] Most CEOs, moreover, themselves emphasize personal, rather than business, reasons for getting involved with corporate philanthropy: a personal desire to contribute to a worthy organization, a personal sense of ethics, a personal background in social causes. All of this suggests that when CEOs do get involved with their company's giving programs, they may be eager to put their personal stamp on them.[20]

Staying close to the CEO, but not too close, is thus a general dilemma for corporate philanthropists, rooted in the distinctive history of what they do and the attitudes of top management toward it. The recent fiscal squeeze, however, exacerbates the dilemma by further undermining the professional autonomy of corporate philanthropy. One corporate philanthropist warned darkly that the old regime might easily come back: If the money and staff of contributions programs were cut too much in the face of hard economic times, he argued, serious grantmaking would become impossible, and the programs would quickly revert to mere check-writing operations and hence become the province of top management again:

> Money's going to be very scarce, staff is going to be even scarcer, which could turn corporate philanthropy offices into check-writing operations and if it becomes a check-writing operation, it'll go back to being CEOs and senior officers picking their favorite organizations and ones that they want to serve on the boards of and so forth.

◆

Looking Good vs. Doing Good

Corporate giving officers never forget for a minute that they are corporate managers and that their giving programs are there to serve the corporation. At the same time, they aspire to helping the corporation in a particular kind of way: Not necessarily by supporting projects that contribute immediately and directly to corporate interests, but by addressing what they see as real areas of social need, by "making a difference" in ways that may help the corporation only indirectly or in the long run.

As we saw in chapter 3, this is evident in the enthusiasm even the most matter-of-fact, businesslike corporate philanthropists convey about the grants in which they take particular pride even when these grants are rather remote from immediate corporate interests. It is also clear from how they talk about grantmaking in general. Recall Mark Peters's contention that the key to corporate giving is "to address the community needs," rather than thinking about immediate payoffs to the corporation. Remember too Wilma Carter's effort to distinguish philanthropy, which improves "societal well-being" and thus "positively affects the bottom line down the road," from sponsorships, in which there is more of an immediate "PR focus." Or Harriet Paulson's argument that corporate philanthropy serves the company, but should not be driven directly by marketing considerations.

To be sure, the distinction being drawn here is hardly airtight. Another corporate philanthropist, Warren Simpson, calls it a "sometimes fine line." Simpson, who has worked in engineering and personnel as well as philanthropy in his thirty-two-year corporate career, ticks off the goals of his giving program as we talk: having a positive impact on the company's communities, "accessing" people and technology, and enhancing "in the long term the ability to market products." Asked to explain how philanthropy might assist marketing, he elaborates:

> We have a lot of products that are marketed to not-for-profit organizations. . . . When our [marketing] people go to a university [for example], we want them to be armed with a knowledge base that includes information about what our contributions have been to the university, what our research grants have done, what our in-kind support to the school has been, not to use that in a heavy-handed, leveraging way, but yet to be knowledgeable about it. So, I spend time with our marketing people making sure they use that information prudently. I mean [laughs], the last thing in the world we want to do is waltz in there and say, "Well, look at all we're doin' for ya. You've got to . . . buy [our] products."

How direct the relationship between philanthropy and marketing ought to be is, to say the least, a bit fuzzy here. Simpson seems to say that

◈

the goal of donations to nonprofit organizations is to get them to buy more of his company's high-tech equipment, then to back off from this claim: It somehow helps if his company's sales staff come to universities armed with information about donations and research grants, but they should use this data "prudently."

The exact relationship was important enough to Simpson that he tried to articulate it more clearly in a follow-up conversation. He emphasized that "we don't make contributions with a goal of selling product" or exacting a "quid pro quo of any kind." Still, he maintained, nonprofit organizations may be more willing to buy the products of a company that has supported them with its philanthropic dollars. Indeed, he argued, nonprofits often want to know this information.

However fine the line between philanthropy as a relatively autonomous activity serving the corporation in a distinct way and philanthropy as a mere adjunct to marketing or public relations, most corporate philanthropists insist on drawing it. The distinction is central to their understanding of themselves and their work.

At the same time, they acknowledge frequent pressures within corporations upon philanthropy programs to yield a tangible, short-term return, pressures that make the distinction hard to maintain. The most common demand is for philanthropy to yield immediate public relations payoffs, hence the phrase "struggle between looking good and doing good."

Some corporate philanthropists see corporate giving as the victim of a general short-term mentality on the part of top management. One manager, who worked extensively in nonprofit organizations and government before doing six years of community affairs and philanthropy work with her company, explains the pressure on philanthropy programs to provide visible, short-term benefits to the corporation by noting acerbically that "the business community has the attention span of two-year-olds" coupled with a prejudice that they know how to do things better than nonprofit organizations. This leads them to a "quick-fix mentality" when it comes to dealing with social problems. (However, she exempts her own company, a "wonderful institution," from the indictment.) Only long-term public/ private partnerships to address pressing societal problems like community development or health care, she argues, can force corporations to expand their attention span.

Fran Lunt criticizes the short attention span of top management more gently, perhaps because she is a career employee with her company:

> I remember sitting in an audience and hearing [our CEO] say that 1989 was going to be our year of education, and at that very moment I remember thinking, "And what's 1990 going to be, our year of AIDS

◆

research, or this, that, or the other thing?" . . . There has been the tendency to say, "Let's just throw money at this issue and get a result and let's move on. . . ."

Other corporate philanthropists diagnose their dilemma more point-edly and fix the blame more narrowly. One argues that "the new corporate managers quite often have a very short-term outlook for results," because the threat of hostile takeovers creates "tremendous pressure to make your stock perform." Philanthropic grants, in contrast, "necessarily and prob-ably correctly have a long-term outlook and long-term impact." Another describes the impact of the specter of takeovers and mergers this way:

> I think [they] make it a lot more difficult for a company to be more altruistic and more longer term thinking. I think a lot of corporate philanthropy managers are having to cook up a lot of programs that have a lot of corporate benefits, some community benefits, but that have sort of their own interests first. They can wave it before the Board, . . . so they'll get refunded. I think that's a huge pressure, and this doesn't allow them to be very creative to get beyond those things that are self-serving.

Mark Peters blames the conflict between looking good and doing good on "communications and public relations people" who feel that "philan-thropy should be driven by public relations values," while "addressing needs and making a difference is kind of a secondary objective." As an example, he notes that his company gets to designate the recipients of some of the proceeds of a yearly charity athletic tournament that it sponsors. Public relations people, he complains, typically want to funnel the money to "organizations with which we can get the most press." His position in contrast is that "we identify . . . what the needs are in the community and tie the distribution of money into some specific needs and specific programs that address those needs." If the company can also generate some publicity around it, he adds, "that's well and good."

Even when corporate philanthropists emphasize the importance of making philanthropy businesslike and tying it closely to corporate inter-ests, they note the downside of strategic giving as well. One spoke enthusiastically about the importance of measuring carefully the impact of corporate grants. Then he added that to expect these measurable results to appear in the short term would undermine the very nature of philanthropy:

> Well, I think that there is a tendency on corporate boards to look for immediate results and I think that we have to guard against that. . . .
> We have to recognize at times that the results can only be observed indirectly at a great distance in time. And if the results orientation were to pressure us to abandon some of the more long-term or riskier

undertakings that we sponsor, I think that would be an unfortunate outcome.

Another speaks positively about how corporate givers have ceased to be mere do-gooders and have developed a more sophisticated sense of how giving can be linked to corporate interests. He adds, however, that this also has its drawbacks: Faced with tough economic times and pressures on profits, corporations may demand that grantmaking show short-term results, as they do with all operations. The most tenacious problems of society, however, require long-term investments that yield results only after a number of years. "If we don't look good, we're not empowered to do good," he notes. The best a grantmaking executive can hope for is to mix a little doing good with a lot of looking good.

Another corporate philanthropist, while denying that the "struggle between looking good and doing good" is a problem at his corporation, still implies it is an issue that he regularly has to address:

> Within our company . . . we're fairly lucky in that we have a senior management that is supportive of the things we do. . . . Because we have a balance of things that are short term vs. longer term, they understand that mix within our program and they're supportive of it. That's not to say that they don't put us through our hoops when we go and ask for money. . . .

Generally, corporate giving officers see the "struggle between looking good and doing good" as a difficult balancing act. One actually talks about

> the balancing act of the need to run a decent program that's got some integrity and some values and priorities, balancing that with your corporation's intense need to be known for what you're doing in the area of giving.

Another speaks at length about the difficulties of learning "to balance the looking good and doing good functions in corporate philanthropy in sensitive, intelligent . . . ways." He describes the situation in this way:

> Corporate philanthropy has two missions, two purposes. One is to serve a social group. The other is to represent a corporate self-interest. They're not mutually exclusive of one another, and the real magic of corporate philanthropy is to be able to serve both purposes well at the same time, and when you can do that, you're really running a good corporate foundation. But it's hard to do and we have to have staffs that are sensitive to those issues, that don't get it out of balance. If you get it out of balance, you're in trouble.

This passage captures the understanding corporate philanthropists have of their dilemma quite nicely: "Looking good" and "doing good" are not

◆

"mutually exclusive," but balancing them is "hard to do" and requires "real magic."

Whatever way corporate philanthropists understand it, the struggle between looking good and doing good is real. The pressure on them from top management to provide visible, short-term benefits to the corporation certainly reflects in part immediate economic conditions and the fiscal squeeze on corporations these have created. However, it also reflects a short-term mentality inherent in American corporate culture.

Robert Hayes and William Abernathy provided the classic analysis of the short-term corporate mentality in a 1980 *Harvard Business Review* article. Reflecting on the fact that the United States seemed to be losing its competitive advantage to Western Europe and Japan, they argued that the culture of top U.S. managers emphasizes short-term cost reduction over long-term investment in new products and technologies, a choice they termed "a broad failure of both vision and leadership." They blamed this short-term mentality on a number of factors from the changing background of CEOs to a relative lack of government and union constraints on corporate behavior.[21]

In a finer grained look at American corporations in the mid-1980s, Robert Jackall made a similar point. Based on in-depth interviews with managers in three major corporations, Jackall argued that the short-term criteria used to evaluate managers and the rapidity with which those on the fast track move through jobs encourage a "take the money and run" mentality that sanctions producing short-term gains for the corporation and that at an extreme may burden the corporation with long-term costs. More important for our argument, this ethos "makes it difficult to sustain organizational commitment to goals defined as socially important."[22] While their explanations differ, a number of other observers have likewise emphasized the short-term mentality of American corporate leaders.[23]

The Not-So-Seamless Web

The complex relationship between corporate philanthropy and senior management and the delicate balance between looking good and doing good are really two different versions of the same underlying problem: Corporate giving programs need a degree of autonomy within the corporation, from both senior managers and the demands of the short-term bottom line; yet powerful pressures threaten to undermine this relative autonomy.

Together these two dilemmas call into question the completeness of the picture that corporate philanthropists painted of their work in chapter 3, the belief that their work is a seamless web and the sincere enthusiasm that they have for their "wonderful job." Both the belief and the enthusiasm take for granted a degree of autonomy within the corporation that is problematic, a fact that corporate philanthropists themselves acknowledge.

The place of philanthropy in the corporation is tenuous partly because of the fiscal squeeze, but not because of this alone. To be sure, corporate restructuring and downsizing in the face of global competition, mergers and takeovers, and a sluggish economy inevitably put pressure on philanthropy budgets, which in turn limits the autonomy of the giving program.

This fiscal squeeze, however, merely exacerbates the underlying problems. Corporate philanthropy began as little more than a "check-writing operation" for the favorite charities of top management; it has risen from these humble beginnings (i.e., professionalized) only slowly and unevenly; and top managements may have strong incentives to reassert personal control over their giving programs. As a result, corporate giving programs inevitably face the problem of too much CEO involvement as well as too little. Similarly, the pressure on corporate philanthropy to offer short-term, visible benefits to the corporation results not only from the immediate fiscal squeeze but from the short-term mentality of American corporate culture generally. Consequently, the struggle between looking good and doing good is inherent to the enterprise.

The impact of the fiscal squeeze on the autonomy of corporate philanthropy, moreover, is exacerbated by the strategies recommended to forestall the budget ax. What the official culture tells corporate philanthropists and what they tell each other is that the keys to surviving corporate cost-cutting are (1) get closer to the CEO, (2) tighten the links between philanthropy and marketing, public relations, and/or human resources, and (3) provide palpable evidence that philanthropy serves the bottom line.

This advice is unexceptionable in its realism: Corporate philanthropy is part of the corporation and especially in hard times must show its worth to the company and work closely with other units. The problem lies less in what is said than in what is not said. There is little recognition that the proposed solutions to the fiscal squeeze may complicate the underlying dilemmas of corporate philanthropy and compromise its autonomy. There is even less attention to how that autonomy might be preserved. Recall that Craig Smith holds out support for Ronald McDonald Houses as an exemplary kind of corporate giving. Temporary accommodations for the families of hospitalized children are undoubtedly a fine thing, but how does corporate philanthropy sustain projects that are less visible or whose impact is more long term?

Here, as in chapter 3, the workaday worldview of corporate philanthropists diverges in an important way from the official culture of corporate philanthropy. This time, however, it does so in a different way. Chapter 3 argued that corporate giving officers lacked in their everyday thinking a broad vision of corporate philanthropy, something that the official culture had. Here, we find they have something the official culture lacks, a partial appreciation of the inherent contradictions of their enterprise.

5

Corporate Giving under Fire I

Planned Parenthood

Upsetting Someone with a Gift

"The last thing we want to do is upset someone with a gift," remarks one corporate philanthropist, whose capacity for understatement I came to appreciate. Since the mid-1980s, however, some corporations have managed to upset a variety of people with their gifts, and upset has led to protest.

Corporations, of course, are no strangers to consumer boycotts and other forms of protests. Groups of all political persuasions have routinely attempted to use the threat of lost sales, demonstrations, letter-writing campaigns, and other forms of pressure to get corporations to change what they produce, how they produce it, where they produce it, or how they market it.

What is relatively new, however, is protest focused not on how corporations make their money, but on how they give a bit of it away. Many of the complaints have come from the Right. The conservative Capital Research Center has routinely condemned corporations for supporting "liberal" public policy groups.[1] The American Immigration Control Foundation has criticized corporate support for such major Hispanic groups as the League of United Latin American Citizens, the Mexican American Legal Defense and Educational Fund, and the National Council of La Raza, because

> these organizations have consistently fought immigration control. They supported amnesty for illegal aliens and opposed sanctions against hiring illegals. They oppose every effective measure to control illegal immigration. All support bilingualism.[2]

Other conservatives have criticized corporate (as well as foundation and government) support for controversial art and the refusal of some corporations (including Wells Fargo, BankAmerica, and Levi Strauss) to support the Boy Scouts because of the latter's anti-gay policies.[3]

◨

Corporate philanthropy also has its progressive critics, though with notable exceptions they do not back up their criticism with threats of boycotts and other economic pressure. The National Committee for Responsive Philanthropy has routinely criticized corporations for not devoting more of their profits to philanthropy and for not being "more responsive to disenfranchised communities" in particular.[4]

Some corporations have managed to catch flak from several directions at once. Philip Morris, whose profits still come mainly from tobacco despite its acquisition of Kraft and General Foods, stands accused of using its grants to nonprofit organizations as a way of cleaning up its tobacco-stained image and neutralizing its recipients in political battles over tobacco. Anna Quindlen, for example, caustically describes the philanthropy of tobacco companies as "money laundering":

> Money made through cigarette sales is tainted by death and disease; money spent by Gay Men's Health Crisis is gilded by good works. It sounds like the title of a self-help book: "When Good People Take Bad Money."[5]

ACT UP, the gay activist group, urged consumers to boycott two Philip Morris products, Marlboro cigarettes and Miller beer, because of the company's support for Senator Jesse Helms. It also urged arts groups to refuse grants from Philip Morris. At the same time, conservatives have condemned the company for those very arts grants, which often go to experimental art.[6]

The most prominent controversy has concerned support for the Planned Parenthood Federation of America and its many local affiliates. In the late 1980s, this support became a bone of contention in many of the few dozen local United Ways that included PPFA affiliates among their recipients.[7] It also became an issue for corporations: Once viewed mainly as a provider of birth control, sex education, and other family planning services, by the mid-1980s PPFA was also seen as a major advocate of abortion rights. What had once been a comfortably "innovative" recipient of corporate largesse became increasingly "controversial" as it moved to the center of the abortion debate. A number of anti-abortion groups helped this along by pressuring corporations to stop their funding with letter-writing campaigns and consumer boycotts. This culminated in 1990 when the Christian Action Council announced a boycott of more than forty corporations alleged to be funding Planned Parenthood. Many corporate philanthropy programs had to deal with the issue in the late 1980s and early 1990s.

◆

Overall, the controversy had little effect on the financial health of Planned Parenthood. To be sure, the organization lost a significant part of its corporate funding and has had trouble attracting new corporate grants. Corporate support, however, has never constituted more than a tiny percentage of donations to Planned Parenthood, and increased individual donations have more than made up for the losses.[8]

Despite the limited impact on Planned Parenthood, the controversy and the boycott tell us a great deal about corporate philanthropy. A number of America's largest corporations did support Planned Parenthood (and many still do) and had to decide whether or not to continue funding. The decisions they made and how they made them are interesting in themselves. They also help to illuminate further two issues central to our discussion so far: the problematic position of philanthropy in the corporation and the role of a common culture and transcorporate networks in the working lives of corporate philanthropists.

To begin, the response of corporations to the Planned Parenthood controversy was twofold and quite paradoxical. On the one hand, those who could avoid the glare of publicity, either because they reached a decision before the boycott began or never got caught in its net, generally stopped funding Planned Parenthood. In a few instances, a pro-life CEO simply mandated that funding end; in others, there was a clear fear of imminent controversy; for still others, it was more of a nondecision or a decision whose rationale had been lost with the passage of time. The dominant theme among all was simply that political controversy was not a place for a corporation to be, if it could be avoided.

On the other hand, with one crucial exception, all those corporations who took the brunt of the storm—the bags of letters, the occasional headlines, and, in the case of banks, department stores, and oil companies, the torn-up credit cards—actually decided to continue funding. Some did so with little more than an apparent shrug; others seemed to agonize over the decision. These corporations too were eager to avoid controversy, but they had a different idea about how to do so. They had other reasons for their decisions as well.

In short, where corporations could decide the issue quietly and hence with few repercussions, they stopped funding Planned Parenthood. Where the decision was relatively visible and bound to anger someone, they continued funding. One thing we need to explain is this pattern of *Hidden Attrition* and *Visible Perseverance*.

The Planned Parenthood controversy is also interesting because it effectively separated out the dual goals of corporate philanthropy, doing

◈

good for society and doing well for the corporation. As corporate philanthropists define "doing good," Planned Parenthood is certainly a meritori-
ous organization to support. They agree that teenage pregnancy and
sexually transmitted diseases are major social problems, that sex education and pregnancy prevention programs are important social services, and
that Planned Parenthood is an excellent service provider. No one questions
any of these assumptions. Hence the logic of doing good unambiguously
requires corporations who targeted these issues to continue their support
for Planned Parenthood, whatever the controversy.

Doing well for the corporation, however, *might* dictate a different
outcome. Controversy raises the specter of bad press, or at least not the
glowing public relations pieces that philanthropy is supposed to elicit. It
means a possibly tarnished image. Boycotts raise the threat of lost sales,
which take forms ranging from written threats not to buy the companies'
products to such palpable things as shards of credit cards returned in an
envelope. The logic of doing well, as we shall see, does not unambiguously
dictate discontinuing support for Planned Parenthood but it does at the
very least complicate the decision.

In other words, the Planned Parenthood controversy makes "the
struggle between looking good and doing good" especially visible. In
doing so, it focuses attention as well on the problematic, complicated
place of philanthropy within the corporation in general.

A final important issue is whether corporate philanthropists dealt with
the Planned Parenthood controversy primarily individually or collectively.
Chapter 2 introduced us to the culture of corporate philanthropy and the
transcorporate networks that sustain it. Chapters 3 and 4 showed that these
are palpable realities in the everyday lives of corporate philanthropists, but
that their workaday worldview differs in important ways from the official
culture. How did culture and networks come into play on this issue? Did
corporate philanthropists discuss their decisions with their peers? To what
extent did they share a common understanding of their situation? Did a
"right" way to deal with the controversy emerge? We shall see that the
culture of corporate philanthropy came into play, but in a distinctly
limited way.

For this analysis of the Planned Parenthood controversy, I went beyond
the sample of forty-three companies drawn from the fifty largest corporate
giving programs, which I have used in previous chapters. I tried to identify
all those among the one hundred largest programs that had had to address
the question of whether or not to continue support for Planned Parenthood
between 1985, when the first signs of organized protest appeared, and

◧

1991, when boycott efforts seemed to peter out.[9] Using a boycott list provided by Life Decisions International (which inherited the boycott from the Christian Action Council), press accounts, and information provided by corporate philanthropists themselves, I came up with a list of twenty-five corporations, sixteen of whom had chosen to continue funding Planned Parenthood between 1985 and 1991 and nine who had not. Twenty-two of these (fifteen continuing funders and seven defunders) agreed to talk. I also asked those corporate philanthropists who had not had to deal with the Planned Parenthood issue whether they recalled supporting the organization any time before 1985.[10]

History of a Controversy and a Boycott

Planned Parenthood was once known primarily for providing birth control and sex education programs, which many corporations could support without qualm. Indeed as late as 1979, in his well-regarded book on corporate giving, Frank Koch of the Syntex Corporation nonchalantly presented support for family-planning organizations such as Planned Parenthood as the kind of blue-chip donation of which any corporation could be proud, right along with supporting the local university, symphony, art museum, or United Way.[11]

In the 1980s, however, all that changed. Under the leadership of Faye Wattleton, who became president of the organization in 1978, Planned Parenthood became one of the leading advocates of abortion rights and thus put itself right in the center of perhaps the most divisive issue in American society. Beginning in 1985, a number of pro-life groups initiated letter-writing campaigns and boycotts against corporations that continued to fund Planned Parenthood. The decision to fund or not to fund Planned Parenthood became politicized.[12]

While the American Life League, the National Right to Life Committee, Rescue America, and other pro-life groups were all involved in some way, the major offensive against corporate supporters became identified with the Christian Action Council (now known as CareNet) which described itself as "the nation's largest Protestant pro-life group" and boasted over 350 "crisis pregnancy centers" in 1992.[13]

The Christian Action Council's letter-writing and boycott campaigns originated with Doug Scott. In 1986, when he was director of Human Life, the Washington state affiliate of the National Right to Life Committee, Scott began to gather a list of corporations contributing to Planned Parenthood and to publicize their names. In 1988, Scott became director of public policy at the Christian Action Council (CAC) and his personal name-gathering effort became a national letter-writing campaign.[14]

In the same year, J. C. Penney stopped funding Planned Parenthood in New York City when it moved its headquarters from that city to Dallas. The next year, Union Pacific stopped its support in response, it said, to "comments from stockholders and other individuals." Scott and the Christian Action Council claimed credit for both. Stockholder resolutions demanding an end to support for abortion rights advocacy groups, however, failed badly at both Quaker Oats and General Electric.[15]

By 1989, many corporations began to feel some heat as first pro-life and then pro-choice letters piled up. The experience of one is fairly typical of those who became major targets:

> We were first approached by the Christian Action Council beginning in October 1989, which asked if we gave to a list of several organizations. . . . And we sent them our annual report. Planned Parenthood was on there, and several of them were on there. . . . And there were several interim communications and around the same time we began to get some letters I think orchestrated by them.
>
> I must have stopped counting, but as of June 13, 1991, from the time I first began getting letters, which was the fall of 1989, I had received 2,218 letters of which 58 percent were asking us to stop . . . 42 percent were saying "keep it up, good work."

Another gave the following account:

> Doug Scott called asking rather nicely about our giving practices. . . . He wanted to know did we fund abortion clinics. I told him we did not and haven't. . . . I said, "However, though, we do fund a program . . . under which people receive training [in teaching sex education] from Planned Parenthood." Boy, Doug just jumped right on that and it seemed to bother him, so he wrote me back a letter saying he wanted a commitment from us to no longer fund that program and further, I think, to not do it for at least five years, because he was going to announce us as being supporters of abortion clinics . . . and he would put us on a list that would be distributed nationally to a number of organizations, all of which are in the same network.

Later, he added, "we started getting really terrible letters that came to both myself and the chairman of the company. Some of them were very spiteful . . . comparing him to Hitler and so on."

For all the efforts of Scott and the CAC, the Planned Parenthood issue remained largely a low-key one, dealt with primarily in the privacy of corporate offices, until March 1990, when a bombshell hit: The AT&T

◇

Foundation, one of the oldest (twenty-five years) and largest ($50,000 a year) corporate funders of Planned Parenthood, announced it would no longer support the organization.

AT&T's grant had gone to programs to reduce unintended teen pregnancies, part of a larger effort to "address some of the serious social and economic ills children face," as Reynold Levy, foundation president, put it in a letter to AT&T employees. The grant did not fund abortions or abortion advocacy and was not meant to take a position on abortion; however, Levy noted, "increasingly many employees, customers, and share owners—on both sides of the abortion issue—have interpreted it as such."[16] Because Planned Parenthood's role in abortion rights advocacy had been increasing, there seemed to be no way of separating AT&T's support for the organization's teen pregnancy programs from taking a position on abortion. The abortion debate is "no place for our corporation to be," Sarah Jepsen, executive director of the foundation, told the *Chronicle of Philanthropy*.[17]

Planned Parenthood struck back angrily and loudly. The organization took out full-page newspaper ads entitled, "Caving into Extremists, AT&T Hangs Up on Planned Parenthood." It cancelled a major contract with AT&T for a new phone system, and it began a direct-mail campaign to urge its supporters to repudiate AT&T's action.[18]

Planned Parenthood accused AT&T of allowing "fanatics to dictate its corporate policy" and of betraying their long relationship. AT&T, it said, had assured Planned Parenthood that all was well, even as the phone company deliberated for several months on the fate of the grant and had not communicated the final decision personally before the press got hold of it. (AT&T admitted it might have handled the matter better, but expressed its own indignation at Planned Parenthood for trampling on their long relationship with its combative public response.)[19]

The Christian Action Council seemed to know of the decision before Planned Parenthood did and swiftly claimed another victory.[20] The press agreed, and what the AT&T Foundation had regarded as a high-minded effort to rise above the abortion issue became routinely typed instead as a capitulation to anti-abortion pressure groups. Rather than getting out of the abortion debate, AT&T was in deeper than ever.[21] Several years later, Jepsen drew the following lesson: "In an emotionally charged issue you really cannot win."[22]

Other corporate supporters of Planned Parenthood now found themselves in a no-win situation, in which any action would be regarded as taking a position on a divisive issue. Continuing support would be seen as

◆

affirming Planned Parenthood's position on abortion, as surely as stopping support would be seen as opposing that position. Some corporate grant-makers claimed they wanted to stop funding Planned Parenthood, but they feared that any public action "would be suicide," placing them in the "sights of Faye's 48-inch guns," as one grantmaker anonymously put it. Of course, some corporations weathered the storm with equanimity. Despite some 10,000 letters and pickets at its Red Lobster restaurants, General Mills publicly reaffirmed its support for Planned Parenthood. Still, being in the middle of the abortion debate was a place that few corporations would freely have chosen to be.[23]

The Christian Action Council, in contrast, could not have been happier; its cause was firmly in the media spotlight. After claiming the AT&T decision as a success for its letter-writing campaign, it named American Express its next target. On August 8, the CAC called a press conference to announce that its letter-writing campaign would become a consumer boycott of forty-four corporations identified as supporters of Planned Parenthood.[24] Writing in the *Pro-life Advocate*, Thomas Glessner, CAC executive director, proudly announced that fifteen corporations had heed-ed his organization's call to "get out—and stay out—of the abortion business" by ending their support for Planned Parenthood. He named but five of these: J. C. Penney, Eastman Kodak, Union Pacific, AT&T, and Federated Department Stores, but presumably they included as well Xerox, Rockwell, AMP, and Meijer, all of whom were quietly dropped from the boycott list shortly after the press conference.[25]

Publicly, the CAC claimed that all it wanted was a level playing field in which corporations did not support organizations on either side of the abortion issue. "We ask corporate America to be neutral," Doug Scott wrote to the *Chronicle of Philanthropy*.[26] "We simply want companies to stay out of this controversial issue," announced a CAC press release, "but for some reason Planned Parenthood thinks neutrality can only be reached when they are funded and pro-life groups are not."[27]

To their supporters, the boycott leaders explained more candidly that they sought to damage Planned Parenthood, not so much by cutting the organization's small amount of corporate funding, but by attacking its legitimacy and tying up its time and energy in crisis management. As Scott put it in the *Pro-Life Advocate,*

> If corporations are making Planned Parenthood ineligible for funding, there must be something wrong with this organization. Besides, successful efforts to defund Planned Parenthood infuriate its leaders causing them to spend more time working on this issue and less time damaging the lives of our children.[28]

◆

The boycott announcement did not get the attention the CAC had probably hoped, because it coincided with the beginning of the Gulf War. About a month later, however, events at the Dayton Hudson Corporation put the Planned Parenthood controversy back into the headlines.[29] On August 2, the Dayton Hudson Foundation had quietly told Planned Parenthood of Minnesota that it was ending its support because it did not want to be part of the national abortion debate. The corporation did not make the decision public immediately nor did Planned Parenthood respond in any visible way. Indeed, Dayton Hudson was on the CAC boycott list published a few days later.

On August 31, however, the action somehow became public. In the ensuing week, a firestorm of protest erupted in Minneapolis, the corporation's headquarter city, and beyond. The Minnesota Women's Consortium organized a protest rally and threatened a holiday season boycott. Local residents led by the mayor's wife returned credit cards and angrily confronted store employees. Nonprofit organizations, who a few years earlier had spearheaded the successful opposition to a hostile takeover of Dayton Hudson by Dart Industries, expressed a profound sense of betrayal. The Comptroller of New York City (whose employee retirement system owned considerable Dayton stock), the president of Bryn Mawr College (a corporate board member), and even the great-grandson of the company's founder all protested the decision. On September 7, the Dayton Hudson Foundation announced it would reconsider its decision in response to the level of concern expressed by the community. On September 20, it restored the $18,000 grant, saying that it was "satisfied that we can make this grant without taking a position on abortion."[30]

After fall 1990, the Planned Parenthood controversy largely disappeared from the headlines and reverted to an issue corporate giving programs could agonize over in the quiet of their offices. The next summer, Scott left the Christian Action Council, a victim of budget cutbacks, and founded Life Decisions International (LDI) to continue the boycott. In June 1992, he claimed that twenty-two companies had agreed to stop funding Planned Parenthood, an addition of seven in two years. He would name only one of these additional seven, Pioneer Hi-Bred. The rest, he said, had agreed to stop funding Planned Parenthood on the condition that their names not be publicized. That way they could be dropped from the boycott list while giving Planned Parenthood an innocuous reason for why their funding stopped. Overall, however, Scott pictured the boycott effort as quite low-key, though he expected it to pick up. Once he had left the CAC, he said, "things started going downhill in terms of follow-up" on the boycott targets. "There really hasn't been a concentrated effort to really

◆

push this for a year."[31] Indeed, nearly all the corporations in the current study who had received large numbers of protest letters reported little activity after 1991.

Hidden Attrition

AT&T was a big exception: Most corporations who stopped funding Planned Parenthood did so quietly before the controversy reached its peak in 1989 and 1990. Grants to Planned Parenthood slipped away imperceptibly through the 1980s; by the end of the decade, Planned Parenthood reported that its corporate grants were only about half of what they had been in the 1970s.[32]

One senior corporate philanthropist, executive director of his company's foundation for thirteen years and associate director for two years before that, bluntly acknowledged ending support for Planned Parenthood early on, specifically because of the abortion issue:

> We did [support the organization] at one time until Planned Parenthood adopted the policy of abortion as a means of birth control. At that point we dropped them. . . . I'd say 1984 maybe.

Another recalled terminating support for a Planned Parenthood affiliate "at least ten years ago, maybe fifteen," because, he said, they seemed to want general operating grants rather than ones earmarked for specific projects like sex education:

> We contributed to a fund that they had to educate women about their sexuality. They at some point decided that they weren't going to be told how to use money that they were raising and they called our bluff. They found we weren't bluffing; you either use it that way or we weren't going to give them anything. We haven't contributed to them since.

Overall, however, most current corporate giving officers can shed little light on what happened in the early 1980s, since few were on the job then. Still, a simple contrast tells the story sufficiently well. Among the forty-three giving officers with whom I spoke from the top fifty corporate giving programs, three acknowledged ending sustained programs of support for Planned Parenthood prior to 1985, and another ten mentioned having given one-shot support to Planned Parenthood sometime before 1990 for such things as capital campaigns. *None,* however, mentioned starting an ongoing program of support for Planned Parenthood since 1985; and none mentioned any one-shot grants in the early years of the 1990s. The long-term attrition is perfectly clear: If corporations could go quietly, they did.

◆

The same held true for those who stopped sustained programs of support *after* 1985: All but one (AT&T obviously) did so quietly without the prodding of letters or boycott threats. Those companies who stopped funding Planned Parenthood after 1985 did so for a number of reasons, but apprehensions about the impact of controversy on the corporation's well-being always lay close by. Two corporate philanthropists explicitly said they did so because they believed that being involved in the divisive abortion issue was bad for the company and unfair to employees and stockholders. One of these, who didn't know her company was on a boycott list until well after the decision was made, put it this way:

> We had made a decision back about I think it's been two years ago [i.e., sometime in 1990]. . . . I think it was General Mills that had such a problem with Planned Parenthood. And at the time that happened, although we don't deal with what we would typically think of as consumer products, we did realize that it has caused them a fair amount of problems so we made the decision . . . that we were not going to approve recommendations specifically to Planned Parenthood. Not because we disagree with their practices or any of their programming but rather because we're dealing with shareholder investments. We really had to stay away from those kinds of controversial organizations.

Another two corporate giving officers said the directive to stop funding came directly from the CEO, acting more out of strong personal pro-life beliefs than out of concern for the impact of controversy on the corporation. One put it bluntly:

> He [the CEO] stopped it. . . . He felt very strongly about that issue and even though people explained [the grant] was not in any way connected to abortion, he just said no. So that's where that went.

She added that given the controversy surrounding Planned Parenthood, her corporate giving program would be unlikely to start supporting the organization again even if her corporation got a new CEO who was indifferent to the abortion issue.

In another case, the grant to Planned Parenthood was from a local plant site, not from corporate headquarters, and ended automatically when that plant shut down. Here too, the corporate giving officer emphasized that she would not consider resuming funding, because Planned Parenthood was identified with the abortion issue:

> Our position is not to support controversial organizations. We have shareholders and stakeholders on both sides of the issues and it's not up to us. We believe that's a personal decision and our corporate dollars cannot support personal decisions one way or another. There

◈

are enough problems out there that people agree on . . . and that's where our dollars should focus.

Still another corporation stopped supporting Planned Parenthood in 1987, the giving officer claimed, because all of his foundation's grants are of limited time duration. He added, however, that his company would never fund them again.

Howard Rollins, head of philanthropy for a major pharmaceutical company, spoke frankly and at some length about his corporation's aversion to controversy:

> Our giving program is a strategic tool, if you will, for the company. It is used to advance the mission of the company. It is not intended to be necessarily a lever for social change. I mean there are large private foundations, there are wealthy individuals and there's a big thing called the federal government that does that pretty effectively. So we don't set out to create controversy and frankly that would probably be a disincentive for our management to continue to increase our budget. They're not looking to have [the company's] name associated, frankly, with causes on which there are strong feelings on either side, because you're going to alienate probably 49 percent or 51 percent of your shareholders, employees, or customers. It's not a very good business decision. For us to come out strongly in favor of Planned Parenthood, for instance, would polarize a large minority probably of shareholders, customers, and employees and frankly would be very distracting for our management.
>
> I don't think it's very good business to set about making grants which are going to end up being written about, talked about, in the media in a contentious way. . . . We do look for funding opportunities which would be viewed as popular and would be reported on as progressive but not controversial. There's a difference there.

Why fund Planned Parenthood, Rollins continued, when his company could use the same money to put vans on the streets of poor neighborhoods to immunize children and provide well-baby care?

In other words, as several of Rollins's peers said in chapter 3, corporate philanthropy plays by different rules than private foundations or other kinds of donors. It is, after all, a "strategic tool," used "to advance the mission of the company," not a "lever for social change." Senior management would frown on grants that polarize society and are reported by the media in a "contentious way." Why run this risk, when there are plenty of "progressive," noncontroversial grants around?

This attitude makes perfect sense for any corporate philanthropist; it simply reflects the realities of the organization for which they work and their relationship to it. Indeed several corporate giving officers expressed skepticism that any corporation would initiate support for Planned Parenthood as long as it remained controversial. One, whose company decided to continue supporting Planned Parenthood, nonetheless said he "would be real surprised if any other corporation that hasn't funded it would decide to do so now." Another, whose company stopped funding, also doubted that "anybody would right now initiate something with Planned Parenthood, if they haven't done it before." It wasn't simply the specter of "people ripping up their charge cards," she added. (She probably had Dayton Hudson in mind, though this could apply as well to any financial institution, department store, or oil company.) Even companies who do not produce consumer products and hence could not easily be boycotted still would have to "spend three and four months full-time addressing letters" and the like.

In short, given the controversy surrounding support for Planned Parenthood, it made perfect sense for any corporation to get out, at least if it could go quietly, before the letters started and the press got wind of things. What made the situation easier for five of the seven corporations who terminated support after 1985 was that the grants in question were peripheral to their giving programs—or so their giving officers said in retrospect. The money had come not from corporate headquarters, but from a division of the company or a local facility. Or, it had come from unbudgeted discretionary funds. As a result, corporate philanthropists could reasonably claim that support for Planned Parenthood was not central to the priorities of the giving program and thus could minimize the significance of terminating funding. The giving officer at one company where defunding occurred on CEO edict noted that their grant to a local Planned Parenthood affiliate had come from discretionary funds and that her program would probably have ended support soon anyway.

> We also said to Planned Parenthood all along [that] we thought the last grant had already been made. It wasn't like we suddenly called them one day and said, "You're not going to get the money." We said . . . we're not dealing with these kinds of things anymore; we're putting more money into focus areas. We're putting more money into other parts of the country.

Some corporations, then, saw little problem with discontinuing support for Planned Parenthood. Controversy endangers corporate interests; there are less contentious ways of doing good; and the Planned Parenthood grant was not central to their philanthropic focus areas. They could get out quietly, and they did.

Their approach to the issue coincided with that of a "silent majority" of corporations which had never funded Planned Parenthood to begin with. One head of a major corporate foundation put it this way:

> We had purposely avoided support to organizations that fall into the general heading "controversial." Planned Parenthood is one. We don't see anything to be gained by that. How I feel personally is one thing, and I support it personally; but I don't feel, nor does our management feel, that it's in the company's interest to become embroiled in the support of an organization that has virtually nothing to do with the core business purpose of the company.

Visible Perseverance

After surveying the reasons some corporate philanthropists give for not funding controversial organizations, it may seem all the more puzzling why *any* corporations continued funding Planned Parenthood and why most did so in the face of a maelstrom of letters on both sides of the issue as well as a boycott threat.

An answer can be found in how corporations justified continuing support. In general corporate philanthropists made three kinds of cases for continued support for Planned Parenthood: the Quality/Fit, Due Process, and Avoiding Controversy arguments.

The *Quality/Fit* argument maintains that Planned Parenthood deserves continued support because it runs programs effectively addressing issues of high priority to the corporate giving program. In particular, this has meant that Planned Parenthood has excellent education programs for dealing with teen pregnancies which fit nicely with some companies' focus on urban poverty or on families and children.

The *Due Process* argument asserts that corporations need to maintain the integrity of their grantmaking procedures by keeping them apolitical and by not ceding control over them to outside groups. To stop funding Planned Parenthood in the context of political controversy would effectively make an ideological "litmus test" part of grant decisions and limit corporations to funding only those few nonprofit organizations that do not run afoul of any political position. It would also create the appearance of capitulating to anti-abortion forces, encourage other outside pressure groups to try to influence grantmaking, and thus give these groups effective power over corporate philanthropy. Either way, professional corporate grantmakers would lose the ability to run their programs according to clear goals and guidelines.

Finally, the *Avoiding Controversy* argument maintains that defunding Planned Parenthood, far from getting a corporation out of the abortion

◆

debate, would push it far deeper in and further threaten its image and perhaps its profits. The erstwhile funder would become a "lightning rod" for the high-pitched feelings that the abortion issue evokes on both sides. Better to stay where one is quietly than risk heightened visibility.

Different corporate giving officers used different combinations of these arguments to justify continued funding of Planned Parenthood and reported different decision-making processes concerning the issue. Roughly speaking, the fifteen corporations who decided to continue funding at some point after 1985 fall into two groups.

Five of them, the Deliberators, decided to continue funding only after protracted debate and weighing of alternatives, usually a process in which the corporate giving officer successfully overcame the ambivalence of top management. Giving officers in these companies used all three arguments to justify their final decision, but emphasized Avoiding Controversy. As a result they usually started from the same premises as those corporations who stopped funding, but drew different conclusions.

Ten corporations, the Stalwarts, simply continued funding with little internal debate. They tended to emphasize the Quality/Fit and Due Process arguments. In these companies the corporate philanthropist spent less time convincing top management that continued funding was the right thing and more time simply crafting a tactically suitable response.

Deliberators

The Deliberators describe protracted, often agonizing efforts to deal with the Planned Parenthood issue. One of them is Susan Bond, who at the time of the interview had worked in philanthropy at her financial services company for thirteen years, including five as vice president of the company foundation and one as president. Before that she had worked for nonprofit social services agencies. Bond spoke passionately and in detail about handling the Planned Parenthood issue, which her company initially faced before the AT&T affair. Indeed, she welcomed the interview as her first chance to reflect systematically on what had happened. It was "the most difficult thing I've dealt with since I've been in this job," she said. Elaborating, she emphasized that she had to separate her personal beliefs from her corporate responsibility, handle the polarized feelings on the issue, respond to the large volume of letters and calls, and coordinate all the people whose input shaped the final decision. She talked about being "under enormous pressure" and subject to "a lot of visibility."

Bond consulted the legal department to determine what corporate governance issues were involved in responding to outside pressure and with human resources people to gauge employee opinion. She worked

◆

closely with the senior and executive vice presidents to whom she reports as well as with public affairs people from the corporation's various divisions. She revisited the program her foundation supported, a counseling program for teens in the company's headquarters city.

Out of all this came a consensus that in effect incorporated all three of the basic arguments for continued funding. First of all, everyone agreed, the Planned Parenthood grants fit the giving program's guidelines:

> These are good solid programs that are doing what they say they're doing. They fit into our guidelines. And that was, I think, the first [thing]. I mean, if those things didn't follow, we might have come out differently.

Furthermore, Bond and her colleagues concluded that continuing funding was likely to generate less additional controversy than would stopping:

> We felt that looking at our employee base and cutting down what we felt was our customer base, in many ways the PR thing could go the other way if we withdrew our funding.

Finally, terminating the grant would threaten the integrity of the giving program (and raise issues of corporate governance) as well:

> Once you go down this road of making your choices on the basis of what special interest groups and others want, and not on the basis of what we determine is the best kind of program to have, it's a pretty slippery slope. . . . What seems not to be controversial today might be controversial tomorrow, and I think we're involved in a number of educational initiatives, many of which have a potential for controversy. . . . If we start down a slope where we let these decisions be made by others, it's going to be pretty difficult to end it.

While Bond emphasized all three arguments for continued funding, the argument that, all in all, continuing support generated less controversy than not doing so was pivotal. For one thing, she openly acknowledged that her company would be unlikely to start funding Planned Parenthood had it not already done so, despite how well its programs fit her company's philanthropic priorities:

> Clearly, people would like us to stay away from controversial issues. I mean, clearly, if we were starting over, we wouldn't be seeking out Planned Parenthood. . . . Do you know what I mean? I mean, clearly you don't want to seek out these things.

For another, asked why her company decided to continue funding at about the same time AT&T decided not to, Bond guessed that AT&T got different

◧

advice from sales and public relations people as to how best to minimize controversy:

> I think there was a great deal of pressure from their sales force, and I think in the end they were persuaded that for partly PR considerations and sales considerations, they should stop.

Bond noted with some glee that the wisdom of continuing support was confirmed by all the grief AT&T got for the opposite decision.

Another Deliberator is Frank Davis, who had been director of philanthropy and vice president at a major bank for five years when we spoke. Prior to his current position, he had worked for social service agencies and in academia. For Davis, the debate over whether or not to continue the Planned Parenthood grant pivoted on two very different notions of how to avoid controversy. Several of the senior managers of the bank favored ending the grant. According to Davis, this was partly because a number of them were Pro-Life Catholics, but it was also because

> most of the people were convinced that it was inappropriate for the [corporation] to take a position one way or the other on an issue that there is such heartfelt disagreement about.

Davis himself, in fact, agreed with this position in principle:

> And I happen to agree with that. If [the corporation] hadn't been supporting Planned Parenthood, would we do it now? No. Because there is such heartfelt disagreement about it. You know, we are a corporation. We're not a social organization. We're a corporation. . . . It's not a corporation's business to try to change the social balance.

Unfortunately, the bank was supporting Planned Parenthood, and Davis firmly believed that ending funding would simply insert it more deeply into the controversy and hurt it more, as it had with AT&T a few months before and was doing to Dayton Hudson at about the same time his company was debating the issue:

> It doesn't do [the corporation] any good to be identified with Planned Parenthood. [But] it would do more harm at this point if we cut off support, because we've become part of the argument.

Davis convinced top management not to end the Planned Parenthood grant by canvassing opinion in the company's various units:

> We stopped them from doing it by saying that we have another meeting coming up in a couple of months. Before you act, let's take one more look at this and look at the ramifications of this and poll our business units—you know, too many hours spent on a $15,000

◈

> contribution, but it was the right thing to do. We then did that and
> polled the regional bank and the private bank that handles the wealthy
> people; the credit card people, because they're the ones where most
> of the action occurs in terms of cut-up credit cards, and so forth. And
> all of the market people said, "don't stop funding Planned Parenthood,
> it's crazy."

The specter of headlines in the *New York Times,* he said, was what
ultimately turned around the opinion of the president of the company.

Oliver Peck is a third Deliberator, who had just completed ten years of
heading corporate philanthropy programs, including three at his current
company and seven at a prior one. Before entering corporate giving, he
had worked primarily in corporate government affairs and public issue
research. Peck's first corporation had never supported Planned Parenthood; his current corporation already had been doing so when he came on
board. For him, then, the difference was not merely hypothetical. One of
the more senior and well-respected corporate giving officers, he spoke in
the detached, magisterial way of someone articulating the conventional
wisdom.

As Peck sees it, the dilemma is first of all between funding a worthwhile
program and keeping the corporation out of controversy:

> If I were sitting here as the president of a private foundation, I would
> say that on the merits of the issue, funders are correct in their funding
> of Planned Parenthood if they're trying to prevent . . . disease or . . .
> unwanted pregnancies. I think this is a proper place for funders. It is
> an increasingly risky place for a corporate funder to be and the reason
> is that we have portholes through which critics can pour.

Because the first corporate giving program Peck headed had not supported
Planned Parenthood, there was no way he would have initiated support,
because to do so would be to place the corporation smack in the middle of
the abortion controversy:

> So when you have two warring factions like that, it just seems to me
> that with a million opportunities for a corporation to fund good works
> around the world, to step in between two groups of people who are
> firing machine guns at each other and will shoot anybody who steps
> in between them is a mistake for a corporation to make. So when I was
> president of the X Foundation, even though on the merits of the
> question and the morality of the question . . . I really feel that funders
> ought to be lining up with Planned Parenthood and others who do
> that kind of work, . . . I never put X corporation in the position of
> doing that.

◈

Because Peck's current giving program was already supporting Planned Parenthood when he came on board, however, there was no way to avoid negative publicity and possible adverse consumer reaction. This required a more careful weighing of costs and benefits. He decided to take the "calculated risk" of continuing funding.

To be sure, this calculus could change. Continued support, Peck said, "is worth it in terms of the program. However, . . . if those odds were to change, we'd have to weigh that very carefully, I think." For the moment, however, he seemed satisfied with his position, especially given the negative publicity that rained down on AT&T when it stopped its funding. "The worst of all outcomes for a corporation is to become a lightning rod on the issue, and that is what I feel happened with AT&T."

Both Davis and Peck make the Avoiding Controversy argument by drawing upon themes we have already encountered in the workaday worldview of corporate philanthropists described in chapter 3. In particular, they root their case for avoiding controversy in the unique nature of corporate giving. We are a "corporation," says Davis, not a "social organization" bent on improving society. Hence we should not brook controversy merely to do good. If he were head of a "private foundation," says Peck, he would have decided to continue funding Planned Parenthood purely "on the merits of the issue." As head of a corporate giving program, he had to make dealing with controversy central.

Stalwarts

Stalwarts handled the Planned Parenthood issue very differently from Deliberators. For them continued funding appeared to be a foregone conclusion; the only issue was how best to represent this publicly. Giving officers at these companies betrayed little sense of any debate or agonizing over the issue, of calculated risks or closely calibrated decisions about how best to avoid further controversy. As one admiring peer put it, it was a "no brainer" for them.

Asked whether or not the controversy surrounding Planned Parenthood had come up in discussing how to respond to the hundreds of letters her corporation received, Paula Jonas, who has worked over ten years in philanthropy at a communications company, replied:

> You know, it really hasn't. When we talked about it and shared some of the letters, we just decided that it was an important community service, we had been supporting it for good reasons and we would continue to support it for the same good reasons. It's sort of like you can't please everybody all of the time and the rationale that had gone

◆

into doing the funding in the first place we thought was still very sound.

Support for Planned Parenthood closely fit the priorities of Jonas's giving program:

> We try to do some research when we decide what our focus areas would be. And one of the major areas that we've been supporting for the past three years is early childhood education. And as a part of the research that we did, with respect to early childhood education, I mean the problems of teen pregnancy become very apparent and that's an area that we think kids ought to have knowledge to make the choices that they have to make. And so Planned Parenthood provides that information as do other community organizations.

A second Stalwart corporate giving officer likewise justified her decision to continue support for "education and family planning services for low-income clients" by emphasizing the centrality of this to her foundation's priorities:

> Our foundation places high priority on funding services for families, children and youth. We have a category of grantmaking called "health and social action." So this particular grant hits both the target population and the emphasis on preventive health as we define it in our guidelines.

Grant Porter, who had run philanthropy programs at two companies over eight years after considerable experience in both government and the nonprofit sector, emphasized Due Process arguments. Faced with expressions of concern from his current corporation's sales staff over the Planned Parenthood grant as well as protest letters from outside, he stressed the importance of maintaining the integrity of his giving program:

> I think some organizations have become a little bit sensitive to controversial issues. I think that's too bad. I mean, I think that if you take this aversion to controversy . . . to its illogical extreme, you will in effect neuter corporate philanthropy. . . . You're bound to violate somebody's sense of ethics or morality in almost anything you do.

Porter also underlined the dangers of applying ideological "litmus tests" to corporate giving:

> We don't think it is the right thing to have a litmus test for how any organization approaches the abortion issue, either pro or con. In other words, we are funding programs, not an organization's position on abortion. If we were to have a litmus test that said we will not support any organization who supports abortion or any organization who

opposes abortion, we would then have to suspend the support for Catholic hospitals, for Catholic parochial schools, for a bunch of other organizations that are out there . . . that I suspect have a position on abortion.

To be sure, Stalwarts did not wholly ignore the Avoiding Controversy argument. For example, one emphasized that "giving in" on Planned Parenthood might make her company a magnet for other controversies. "Once you start giving in on this stuff, God knows what could go out of fashion next year," she quipped.

All in all, however, the Stalwarts sound quite different from the Deliberators, from those who have stopped funding Planned Parenthood, and from the silent majority who never have. They seem relatively oblivious to controversy and its short-term impact on corporate interests. What accounts for this? How are Stalwarts different from other corporations?

Two characteristics distinguishing Stalwarts from Deliberators help explain the relative ease with which the former dealt with the Planned Parenthood issue. The first is *structural insulation*. Corporations who do not produce goods or services primarily for a competitive consumer market are less likely than those who do to feel vulnerable to public pressures and hence to be wary of controversial issues that polarize the public. They are thus less likely to agonize over continuing support for Planned Parenthood and to worry in particular about avoiding controversy. Five of the ten Stalwarts are at least partly insulated from consumer pressure, because they do not directly serve mass consumer markets or because they enjoy some protection from competition. They include two financial services companies that serve a limited clientele of institutions and rich individuals, a basic metals company, and two local phone companies. In contrast all five of the Deliberators serve mass, competitive consumer markets, including a major retailer, an over-the-counter pharmaceutical company, and three financial services companies.

The more structurally insulated Stalwarts often discussed the Planned Parenthood issue with a degree of flippancy or braggadocio absent from their peers. One corporate giving officer, whose company produces metals that go into airplanes among other things, had this to say about the boycott threats his company was getting, which struck him as form letters without "heart" or "substance": "They also are fundamentally dishonest, because they say they are going to boycott our products and they have no way of knowing how to do that." Would they refuse to fly on Boeing 747s, he wondered?

Sarah Hilgard, who works for an international bank that manages investments and pension plans for governments, private institutions, and rich individuals, boasted not only that her company's support for Planned Parenthood was larger than any other corporation's in her headquarter city but also that it was for general operating expenses (except abortion services). Most corporate philanthropists, in contrast, usually downplayed the size of their grants and emphasized that they were for specific programs. She also spoke derisively about the protest letters she received:

> I mean we got letters that said people aren't going to buy our cake mixes, they aren't going to use our products. But they weren't people who had any client-consumer relationship with us anyway.
>
> Most of the letters we get say the same thing. The wording is almost identical and they're typically from Indiana, Iowa, Illinois, the "I" states I call them. Idaho.

Her bank, of course, does not produce cake mixes; its clients do not come primarily from the "I" states; it does not even issue credit cards. Indeed, Hilgard credited her company's relative insulation for the ease with which it dealt with the Planned Parenthood issue:

> So, there's been no other real discussion about should we change our policy, should we do something else. I think it's easier, probably, to do that because we don't have picketers downstairs. We don't have people mailing back credit cards or cancelling their charge accounts or their other accounts or something like that. I suppose if that were to happen, we'd have more conversation about it.

A second way Stalwarts differ from other corporations, especially from Deliberators, is their *reputation for social responsibility.* All major corporations emphasize the importance of being good corporate citizens and serving the interests of all their "stakeholders," not just their stock owners. Most probably can point as well to actions that realize this rhetoric. Still, a few corporations tend to have especially strong reputations in society at large for being especially socially responsible (whatever the reality behind this), and they are recognized for this by groups that track such things. They win Corporate Conscience Awards (from the Council on Economic Priorities), Business Enterprise Trust Awards, Harvard George S. Dively Awards for Corporate Public Achievement, or Lawrence A. Wien Prizes for Social Responsibility; or they are listed among the "100 Best Companies to Work for in America."[33] Corporations with a strong reputation for social responsibility are more likely to regard continuing a worthwhile but contentious grant as important to their reputation and to pay less attention to the controversy this might involve. Senior managers in such companies are

◈

less likely to impose their own views on the issue or to need major convincing that continued support in the face of controversy is a good thing.

Six of the ten Stalwarts have especially strong reputations for social responsibility, but only one of five Deliberators.[34] Furthermore, while four of the five Deliberators reported that at least one member of senior management favored defunding, none of the Stalwarts reported having to convince skeptical bosses about the value of continued funding. Overall, nine of ten Stalwarts, but only one of five Deliberators were either partly insulated from consumer pressures or enjoyed a strong reputation for social responsibility.[35]

The impact of reputation was especially telling in the case of one Stalwart corporation, a major consumer products company, closely identified with its products, facing several well-known competitors, and hence eminently boycottable. It faced a greater volume of letters and more pressure than perhaps all but two or three other corporations. Yet Katherine Rose, head of its corporate giving program for four years (and before that a university administrator), described no hesitation in continuing the grant, either on her own part or from top management. A former head of the same giving program confirmed this in a subsequent conversation, as did a colleague at another company in the same city.

Rose justified continued support of Planned Parenthood by emphasizing the damage that terminating funding would do to her company's hard-won reputation with the nonprofit world and the public generally in her relatively progressive and philanthropic city:

> I wouldn't abandon any organization, if they are performing well on the part of services we think are important to the public. I would think twice about abandoning an organization that's delivering that service simply because somebody else out there doesn't like it. I think . . . we would weaken the public trust in us as a philanthropic foundation if we ran scared and abandoned a good organization just because somebody else complained. . . . I think we just have to have clear guidelines and be willing to explain those guidelines to the public and let those give us some backbone. . . . When we've committed ourselves to be a partner in a grants relationship, I think we . . . carry a strong commitment into that relationship, and . . . if we were to run away from funding organizations because somebody complained, I think the nonprofit sector should have reasons to distrust us. . . . So we want credibility with the nonprofit communities, we want the confidence of the public, and we want to do some good and solve some community problems.

◈

Yes, Rose added, consumer boycotts were a serious issue at a company like hers. Still, her company had accrued a reputation for "dedication to community" and "commitment in providing the strongest services in the fairest way." She could best serve her company and its competitive position by maintaining this reputation, not by fleeing from the specter of a consumer boycott.

Controversy and Corporate Philanthropy

Problematic Position in the Corporation

We began this chapter with an apparent paradox: Why did corporate supporters of Planned Parenthood who faced significant public pressure to stop their funding usually continue, while those who faced little or none stopped? How the problematic position of philanthropy in the corporation (serving corporate interests and cultivating the support of corporate leaders while maintaining a degree of autonomy) came into play is central to the answer.

Corporate philanthropists who had the luxury of dealing with the Planned Parenthood issue outside the spotlight had a relatively easy time of it. They could avoid controversy and thus avoid damage to the corporate image simply by ending funding. No fine-grained calculations or agonizing deliberations were necessary. Because they were not under external pressure to stop funding, the decision to do so usually carried little risk to the integrity of their program or their own authority. (Of course, two corporate philanthropists stopped funding Planned Parenthood in response to CEO edict, but that was clearly unavoidable.) Furthermore, the grants in question were usually peripheral to the giving program's priority areas and thus terminating them did not raise questions about the seriousness of their philanthropy. Casually made, they could be casually unmade. Since ending support for Planned Parenthood did not strike at a central giving priority, the corporate philanthropists in question could plausibly argue that they could do good in plenty of ways that didn't brook controversy and threaten corporate interests—a claim that resonated as well among the "Silent Majority" of corporations that had never funded Planned Parenthood to begin with and thus could look at the matter as spectators.

In short, for those who could defund quietly (as well as for the mass of nonfunders), serving corporate interests pointed unambiguously to getting out (or not getting in), while defending the integrity and autonomy of the giving program simply did not become an issue.

◈

Corporate philanthropists caught in the spotlight of publicity also were concerned with avoiding controversy and a damaged corporate image, but they decided, often after considerable debate, that continuing support for Planned Parenthood would more likely preserve the corporate image than would stopping. Certainly those who made their decision after the AT&T affair in the spring of 1990 had a powerful exemplar of how *not* to shield themselves from the fallout of the abortion controversy. In contrast to corporations who could terminate support quietly, those in the glare of the boycott faced potential public relations costs if they stopped funding. For both groups of philanthropy programs, making the corporation look good, or at least keeping it from looking too bad, was a critical factor in their decision.

There was often more to the decisions than this, however, especially for those corporations we have called Stalwarts. Corporate philanthropists caught up in the spotlight of controversy had to worry as well about the impact of terminating support for Planned Parenthood on the integrity of their programs and their own managerial authority. These concerns, in effect, underlay the Quality/Fit and Due Process arguments. Those corporations relatively insulated from competitive consumer markets or having especially strong reputations for social responsibility to protect found these arguments especially compelling. Most had funded Planned Parenthood to begin with as part of a major priority area such as families or health care. In doing so, they had in effect claimed to have used their special professional expertise as corporate giving officers to identify pressing social problems and to choose good programs that deal with those problems. To terminate funding in the face of external pressure would inevitably compromise their authority and call into question the seriousness of their efforts to do good.

The concerns corporate philanthropists had with maintaining the integrity of their giving programs and their own professional authority in the face of the Planned Parenthood controversy make sense given their inherently problematic position in the corporation. On the one hand, corporate giving programs have to serve corporate interests in immediate, palpable ways, especially by enhancing the company's public image. Ignoring these demands would quickly marginalize any corporate giving program. They also need to cultivate assiduously the support of top management. Unless the CEO buys into the idea of philanthropy and the goals of the giving program, it will be a prime target for budget cuts. On the other hand, corporate giving programs need a degree of autonomy and distance from immediate corporate interests and the demands of top

◈

management. To devote themselves wholly to serving immediate corporate interests risks destroying the distinctiveness of corporate philanthropy programs and making them mere adjuncts of public relations, marketing, or human resources. To get too close to top management threatens to reduce corporate philanthropy to a mere "check-writing operation" for the favorite charities of top management. Both situations threaten to undermine the claims of corporate philanthropists to a distinctive authority and expertise and hence a unique role to play in the corporation. In doing so, they also violate what corporate philanthropists value most about their work, the ability to do some palpable good for society while serving corporate interests in the long term.

In short, some of the most important reasons corporate giving programs offer for continuing grants to Planned Parenthood in the face of controversy address precisely those problems inherent in giving money away for a corporation. In this context, ending a grant in the face of well-publicized external pressure may be exactly the wrong thing to do.

The Common Culture

Corporate philanthropy has a distinctly social dimension, as we have seen in earlier chapters. Corporate philanthropists participate in a network of relationships with their peers at other corporations. They talk frequently with their colleagues, partly through national organizations sponsored by the Conference Board and the Council on Foundations. In understanding themselves and their work, they draw upon an official culture that helps define why corporate giving is important, what it should support, and how it should be organized. They have a common understanding of their enterprise. What impact did all this have on how individual corporations dealt with the Planned Parenthood issue? We have said that no corporate giving program is an island. How does this claim apply to the case at hand?

Corporate philanthropists certainly discussed the Planned Parenthood issue with each other and compared notes. At the very least, it was a matter of misery loving company, but it was more than that. Because dealing with controversy is not usually part of their everyday repertoire, they often had to think through how to respond from scratch. In these circumstances, the commiseration and advice of peers was especially important. As one put it, "No one wants to be out on a limb alone."

As a result, the major players in the controversy knew about each other. This was true not only locally but nationally: Corporate philanthropists in New York City, for example, knew what was going on in Minneapolis, or Seattle, or Cleveland, as well as at home. This was partly because both the Contributions Council of the Conference Board and the Corporate

◆

Grantmakers Committee of the Council on Foundations discussed the Planned Parenthood issue and other controversies. This also allowed many corporate giving officers not involved with the issue to keep abreast of it.

These discussions help explain why corporate philanthropists had a common set of arguments for framing the Planned Parenthood issue. To be sure, individual corporate giving officers drew upon these arguments in different ways, but they shared a common language for managing controversy.

Conversation among corporate philanthropists also reinforced the solidarity born of a shared crisis. Corporate giving officers sympathized with the plight of their embattled peers, irrespective of whether or not they themselves had to deal with the issue or of how they handled it. Peck's image of corporations caught between "two warring factions . . . firing machine guns at each other" captures this sympathy nicely: Corporate philanthropists saw themselves and their peers as hapless victims of a war between Planned Parenthood and the Christian Action Council. They hardly ever criticized how a particular corporation handled the issue, though a few who decided to continue funding took quiet pleasure in handling the issue better than AT&T.

If sharing experiences gave corporate philanthropists a common general frame and a degree of solidarity on the Planned Parenthood issue, it gave them little direct advice about whether to continue or terminate funding in the face of controversy.[36] One giving officer talked about her extensive contact with peers on the issue: "I have been free to pick up the telephone and call my colleagues and share my experiences and, say, find out from them their experiences." Indeed, she "gained strength by talking with fellow staff people in other companies." Yet when asked what consensus had emerged from such discussions about continuing or terminating support, she seemed uncertain, alluding simply to "a wide variety of opinion."

Others were quite certain that no consensus was ever reached, because the conversations were simply not of that nature. Yes, it was useful to compare experiences, they said, but the underlying assumption of all discussions of corporate giving is that each corporation goes its own way. As one corporate philanthropist put it,

> Every company really ends up handling it according to its own corporate culture. And the lessons were so different because the experiences were so different and the management was so different.

Another emphasized more generally that his experience at both the Conference Board and the Council on Foundations led him

◧

to greatly value the diversity and independence that each of the members brings to any discussion that takes place at meetings. . . . I find the difference in programs to be a significant contribution to my continual learning efforts. Each company must conduct its program in the best interests of many stakeholders, such as their company, their employees, and the communities in which they operate.

In short, the corporate response to the Planned Parenthood controversy was collective (not simply individual), but only to a limited degree. Corporate philanthropists thought out the issue in a shared language, they compared notes with each other, and they enjoyed a strong sense of solidarity. However, at no point did they develop a collective answer to the fundamental question: whether or not a corporate giving program should continue funding a program that becomes controversial. Indeed the consensus was that this question should not have a collective answer; it ought to be up to the individual corporation.

Once again, we see that although the culture of corporate philanthropy is certainly a palpable presence in the lives of corporate giving officers, their everyday thinking diverges from or goes beyond it in important ways. Chapter 3 showed that although the culture of corporate philanthropy includes broad or classwide justifications for corporate philanthropy, the workaday worldview of corporate philanthropists generally does not. Chapter 4 demonstrated that corporate philanthropists have a more complex understanding of the problematic nature of what they do than does the official culture of corporate philanthropy. Now, the Planned Parenthood controversy illustrates how circumscribed collective discussion and consensus in corporate philanthropy is. Corporate philanthropists may compare notes and offer each other support, but ultimately it is expected that each go her or his own way.

And Where Is Politics?

Throughout the Planned Parenthood controversy, corporate philanthropists maintained that they were apolitical. AT&T insisted that terminating its grant to Planned Parenthood was not a rejection of the organization's support for abortion rights; it was an effort to avoid taking a position on abortion. Corporations that continued their funding argued that they were not in any way supporting abortion or Planned Parenthood's advocacy of abortion rights. They were merely funding family planning, teen pregnancy, or sex education programs that happened to be run by Planned Parenthood, which happened to be a major proponent of abortion rights. We are "funding programs," they maintained, not applying ideological "litmus tests" to organizations.

◈

Few people outside the corporate world bought this argument. Hardly anyone, whether pro-life or pro-choice, could so neatly separate support for Planned Parenthood's non-abortion programs from support for abortion rights, which was precisely why corporate philanthropists found themselves in such a mess. Pro-choice groups condemned AT&T and applauded American Express and General Mills; pro-life groups did the opposite.

Indeed, corporate support for Planned Parenthood programs does have an implicit politics to it. Supporting any programs of Planned Parenthood implies that it is all right to fund the other services offered by an organization that also supports abortion rights and provides abortions. This in turn implies that providing access to abortion, if not wholly right, is at least not so wrong as to stigmatize the abortion provider and put them beyond the pale of respectability. It means, in other words, that abortion is not murder or another evil of similar magnitude. If corporate support for Planned Parenthood is not necessarily pro-choice, it is certainly *not* pro-life.

More generally, neutrality (i.e., a formally apolitical stance) often has its own politics. This is an insight worth keeping in mind as we turn to the general issue of the politics of corporate philanthropy. As with support for Planned Parenthood, corporate philanthropists argue that none of their grants are meant to be partisan or ideological. They are meant instead to do good in generally acceptable ways. As we saw in chapter 3, moreover, corporate philanthropists generally avoid spelling out a general social vision of any kind or a sense of how corporate philanthropy fits in the general political strategy of business. In other words, they avoid any kind of general classwide rationality, at least apparently. Still, what is true for the Planned Parenthood issue may be true for corporate philanthropy in general: Neutrality may have its own politics. Teasing out the politics of corporate philanthropy from behind the facade of neutrality and pragmatism and identifying its role in corporate politics generally are the tasks of the next two chapters. We begin with another controversy, this one pitting corporate philanthropy against the conservative Capital Research Center.

6

Corporate Giving under Fire II

The Capital Research Center

Perhaps an Incredible Notion

"American businesses are helping finance public policies that erode the American free-market economy and its underlying normative system of individualism, self-reliance, and self-responsibility." American businesses subverting themselves? Perhaps an incredible notion. Nonetheless, this claim has been made every year since the mid-1980s by the conservative Capital Research Center (CRC). The Center backs up its claim with an annual volume documenting the giving practices of America's largest corporations.

If attacks on big business from the Right seem ironic, it is, as we have seen, a common irony. The boycott of corporations supporting Planned Parenthood came from the Right. So has protest over support for Hispanic groups deemed too supportive of illegal immigration or for artistic work deemed pornographic. So did the furor over the refusal of a few corporations to fund the Boy Scouts because of their anti-gay policies. To be sure, corporate philanthropy has its critics from the Left too, but this criticism does not exude the same bitter sense of betrayal.

What is puzzling about the CRC's challenge to corporate philanthropy in the first instance is that it happens at all. Perhaps, one can understand anti-abortion groups criticizing a few corporations for supporting Planned Parenthood. The CRC, however, aims considerably more broadly, criticizing most major corporations for being too liberal overall in their philanthropy. Isn't big business conservative? Aren't conservatives pro-business? Why don't big business and the Right get along better?

What is also puzzling about the CRC's challenge is that it has fallen flat. Year after year it has sent corporate CEOs the message that their giving programs have been taken over by liberals and even radicals. Every year the *Wall Street Journal* takes up the cry as do other media outlets favored by big business. After the Republican victory in the congressional elections

◆

in 1994, new House Majority Leader Richard K. Armey added his voice as well. One would expect the image of the perfidious corporate giving officer to resonate in the minds of top corporate management; as one corporate philanthropist noted, top corporate managers are always ready to suspect that "those fools over there in corporate contributions" are "a bunch of do-gooder, probably left-of-center people." Yet, according to the CRC's own data and the reports of corporate philanthropists themselves, the charges have made few waves.

The solution to both puzzles is the same. Conservatives are at loggerheads with corporate philanthropy because the two have very different visions or ideologies of the proper role of big business in American politics. I shall call these visions the Conservative and the Pragmatic, and one point of the next two chapters is to spell out what they are and to examine how they conflict (but also in a broader sense work together). The Conservative Vision, exemplified by the CRC, pictures big business as embattled in a political world composed of enemies bent on destroying or at least hobbling it. Corporate philanthropy ought to be a weapon in this battle. The Pragmatic Vision, implicit in corporate philanthropy, pictures large corporations as competing relatively amicably in a polity of diverse interests, with whom alliances can be made, bridges built, understandings reached. Corporate philanthropy is merely one way of doing this.

Similarly, the CRC's challenge falls flat precisely because it flows from assumptions so alien to those underlying corporate philanthropy. Both the Conservative and the Pragmatic visions play an important role in the corporate world. Indeed, the changing mix of the two is a key to understanding the distinctive presence and power of big business as a political actor. In corporate philanthropy, however, the mix distinctly favors the Pragmatic Vision. Both top management and corporate giving officers take its assumptions for granted and find the alternative vision out of place. The Conservative Vision is thus articulated largely outside the corporate world by the CRC.

The most important point here is that corporate philanthropy is in fact informed by a broad vision of the place of big business in polity and society. In our discussion until now we have seen precious little of this broad vision, what we have called "classwide rationality." To be sure, the culture of corporate philanthropy, the ensemble of practical and philosophical writing aimed at corporate philanthropists and their bosses, has historically articulated such a vision at points, but it has primarily encouraged corporate giving programs to tie themselves closely to the strategic interests of their own corporations. Indeed it encourages individualism

◆

among these programs to the extent of not prescribing how they should act even in the face of crisis, such as the Planned Parenthood controversy. In their everyday view of their work, moreover, individual corporate philanthropists hardly have the luxury of articulating a broad vision, especially given the pressures to serve the interests of their own companies in direct, palpable ways. More generally, they avoid anything that smacks of politics, partisanship, or ideology.

As we have suggested, however, neutrality can carry its own kind of political vision; pragmatism, its own ideology. A political vision lies implicit in the everyday practice of corporate philanthropy and becomes explicit when that practice is challenged in the way represented by the Capital Research Center. By examining this controversy, we can now articulate that Pragmatic Vision.

Chapter 6 examines the CRC's critique of corporate philanthropy in the context of the Right generally, the corporate response, and the underlying conflict of visions. Chapter 7 even spells out the broader significance of these conflicting visions for a theory of corporate politics.

Capital Research Center on the Attack

The CRC and Corporate Philanthropy

The Capital Research Center has been one of the most persistent critics of corporate giving in recent years.[1] It was founded in 1984 by Willa Johnson, who had been a senior vice president at the Heritage Foundation and had served briefly as associate director of personnel in the Reagan White House. Johnson stepped down in 1994, and Terrence Scanlon, vice president for corporate relations at the Heritage Foundation and chairman of the Consumer Production Safety Commission from 1984 to 1989, took her place.[2] The CRC's annual budget rose rapidly from $69,000 in 1984 to $380,000 in 1988 and $1.1 million by 1994.

The CRC is an integral part of the growing conservative political and intellectual network. Much of its money has come from private foundations that have played a central role in building conservative policy groups generally, including the Sarah Scaife Foundation, the John M. Olin Foundation, and the Adolph Coors Foundation.[3] Its executive committee has included such conservative luminaries as Midge Decter, Richard Allen, R. Emmett Tyrrell, Jr., and Ernest Lefever. Its yearly critiques of corporate philanthropy boast introductions from the likes of William Simon, Pete Du Pont, and Malcolm S. Forbes, Jr. Its publications receive attention in the

◆

Wall Street Journal, National Review, Forbes, and *Human Events,* as well as from conservative columnists. After the 1994 elections, the CRC's ideas became integral to the case for the Contract with America.

The CRC's attack on corporate philanthropy presumes a broader critique of the contemporary nonprofit sector and the philanthropic culture that dominates it. Johnson states the purpose of the CRC as providing "new alternatives to the hitherto-dominant culture of philanthropy in America."

> Today, a unified, sophisticated, and well-funded philanthropic elite is dedicated to imposing on us the doctrines of "progressive" philanthropy, doctrines that would reorder our political, economic, and cultural priorities. This movement, driven by a bankrupt ideology long since disproved by history, would impose its own standards of "social justice," based on more involvement of government in philanthropy and more involvement by charities in politics. It has lost faith in traditional American values of individual responsibility and free choice, to say nothing of diversity in the marketplace of ideas.[4]

Johnson argues that the philanthropic and nonprofit world is dominated by "a culture informed largely by those who would use the resources of the nonprofit world to expand the power of government," rather than seeking to make nonprofit organizations alternatives to government.[5] In a similar vein, the CRC's Marvin Olasky laments: "Is this what philanthropy has become—a lobbying operation for the expansion of government programs?"[6]

The CRC's overall goal is to replace the prevailing "philosophically and morally bankrupt" culture and to undercut the power of "philanthropists who have made peace with governmental growth." They seek to revive what they view as an older notion of philanthropy. As Johnson writes,

> I would like to think that what we are seeing is a reawakening of the individual's sense of his ability to be responsible for his own problems and, when so moved, those of his neighbors without interference from tax-supported social engineers.
>
> That is what philanthropy should be.
>
> Philanthropy means individuals responding freely to the needs of those who truly need our help. . . . Charity is one of the great virtues; but it is an attribute of the individual, not of the collective.[7]

The problem with the nonprofit sector, in other words, is that it is too entangled with government: It relies too much on government funding and spends too much time advocating further expansion of government.

◈

Leaders in the nonprofit sector, it is argued, "deemphasize support for traditional charities" and "shift philanthropy's financial resources to nonprofit advocacy groups, especially those that actively promote welfare state programs."[8] Thus traditional charity, which not only sought to alleviate suffering but also to restore personal independence, is replaced by welfare state programs that perpetuate dependency.

In this vein, CRC writers have criticized a number of elements of the nonprofit sector. James T. Bennett, for example, castigates organizations such as the American Heart Association and the American Cancer Society for engaging in too much political advocacy (mostly regarding legislation regulating smoking) and not enough charity (support for research and education).

> No amount of alchemy can transmute political advocacy into charity.
> . . . The fundamental question is deceptively simple: Is the ultimate
> goal of America's three largest health charities to benefit the public or,
> through campaigns of political advocacy, to advance the narrow
> interests of their own leaders and the medical establishment?[9]

Carl O. Helstrom III sounds the alarm over changes in workplace fundraising. He decries the efforts of the National Committee for Responsive Philanthropy to open up workplaces to alternatives to the United Way of America, federated campaigns that provide support largely to "political advocacy groups" rather than "charities." He also criticizes the United Way for responding to this challenge by providing its own kind of access for advocacy groups (through donor option) and by "altering its public image from that of workplace fundraiser to one of spokesman and policymaker for traditional and nontraditional charities alike."[10]

Marvin Olasky takes the Council on Foundations and its president, James A. Joseph, to task for promoting "politically correct" causes. He criticizes the Council for emphasizing "not what foundations could do individually to advance their unique missions, but what they could do collectively to push government toward assumed goodness."[11]

The CRC's most visible, persistent criticism has been aimed specifically at corporate philanthropy in a series of volumes entitled *Patterns of Corporate Philanthropy*, which have appeared yearly since 1987.[12] These books accuse corporations of reinforcing the unholy mixing of nonprofit sector and government by supporting nonprofit groups that advocate for more government funding of the nonprofit sector and for expanded government generally. The 1990 edition argues that "American businesses are helping finance public policies that erode the American free-market economy and its underlying normative system of individualism, self-

◆

reliance, and self-responsibility."[13] And the 1988 edition warns that "the fruits of free enterprise" are going to those "whose purpose is the replacement of capitalism by a utopian collectivism."[14]

In other words, American corporations tend to support liberal public policy groups that favor "more government . . . planning, regulation, income redistribution through the tax system, and increased restraint on . . . private sector economic activities" over conservative public policy groups that are skeptical of government's ability to solve social problems and advocate "greater reliance on individual initiative and self-responsibility and less regulation of the market system."[15]

To document their claims, the CRC annually solicits information on corporate giving from the *Forbes* 250 corporations (receiving usable information from 129 of those companies for their 1994 volume). It then identifies all grants going to nonprofit organizations who engage in public policy advocacy (more than three hundred organizations in the 1994 volume). The CRC classifies each of these organizations on a scale from one to eight, with one to four designating various degrees of liberalism (from radical left to center left), six to eight designating various levels of conservatism (from center right to radical right), and five being middle of the road. Finally, it places corporations on the same scale based on the average ranking of the organizations that receive its dollars. It translates corporate numerical rankings into grades ranging from A (6.5 or higher) to F (below 3.0).

The results vary little from year to year: The corporations in the study give about $30 million a year to public affairs groups, with about 60 to 65 percent going to left-of-center groups and about 30 percent to right-of-center groups. Few, if any, corporations have gotten an A. Only 10 to 15 percent at most have gotten a grade of B (scores of 5.5 to 6.4), while 60 to 65 percent typically have gotten Ds or Fs (scores of 4.4 or below).

The 1994 volume, edited by Stuart Nolan, reports that of $36.4 million in corporate contributions to "nonprofit advocacy groups," 74 percent went to liberal organizations, only 22 percent to conservative ones, a ratio of 3.42 to 1. Among the forty-three corporations that gave at least $250,000 to such groups, only one, Eli Lilly, received an A. None got a B; nine got a C; the rest got Ds or Fs.[16]

In addition, each report provides numerous specific examples of individual corporations supporting groups that are alleged to be its enemies. The 1994 volume castigates oil companies for supporting the Audubon Society and the National Wildlife Federation, which oppose exploration in the Arctic National Wildlife Refuge; insurance companies

◆

and other large corporations for funding the Children's Defense Fund, which promotes national health insurance, expanded welfare programs, and a "nationalization" of vaccine distribution; and both automobile and oil companies for supporting the Alliance to Save Energy, which supports a gasoline tax of fifty cents per gallon.[17]

The CRC does not systematically explain why corporations are so stupid or so perfidious as to support those who seek to undermine capitalism, but several of its authors suggest that corporate contributions programs have been captured by outsiders from the nonprofit sector. CEOs, corporate directors, and top management fail to play an active role in corporate giving, thus leaving it, in the words of William Simon's introduction to the 1988 volume, to "the foundation world's professional managerial elite to define for them what is 'right.'"[18] In the 1992 volume, Olasky asks the dark question:

> What if top executives (often politically conservative) and contributions managers (often politically liberal) are unevenly yoked? What if contributions managers are working not in the corporate or public interest, but in their own ideological interest?[19]

He talks of "philanthropic trade groups" and "contributions officers who come from government or nonprofit groups" taking over corporate giving.[20]

The CRC's case against corporate philanthropy, we should note, can be criticized strongly on at least three grounds. First, donations to public policy groups of *any* political persuasion are but a small percentage of all corporate giving. Thus the $36.4 million in contributions to such groups reported in the 1994 volume amounts to less than 4 percent of the roughly $1 billion the 129 corporations studied gave away. Eli Lilly wins the accolade of "best" corporate giver based on only 1.5 percent of its grants, while Coca-Cola earns the top corporate "misgiver" distinction based on only 2.9 percent. Public policy grants thus in no way capture the overall thrust of corporate giving programs.

Second, corporate philanthropists are rarely the outsiders the CRC takes them to be. As we saw in chapter 3, most come from within the corporate world and are oriented strongly to their own company. Their contacts outside their firm are largely with other corporate philanthropists; few have strong ties to the nonprofit sector. In addition, hardly any have explicit ideological agendas of any kind. They are motivated instead by a desire to serve their corporations in a palpable way (if only to preserve their jobs and budgets from the next round of downsizing) mixed with an

◆

eagerness to do small bits of good. If they were "ideological liberals" who had the power the CRC ascribes to them, it is inconceivable why they direct such a small percentage of their overall philanthropy to liberal public policy groups.

Third, the CRC tends to define liberal and conservative asymmetrically. Conservative groups tend to be those groups with a distinct commitment to a conservative agenda. Liberal groups tend to be all those that seek to use government in any way to pursue a goal or a group interest. Thus, the CRC includes among liberals all major environmental groups (including the Nature Conservancy), all major representatives of minority groups (not only African American and Hispanic, but Jewish and Asian American as well), the major representatives of the nonprofit world (the Council on Foundations and Independent Sector), the League of Women Voters, and most interestingly, several business groups as well (Council on Foreign Relations, Committee on Economic Development, the Foreign Policy Association, Trilateral Commission, National Alliance of Business).

The CRC and the Right

It would be wrong, however, on the basis of these criticisms to dismiss the CRC out of hand, because their arguments on corporate philanthropy and the nonprofit sector have had broad influence on the Right and hence in American politics, especially after Republican victories in the 1994 congressional elections. The 1994 edition of *Patterns of Corporate Philanthropy* went out to corporate leaders with a cover letter signed by new House Majority Leader Richard Armey, accusing big business of being "firmly behind the welfare state."[21] *The Tragedy of American Compassion* by former CRC staffer Marvin Olasky made it to House Speaker Newt Gingrich's celebrated reading list and has become central to the conservative case against government support for the poor.[22] Indeed, the CRC is but one part of a "growing network of conservative policy groups" that, according to the *Chronicle of Philanthropy,* "has gained unprecedented influence in setting the congressional agenda on charity policy." Other groups helping to shape this agenda include the Competitive Enterprise Institute, the New Citizenship Project, the National Center for Policy Analysis, the Center for Effective Compassion, and the Heritage Foundation.[23]

In making the case for the Contract with America, conservative leaders have echoed the critique of the nonprofit sector offered by the CRC and these other groups. They have argued prominently for replacing government social welfare programs with private charity, which, they argue, is more efficient and more likely to demand that recipients change their behavior, take responsibility for themselves, and cultivate self-discipline. In *Restoring the Dream,* House Republicans draw the following contrast:

> When the Salvation Army takes care of the homeless, the organization requires the recipients of the aid to get up in the morning, make their bed, wash their dishes, earn their keep, and look for a job. It tries to build up the homeless person's self-esteem and sense of personal responsibility. Behavioral improvement is a condition of continued aid. By contrast, with government programs the assistance is an entitlement—nothing is asked in return for the help.[24]

In a similar vein, Ralph Reed, executive director of the Christian Coalition, calls for replacing "the failed and discredited welfare state with a community- and charity-based opportunity society" and "the pity of bureaucrats with the generosity of churches and synagogues."[25]

The Right has also broadly condemned the dependence of the nonprofit sector on government. Leslie Lenkowsky, president of the Hudson Institute, describes the financial support nonprofits get from government as a "Faustian bargain":

> In return for all the income and recognition they have received from government, non-profit groups have paid a steep price: a loss of independence.[26]

Beyond cutting government spending for social services both directly and through nonprofit organizations, Congress has debated a number of proposals that conservatives believe would transform the nonprofit sector and reduce its dependency on government: limiting political advocacy of any kind by nonprofit organizations receiving government support; barring advocacy groups from the Combined Federal Campaign, the on-the-job fundraising drive for federal employees; encouraging charitable giving by increasing tax credits or deductions for donations to organizations that serve the poor (or alternatively, a flat tax that would increase charitable giving by reducing the taxes many people pay); a greater role for religious organizations in delivering services to the poor. Above all, conservatives believe that cutting taxes, regulations, and litigation will stimulate the economy sufficiently to increase charitable giving dramatically. As Daniel T. Oliver of the Capital Research Center put it: "We need other initiatives, like deregulation and other policies to encourage freer markets, so that more wealth is created and people have more to give."[27]

The CRC's and the Right's critique of the nonprofit sector, moreover, resonates with a number of more general conservative ideas as well, in

◆

particular the political and cultural failure of big business, the subversive-
ness of intellectuals and the New Class, and the strategy of "de-funding the
Left."

These themes were expressed especially clearly in *A Time for Truth,* a
1978 volume by William E. Simon, former Treasury Secretary and head of
the Olin Foundation, a man who played as great a role as any in mobilizing
corporate support for the Reagan revolution.[28] After arguing at considerable length how government spending, taxes, and regulation threaten
capitalism and economic liberty, Simon issued a clarion call for big
business to fight back. The root trouble, he argued, citing a theme common
in conservative writing, is that a New Class of government bureaucrats,
intellectuals, journalists, and foundation heads hostile to capitalism have
taken power in America and are using that power to undermine business
by expanding the state and spreading anti-capitalist ideas.[29] Political and
cultural power in America, in short, has become at odds with economic
power. Business executives have allowed this to happen, because they
have retreated from politics in the broad sense, because they have become
"more concerned with short-range respectability than with long-range
survival."[30] Worse still, they have contributed to their own demise by
allowing their money to fund this New Class, through grants to universities
and other nonprofit organizations as well as through profit-making cultural
institutions.

What business leaders needed to do, above all, Simon concluded, was
not lobby more energetically for specific legislation or spend more to elect
suitable political leaders, but support the growth of a "counterintelligentsia"
in the foundations, universities, and media that would regain ideological
dominance for big business. Accordingly, Simon issued a series of marching
orders to his peers: corporations must shift their funding to foundations
willing to support conservative scholars and research; they must "cease the
mindless subsidizing of colleges and universities whose departments of
economics, government, politics and history are hostile to capitalism"; and
they must shift their support

> from the media which serve as megaphones for anticapitalist opinion
> and to media which are either pro-freedom or . . . at least profession-
> ally capable of a fair and accurate treatment of procapitalist ideas,
> values, and arguments.[31]

In short, Simon and many other conservative writers in the 1970s sought
to alert corporate leaders that preserving their economic power required
maintaining cultural hegemony.

◆

Simon's call for big business to do battle with the New Class (and the similar ideas of the CRC) reflects long-standing ideas on the Right. The idea that intellectuals and cultural elites generally are a subversive rather than a conservative force goes all the way back to Edmund Burke's critique of the French Revolution. The claim that capitalism has won the economic battle only to lose the cultural war harks back to Joseph Schumpeter's 1940s classic, *Capitalism, Socialism, and Democracy.* The American Right has combined the two ideas since at least the early 1950s, when the young William F. Buckley, Jr., in *God and Man at Yale,* roundly condemned the professors at his alma mater for being anti-capitalist and urged his fellow alumni to withhold their support.[32]

The claim that intellectuals and the New Class generally are the force behind the expansion of government's role in the economy and the decline of middle-class values (individual initiative, responsibility, and self-control) underlies the "culture wars" that the Right has fought over the last two decades against the universities, the artistic and literary world, Hollywood, public school textbooks, and other enemies.[33] As William J. Bennett puts it,

> Why is there a battle about our culture? Part of the answer lies in understanding that there is a fundamental difference between many of the most important beliefs of most Americans and the belief of a liberal elite that today dominates many of our institutions and who therefore exert influence on American life and culture.
>
> The elite are most often found among academics and intellectuals, in the literary world, in journals of political opinion, in Hollywood, in the artistic community, in mainline religious institutions, and in some quarters of the media.[34]

One key to winning the culture war and defeating the liberal elite, conservatives agree, is defunding the Left, cutting its financial support from foundations, corporations, and especially the government. In 1981, New Right activist Richard Viguerie argued that

> For more than a decade, the Left has relied on government subsidies to finance its activities. . . . My estimate is that 70 percent of the Left's financing comes from the government. While liberals loudly claim to represent the people, they are primarily financed by compulsory tax dollars.[35]

Viguerie went on to laud the Reagan Administration for "de-funding the Left" by attempting to cut a myriad of government programs. Ever since, conservatives have sought to cut federal support for organizations deemed

◈

outposts of the liberal elite: the National Endowments for the Arts and the Humanities, the Legal Services Corporation, the Corporation for Public Broadcasting, and the like.

Corporations on the political and cultural defensive, a subversive New Class, the need to defund the Left, and the importance of re-establishing the independence of the nonprofit sector—all these themes are both central to the conservative view of American society and implicit in the Capital Research Center's attack on corporate philanthropy. As the CRC pictures American society, corporations face a world of enemies, especially intellectuals and other elites in the nonprofit sector, bent on destroying it or wounding it seriously by expanding the power of government and undermining middle-class values. Under such circumstances, it is inconceivable that corporations should support a nonprofit advocacy group that in any way seeks to expand the power of government or is in any way critical of big business. Corporate philanthropy should instead join the culture war against liberal elites in the nonprofit sector.

The Corporate Response

The Capital Research Center directs its message to top corporate management, whom it sees as potential allies in the battle against the philanthropic elite and their culture. It routinely sends copies of its yearly study to CEOs; these copies often are accompanied by letters from prominent conservatives, including former Republican Cabinet secretaries William Simon and Donald Rumsfeld, and most recently House Majority Leader Armey.

Although the CRC clearly hopes to awaken slumbering CEOs and send them rushing to rein in their errant giving programs, nothing of the sort has happened. Corporate giving programs have not changed their public policy funding, and corporate philanthropists have not come under serious fire from the top.

Indeed, the CRC does not claim to have had an impact on corporate giving, emphasizing instead only the attention the media pays to their studies of corporate giving.[36] Data presented in their 1992 volume, moreover, show no change over the previous five or six years in the grades corporations have received for their giving. Their first study gave 60 percent of the corporations grades of D or F and another 26 percent Cs; the 1992 study gave 66 percent Ds and Fs and 24 percent Cs. The CRC's lack of impact led William Simon to lament in the preface to the 1992 study:

◆

"Nothing would make me happier than to be able to say that the last four years have witnessed a reversal of this sorry picture. I cannot."[37] The 1994 report, once again noting a lack of progress, lamented caustically:

> It is clear that too many corporate executives just don't get it. The trends in corporate philanthropy have not improved during the eight years Capital Research Center has conducted this study.[38]

One of the only top executives to speak out on the subject, J. Richard Munro, chair of the executive committee of Time-Warner, criticized the Capital Research Center in 1991 for giving low ratings to "companies most would regard as having exemplary public service programs such as AT&T, American Express, Mobil, and General Motors" and cautioned corporate executives to "analyze criticism of their giving carefully before reacting."[39]

Corporate giving directors report getting hardly any flak from top management as a result of the CRC's annual reports. The only exception was at a corporation whose "liberal" giving record had been mentioned on both national and local radio talk shows. "Everybody in the company" seemed concerned for a time, the corporate giving officer said. However, a memo noting that the rating was based on less than 1 percent of the giving program's grants and pointing out that many of the allegedly left-wing recipients were really not so radical sufficed to quiet the internal fuss.

More typical is the response described by another corporate philanthropist whose giving program consistently makes the CRC's top ten list of corporate misgivers. The first year, when the CRC's report came to top management along with letters signed by Simon and Rumsfeld, "letters just flooded to us" from "the CEO and the President and the Chief Counsel and the Directors" saying, "What on earth are you doing? Look at what these people say! What's to this?" The corporate giving officer replied with a memo noting the other prestigious giving programs that had been pilloried by the CRC and detailing some of the grants for which his company had been criticized. As it turned out, one of them was to the Aspen Institute, on whose board the Chairman of the corporation sat. In this way, the corporate giving officer portrayed the CRC's report as "only espousing a point of view for which they have no justification." In subsequent years, inquiries from the top dwindled away. This corporate philanthropist concluded from the vantage point of early 1993 that "the Capital Research Center has been neutralized."

Others tell similar stories time and again. One corporate giving officer reports that when top management first received the CRC report,

> I had maybe three or four inquiries and I wrote a three-page response and people called and said thanks very much and that's it. And the

◆

> next year I got one inquiry and I pulled that [response] out and
> updated it and sent it back and since then I haven't heard anything.

The most striking example of the failure of the CRC to get a rise out of top management comes from a corporate philanthropist whose corporate board included Donald Rumsfeld himself. She described a request from her Chairman to identify the grants the CRC found offensive and to compare the company's giving program with that of other companies. She responded with a "white paper" defending the giving program, and that was that: "There was never a challenge in any of the questioning that said, 'You need to do something different.'"

Corporate philanthropists dismiss the CRC with a casualness that conveys no sense of feeling threatened. "They are a joke," says one corporate giving executive; others label it as "ridiculous," "pathetic," "pretty bizarre," "nonsense." The director of corporate giving at a company that received a relatively good (i.e., conservative) rating from the CRC says he is "pretty embarrassed" by that fact. Managers whose giving programs perennially receive bad ratings take satisfaction in this fact. One "took great pride in making their list" of corporate misgivers and mentioned getting a congratulatory memo from top management. Another comments on her program's "D" rating:

> We're in good company. A lot of companies that I have the utmost
> respect for [in regard to] their charitable giving are also in the "D"
> category.

Others express mock dismay at not getting a sufficiently bad grade. One terms herself "offended that last year we were not one of the top ten offenders." Many of the most dismissive of the corporate philanthropists, moreover, are insiders with long careers in their companies, not outsiders from the nonprofit sector.

The casually dismissive response reflects not only the lack of heat from the top but also the sense of being "in good company." The CRC attacks not a few corporations for a particular kind of grant, but nearly all corporations for a wide range of public policy grantmaking. Sharing the attack with AT&T, American Express, ARCO, and other luminaries of the corporate giving world turns criticism into accolade and also reinforces the sense that the CRC stands beyond the pale of respectable opinion. As one corporate giving officer puts it,

> In their view, [my corporation] and Xerox and IBM and Johnson &
> Johnson and every other company that is typically thought by the
> rational world as being responsive and innovative and creative and
> helpful is too far liberal.

◆

By attacking exemplary giving programs, the CRC takes on the whole culture of corporate philanthropy. As a result, the CRC appears to defy common sense, or at the least the common sense understanding corporate philanthropists have about what corporate giving is all about. They "lacked credibility in responsible circles," as one put it.

When corporate giving officers try to explain what exactly is wrong with the Capital Research Center and its criticism of them, they keep coming back to one general characterization. The CRC is ideological and dogmatic; it has preconceived notions about corporate philanthropy and cooks its data accordingly. By contrast, they imply, corporate philanthropy is not ideological.

Corporate philanthropists illustrate the ideological, dogmatic bent of the CRC in several ways. For one thing, one corporate giving officer points out, "their definitions of who is Right and who is Left are pretty bizarre." Several have pet examples of solidly mainstream organizations, often supported by top management itself, that the CRC tars as liberal. We already have the example of the Aspen Institute. Another corporate giving officer gave the League of Women Voters. A third mentioned the Foreign Policy Association, noting with considerable mirth that her corporation's president "has been a member of the board of the Foreign Policy Association and his predecessor had been a member." He might regard the organization as many things, "but left of center wouldn't have been one of them."

Other corporate philanthropists note with obvious irritation that the CRC rates their giving programs on the basis of a tiny percentage of their grants. They take this as further evidence of the ideological rigidity of the CRC, its penchant for imposing preconceived ideas on the data. As one says,

> To put it bluntly, I believe they decide what their answer is and then try to torque their responses to meet their very extreme bias. I mean, they take, in our particular situation, somewhere between $1\frac{1}{2}$ and 2 percent of our total dollar grants annually and on that basis they then proceed to determine by their litmus test and their measurement tool whether you're right, moderate, left of center, etc. It's some of the lousiest junk I've seen anybody put out.

Because of its ideological rigidity, the CRC is impossible to engage in dialogue, corporate giving officers say. As one puts it,

> It's been our experience over the years that it really doesn't matter what you tell them. You can try to explain things. We've tried to do that in the past, but from my perspective and sharing the feelings of others whom

◆

I've talked with, it doesn't really matter what you say to them . . . they're going to print it the way that they want to.

The most striking manifestation of the CRC's dogmatism in the eyes of corporate philanthropists, however, is the organization's "failure" to understand that corporate philanthropy funds projects, not organizations. The CRC believes that by funding a project of an organization, a corporation is supporting and endorsing its overall goals and activities. For corporate giving officers, in contrast, the distinction is crucial: By funding a specific project, one is not in any sense endorsing a whole organization; nor is one agreeing with everything they believe. One corporate philanthropist, for example, seemed genuinely perplexed by criticism of a grant her corporation made to the American Friends Service Committee, which receives a CRC rating of 2 (Left). The grant, she explains, supports a program

> at an alternative high school, which brought Hispanic kids who had dropped out of high school back into school. It's hard to quarrel with getting kids back into school. It happened to be that they [the American Friends Service Committee] were the local service organization that was doing the work.

Generally speaking, corporate giving officers argue, it is unrealistic to expect that any nonprofit organization would see eye-to-eye with a corporation on all issues. As one notes, "there isn't going to be an absolutely consistent philosophical or ideological or political convergence of minds. That's not the way it works." In the words of another:

> Many organizations in my view give to nonprofits for specific projects knowing that those nonprofits in other parts of their institutional activities may take views . . . opposed to those of the giver. . . . We have in our grantmaking consciously recognized that some organizations do good work that we wish to support, but at other times would take views that are not supportive of the company or the industry.

To see how this attitude holds up when one gets down to specifics, I asked a number of corporate philanthropists about the Children's Defense Fund. The CRC places this organization near the far left of its political scale with a rating of 2 and has flagged support for it as a major example of corporate misgiving. Corporate giving officers reply by defending the Fund's programs even while noting ideological disagreements with it. One says,

> The Children's Defense Fund is a good organization. They probably endorse public policy that would go beyond what either I or the company would personally endorse. . . . But that doesn't mean that the

◆

core programs of that organization aren't well thought out or undertaken. So we continue to support them.

Another corporate philanthropist, who runs the giving program of a major
insurance company, makes a similar point but takes it a bit further. Asked
if there is a basic ideological conflict involved in insurance companies
supporting the Children's Defense Fund, given the latter's support of
national health insurance, she replies,

> No, I don't believe that. It's the same thing as with abortion. Do we
> want to have a litmus test on how every institution we support
> proposes to address national health insurance or health care? Can't do
> it. You can't live like that. You can't just live with only an ideologically
> pure sense of collaboration. You know, in part one of the wonderful
> things about . . . corporate philanthropy is the ability to build bridges
> with people who are in organizations who don't necessarily share
> every single viewpoint. In the case of what we're doing with the
> Children's Defense Fund, their work on childhood poverty is very
> important. Do we go do a litmus test and say, "Do you believe A, B, C,
> D? You know, you've got to be ideologically pure in A, B, C, D." No!

Ideological purity, in other words, is both impossible and undesirable. The
implicit assumption is that corporations live in a pluralistic political
world, in which ideological convergence is not to be expected. The
untidiness of this world is simply taken for granted and not seen as a
problem. Indeed, one of the special functions of corporate philanthropy
in this kind of world is to "build bridges" between the corporation and
nonprofit organizations.

Reflecting more broadly on the place of the corporation in society,
another corporate giving officer notes with a smile that conflict is simply a
fact of life for corporations in all their dealings, so why should philanthropy
be any different?

> You know, [the CRC] gives examples of organizations that some of us
> fund who also might sue a corporation. You know, well, we are
> involved in law suits and arguments, [laugh] and lobbying and stuff
> like that as a company . . . all the time with groups. We do business
> with groups that we don't agree with on everything. . . . I don't think
> there's anything wrong with companies being associated with groups
> that they don't agree with on every single issue at every given time.

Conservative and Pragmatic Visions

The clash between corporate philanthropy and the Capital Research
Center is not just about what is or is not liberal or whether one can

◈

legitimately distinguish funding projects from supporting the organizations that run the projects. It is fundamentally about different basic understandings of the place of business in American politics and society. Both understandings are pro-business, but they differ starkly on what business has to do to survive.

The Capital Research Center takes a Manichean view of the place of business in American society: American politics is a battle between pro- and anti-business forces, between those who support free-market capitalism and those, especially the New Class, eager to expand government control of economic life. There is little middle ground. In such circumstances, corporations need to distinguish friends from enemies and when it comes to philanthropy, support only the former. The CRC espouses a *Conservative Vision*.

Corporate giving officers, speaking for the approach that their corporations take to philanthropy, hold a very different view of things. In this view, a kind of *benign pluralism* reigns in American politics. What corporations face is not a world of enemies but a cacophony of groups pursuing a variety of interests and goals. Corporations may disagree with these groups, but few truly threaten them. Above all, conflict and disagreements are simply facts of life that undercut any attempt to be ideologically pure. Indeed, the key to survival in this benignly pluralist world is bridge-building, dialogue, and cooperation. To be combative or overly ideological would merely create enemies and misunderstanding where none need exist. Supporting organizations that the corporation may disagree with is not only inevitable, it is of value to the company. Corporate philanthropists, in short, implicitly endorse a *Pragmatic Vision*.

One corporate giving officer in fact talked explicitly about the pragmatic role of corporate giving:

> Some of the organizations we fund may take a view that the government ought to do something. I think Capital Research feels that the government shouldn't be in various things. And certainly to some extent I agree with them. But government is here and the majority of people do feel there are certain things government should do. . . . So whether you agree with it or not, that's still a pragmatic role. And what I'm saying is that you may support people who may have different views than you have on certain issues.

Society, in other words, is not quite the way this executive (or presumably his corporation) would like to have it, but facts are facts: Government is here to stay, because plenty of people want it that way. It is foolish therefore to take too ideological a stance when it comes to philanthropy.

In a benignly pluralist society, corporate giving officers assert, under-

◧

standing and communication are important. By implication, one important purpose of philanthropy for the corporation is precisely to provide these things. If "building bridges" by supporting a variety of nonprofit organizations is healthy for the corporation, disdaining to do so out of ideological rigidity is downright dangerous. As one says,

> I think from a strategic point of view in a pluralistic society like ours that no company can afford to paint itself into some ideological corner. And you need wide understanding and you need communication with a lot of people. . . .

Several other corporate philanthropists make similar points. One notes simply, "We have a pluralistic society and need to be plugged into various ways of thinking." Another puts it this way:

> I think it's healthy to have relationships with people, with organizations, and so on, that you don't agree with on everything, that you can hear from, that know what's going on.

What all this relating, communicating, and understanding ideally provides the corporation is *access* and *alliances*. Among other things, philanthropy allows the corporation's voice to be heard in places where it otherwise might fall on deaf ears. It also plants the seeds of partnerships that may transform a potentially antagonistic relationship between the company and outside interests.

One corporate giving officer, who had previously been a lobbyist for his corporation, explains the idea of access by drawing an implicit analogy between philanthropy and his former function. Asked why corporations might occasionally fund projects of nonprofit organizations with which they disagree politically, he replies:

> What we have found is even for moderate to liberal kinds of groups you're probably better off working on the inside than you are on the outside. When I was lobbying I went before many a legislator . . . that I knew wasn't going to vote my way. But all I wanted them to do is listen to me. And down the road it might just trigger a little doubt in their minds. . . . If I got my facts on the floor . . . I had to affect their reasoning somewhere down the road, and that's why I think it's important even where we think the group's position is in opposition to ours that we at least get a voice in.

Supporting nonprofits, like lobbying a legislature, is a way of "working on the inside."

Several corporate givers give environmental groups as examples of how philanthropy might build alliances and mitigate potentially dangerous conflict. One, who works for an oil company, explains the benefits of carefully discriminating support for environmental groups:

> There are some environmental groups that it's in their interest to bash us. Regardless of what we say or do, it's never enough . . . [but] we [also] know environmental groups that we can work with. Many, many times they do not agree with legislation or regulations but we're able to work with them in terms of projects that are for the benefit of the community. . . . And when we can work on that kind of a project together, I think it helps in building a sense of goodwill and credibility that maybe then can spread to discussion of other areas.

From this perspective, corporate philanthropy ideally is a foundation on which the corporation can build "goodwill" and "credibility."

The corporate giving officer of a forest products company makes a similar point about her giving program's selective support for environmental groups. "It is important to partner with environmental organizations," she says, "so we can arrive at win-win solutions to the problems we face." Like her oil company colleague, she distinguishes between "balanced" environmental groups, worthy of support, and "polarizing" ones, who presumably are not.[40]

Conclusion

Through much of this book, we have been searching for an ideology, a broad vision of the relationship between big business and society within which corporate philanthropy might take on a significance that goes beyond its contribution to its particular company. We began by showing that corporate philanthropy has a strong collective life. It is not simply the sum total of individual corporate giving programs; rather it has as well a common culture and a network of transcorporate ties among corporate giving programs. Individual corporate philanthropists share this common understanding and participate in that network.

Yet, this collective life, it seemed, did not consistently yield the broad vision for which we were looking. Sociologist Michael Useem has argued that the collective life of corporate philanthropy encourages a "classwide rationality," an understanding of corporate philanthropy as serving the interests of big business as a whole, partly replacing a "company rationality," an orientation toward the interests of the individual corporation alone.[41] We found relatively little of this "classwide rationality," or any broad vision of how corporate philanthropy fits into the broader relationship between big business and society. The official culture of corporate philanthropy (i.e., writing directed to corporate givers themselves) does articulate broad, classwide rationales for corporate giving, but it devotes considerably more space to spelling out and cultivating the relationship between the individual giving program and its company. Corporate giving officers themselves have precious little space to articulate broad visions of what they do, given the day-to-day pressures they face within their firms and thus rarely do so. The few who do ironically are those with strong ties not only to the culture of corporate philanthropy but to the nonprofit sector as well.

In this chapter, however, we have finally found this ideology, embodied in what we have called the Pragmatic Vision and its central notion of benign pluralism. It forms part of the implicit common sense of corporate philanthropy and thus informs how corporate philanthropists think about their work even when they don't refer to it directly. It gets articulated only as corporate philanthropists respond to attacks from the right-wing Capital Research Center. The fundamental clash between the Pragmatic Vision of corporate philanthropy and the Conservative Vision of the CRC helps explain the bitterness of the attack and of the corporate response.

The significance of the Pragmatic Vision goes well beyond corporate philanthropy. It is an important part of corporate politics generally. To understand this role, we need to go beyond the obvious ways that Pragmatic and Conservative visions collide to examining the more subtle ways in which they mix and complement each other. This mix, chapter 7 will argue, is one key to what is distinctive about the political role of big business in American society.

7

Corporate Philanthropy and Corporate Politics

◆

The clash between corporate philanthropists and the right-wing Capital Research Center, examined in detail in chapter 6, comes down to a conflict between different political understandings of the place of big business in American society. Corporate philanthropists hold a Pragmatic Vision, rooted in the idea of benign pluralism. In this view, corporations confront a social world in which they face diverse interests with whom conflicts can be worked out amicably, not bitter enemies who must be conquered. The key to prospering in this world is "building bridges," establishing clear lines of communication, maintaining access. Corporate philanthropy is a way of accomplishing this with the organizations of the nonprofit sector.

The Capital Research Center, in contrast, sticks to a Conservative Vision that pictures a social world in which big business faces many enemies bent on destroying it or at least limiting its power; primary among these is the New Class, liberal cultural elites in the media, government agencies, universities, the arts and humanities, and the nonprofit sector generally. Bridges, relationships, and access in this kind of world are grotesquely out of place. Corporations have to use their resources to defeat their enemies and create a society more favorable to their interests. Corporate philanthropy ought to be a weapon in this battle, funding nonprofit organizations that are resolutely conservative in their outlooks and avoiding those marked with liberalism of any kind. This Conservative Vision is not idiosyncratic to the Capital Research Center; its basic themes resonate across the Right generally, as chapter 6 documented.

The immediate significance of this conflict is that it reveals that corporate philanthropists, despite their resolute commitment to their individual corporations and their claims to be nonideological, have a distinctly political understanding of the way in which corporate philanthropy serves the general interests of big business in American society. In other words, they possess what we have called a classwide rationality, even though they rarely articulate it. Indeed, the themes they emphasize in rejecting criticism from the Capital Research Center resonate with those

◧

stated by corporate leaders since the early 1950s in justifying the expansion of corporate philanthropy as a way of increasing the legitimacy of big business generally, strengthening the nonprofit sector, and limiting the sway of government.

The distinction between Pragmatic and Conservative visions has implications of considerably greater importance and broader significance as well. To get at these, we need to revise our understanding of the relationship between the two visions. So far, we have pictured them as diametrically opposed to each other. We have located the Conservative Vision largely outside the corporate world in an independent conservative movement, which has appeared largely in conflict with big business.

There is some truth to this picture, at least with regard to corporate philanthropy, but overall it is misleading. A more accurate understanding of the relationship between Pragmatic and Conservative visions (and between big business and the Right) and of its broader significance includes the following points:

(1) Although the Pragmatic Vision predominates in corporate philanthropy, elements of the Conservative Vision are also present. That is, the Conservative Vision does not reside wholly outside corporate philanthropy. Corporations do identify some nonprofit organizations as enemies and some activities as anti-business. They circumscribe their giving accordingly.

(2) A mix of Pragmatic and Conservative visions also characterizes other areas of corporate political activity, notably contributions to political candidates through political action committees.

(3) Although Pragmatic and Conservative visions imply very different political strategies for big business, they are not wholly in conflict. At a deeper level they often complement each other.

(4) Because corporate politics mixes Pragmatic and Conservative strategies, the relationship between big business and the Right as an organized political movement is a complicated one, a mixture of conflict and alliance. The conflict between corporate philanthropy and the Capital Research Center mines a real vein of hostility between big business and the Right, but that hostility is only one side of the story. Big business has played a major role in pushing American politics to the right, especially during the late 1970s and early 1980s and again with the 1994 elections.

(5) The mix of Conservative and Pragmatic strategies captures what is distinctive about the power of big business in American society. The changing mix of these strategies over time, moreover, is a key to the changing nature of corporate politics. When the conservative strategy

◙

dominates, as in the Corporate Conservatism of the late 1970s and early Reagan years, corporations organize in a broad way to push American politics to the right. When the pragmatic strategy dominates, big business accepts the political world as it is and seeks broad influence within it. Usually both are active to some degree. Together they give big business a distinct kind of influence that few observers have appreciated. The pragmatic strategy in particular gives big business a kind of power that is often not fully appreciated.

This chapter develops these themes by looking first more closely at how Pragmatic and Conservative visions play out in corporate philanthropy and then at their role in corporate contributions to political candidates. Finally, it uses these ideas to develop an overall conceptualization of the political power of big business in American society that provides a distinctive take on how American corporations occupy a privileged political position. In doing so, it will sometimes substitute the terms "Corporate Pragmatism" and "Corporate Conservatism" for "Pragmatic Vision" and "Conservative Vision."

Pragmatism, Conservatism, and Corporate Philanthropy

At the core of the Pragmatic Vision are the ideas that corporations and nonprofit organizations are potential allies and that corporate philanthropy is a way of building relations between the two. In chapter 6, we heard corporate giving officers allude to these ideas in response to attacks from the Capital Research Center. On a more general level, Reynold Levy, president of the AT&T Foundation, has articulated the importance of "relationships" to corporate philanthropy especially well. In a 1989 essay, he argues that "philanthropy should be approached as a long-term investment that stimulates and reinforces the overall [corporate] relationship with nonprofit institutions." It is a way to build "stable and mutually beneficial relationships between the corporation and its nonprofit allies."[1]

These ties are important for several reasons, Levy argues. First, "the more services nonprofits provide, the less government is required." Second, the nonprofit sector is a major economic force to which no corporation "can afford to pay less than full attention." Third, nonprofit organizations and their leaders command the "power of public respect" and constitute "a set of highly influential shapers of public opinion." Fourth, the nonprofit sector broadly defined has been the source of the great social movements of American society. Corporations either can deal with these movements after they have crystallized as problems or "can interact with

◆

these organizations and their issues before they become forces to be reckoned with on their own terms."[2]

For all these reasons, Levy strongly recommends that recipients of corporate largesse be seen as "potential partners, consultants, and allies" and that philanthropy be seen as "an open door for access, one route by which this constituency can be reached and meaningfully engaged."[3]

One way of clarifying the relationship between corporate donors and nonprofit recipients described in the Pragmatic Vision is to see corporate donations as *gifts*. This is not to say that they are purely altruistic, made with nothing required in return. Gifts of any kind are rarely this simple. Calling them gifts simply signals their difference from economic or market transactions. In an economic transaction one thing is directly exchanged for another; it can be and often is an isolated interaction. You give me a quarter; I give you a newspaper. That's all there is to it; our relationship need go no further. The transaction does not require us to be friends, relatives, or lovers.[4] It invokes no obligations or expectations about future interaction.

In contrast, gifts are exchanges in which there is no immediate quid pro quo; they usually flow from, create, or sustain deeper relationships. They evoke or reinforce a set of norms or understandings about how giver and recipient ought to treat each other. As a result, they activate or reinforce powerful obligations and expectations, which may involve reciprocity at a future date or simply a general way of treating the giver.

I give you a book for your birthday. You are not expected to pull out your wallet and pay me for it or to run out immediately and buy me something of similar value. Indeed to do so would be grossly inappropriate; it would represent a total misunderstanding of what a gift is. However, if I consistently give you gifts for your birthday and for holidays, and you never reciprocate (even though I know you are able to do so), our relationship is likely to become strained. More important, if I give you gifts, and you treat me badly, not the way friends or relatives or lovers are supposed to treat each other, I am likely to feel that the terms of the gift have been violated, though no such terms were ever articulated. My gift asserted that we were friends; your actions violated that understanding.

Corporate philanthropy is a gift in this sense. It does not require the nonprofit organization to do anything immediately for the corporation (other than carry out the program being funded). Corporations usually do not expect the universities or art museums or battered women's shelters they fund to turn around the next day and lobby Congress for legislation the corporation wants.

Indeed, even in the long run, corporations rarely seek or get a specific

◈

quid pro quo for their donations. A prominent progressive critic, known for sharply criticizing corporate philanthropy on a number of grounds, emphasized this in a conversation with me:

> In my history of talking with people about corporate philanthropy I can't think of but one single instance where corporations have ever gone back to their grantees to say, "we need your help now." And that one was the instance of the Dayton Hudson Corporation up in Minneapolis when they were threatened by a hostile takeover and they went to their grantees and said, "Help us get a bill through the legislature so that we can fight off this hostile takeover." And the grantees responded and they got the bill passed. It's the only example I can think of.

Undoubtedly, there are other instances of long-term quid pro quos. For example, in 1994, when the New York City Council proposed a bill banning smoking in most public places, Philip Morris, a major funder of the arts, asked many of its grant recipients to lobby against it, making clear that if the bill passed, the corporation would move its headquarters and grants out of New York City.[5]

Still, the basic point is well taken: What corporations usually expect in return for their grants is not anything specific or tangible (even in the long run), but simply a certain quality of relationship with the recipient. They expect the nonprofit to accept the corporation as a legitimate social and political actor, to listen seriously to its voice, and to air any differences that might arise between them in an amicable, routine way, rather than through confrontation. Like any gift, corporate philanthropy is meant to create or reinforce a relationship, one whose specific, tangible return to the corporation may remain open. These amicable relationships between corporation and nonprofit organizations build upon and reinforce the underlying benign pluralism of American society, in which big business must deal with competing interest groups, but with few real enemies.

The progressive critic mentioned earlier noted that one of his very few corporate supporters has literally insisted on establishing a modest relationship with him beyond simply handing over a check, even though this has never led to any requests for favors.

> We get about $5,000 a year from [a corporation] and in the last four to five years, before I get the check I have lunch with their government relations person. Indeed at some point in time that could make some difference, probably a very subtle difference. I've never been asked to do anything; I doubt if I'll ever be asked to do anything. But at least the link has been established.

Whether or not this critic pulls any punches because of the small

◨

corporate donations he receives, what is more important is that corporations *generally* expect a certain degree of amicability from the nonprofits
they support. This is nowhere more evident than in the Planned Parenthood
controversy discussed in chapter 5. It is not surprising that corporate
philanthropists caught up in the imbroglio would resent the Christian
Action Council and its efforts to boycott funders of Planned Parenthood.
They didn't like having their giving programs politicized and turned into a
potential liability for the corporation. What is striking, however, is that
several of them were even more critical of Planned Parenthood's angry
public response to AT&T's decision to stop funding. The Christian Action
Council's actions were merely a big problem; Planned Parenthood's reeked
of betrayal.

While none thought that AT&T was disloyal to Planned Parenthood by
ending its quarter-century of support so abruptly, several found Planned
Parenthood disloyal to AT&T for getting upset about it. "It does make you
think," one corporate giving officer observed, when an organization makes
a political issue out of a corporate decision to end funding after enjoying
that support for twenty-five or thirty years.

Another was positively livid, his voice rising in anger as he described
Planned Parenthood's full-page ads and campaign to get its supporters to
boycott AT&T as tantamount to blackmail. "There is no way in hell that
they'd ever get funding again" from his company, he concluded forcefully.

Oliver Peck, the senior corporate philanthropist and veteran of two
corporate giving programs already encountered in chapter 5, offered an
especially revealing assessment of the controversy. He criticized the
Christian Action Council and its letter writers. "I have been put off by the
tone of that correspondence," he said. "To me it borders on extortion. You
know, if you stop funding these [programs], we will take you off our list,
and I just, I find that offensive." At the same time, however, he saw both
sides in the abortion debate as equally at fault, referring to them as "two
warring factions," who are "firing machine guns at each other." At points,
moreover, he attacked Planned Parenthood with special anger:

> We saw what happened to AT&T when they started to decrease their
> funding and suddenly . . . the crazier the Right becomes on this issue,
> the crazier Planned Parenthood is getting. Planned Parenthood turned
> right around and even though it had a long relationship with AT&T,
> like a snake bit them, and bit them hard, and in fact took it farther than
> biting them, . . . pilloried AT&T to drum up support among their
> individual supporters.

In effect, he understood the controversy as resulting not simply from a boy-

◈

cott threat issued by pro-life groups, but from the mutually reinforcing craziness of both sides. From this perspective Planned Parenthood was as much to blame as was the Christian Action Council. Indeed, it was more at fault, because it had violated a "long relationship with AT&T."

It is this notion of "relationship" that is important here. Corporation donations are gifts, not market exchanges in which an immediate quid pro quo is necessary. They are instead a way of establishing and reinforcing a certain kind of relationship between the corporation and the nonprofit organization. This relationship carries with it expectations about how nonprofit organizations should behave. To be sure, most corporate philan-thropists would agree that AT&T had handled its decision badly, stopping funding with no prior consultation and letting the decision get to the press before it got to Planned Parenthood. Still, in their view, this public relations snafu did not justify placing full-page newspaper ads attacking AT&T, cancelling a major contract for a phone system, or urging supporters to boycott AT&T. If nothing else, years of funding should buy an amicable relationship between a major nonprofit and a major corporation. Non-profit organizations are not supposed to bite the corporate hands that feed them, even under duress. They are supposed to resolve conflicts with corporations through conversation and compromise. They are not sup-posed to take to the streets, as it were, or even to the pages of the *New York Times.*

The notion of gift not only clarifies the Pragmatic Vision of corporate philanthropy but also helps identify its limits. There are, after all, certain people to whom one simply does not give gifts. Likewise there are limits to the easygoing pragmatism and benign pluralism of corporate giving. The Pragmatic Vision may dominate corporate philanthropy, but a more com-bative conservatism lurks in the background, placing political boundaries on the relationship-building of corporate giving.

Although our focus on the conflict between corporate philanthropy and the Capital Research Center has been useful in identifying the Prag-matic and Conservative visions, it misleadingly implies that the Conserva-tive Vision is wholly alien to corporate philanthropy. In fact, it has a place there and an even bigger one elsewhere in corporate politics.

To be sure, corporate philanthropists talk a great deal about building relationships and bridges to a wide range of nonprofits and decry the dangers of "painting oneself into a corner" in a "pluralistic" society. Even as they do so, however, they recognize the limits to this. Recall the corporate philanthropist in chapter 6 who distinguished environmental groups "we can work with" from those that "bash us," or the corporate

◆

philanthropist who similarly contrasted "balanced" with "polarizing" environmental groups. Each of them clearly is drawing a political line beyond which a pragmatic strategy makes no sense.

Walter George, the especially well respected corporate giving officer we met at the end of chapter 3, grudgingly acknowledged the limits placed on one of his foundation's major priority areas by senior management. The area emphasizes promoting democracy by developing and empowering minority communities and encouraging orderly citizen participation in government. Obviously, he noted, voter registration would be a natural part of this; however, top management has balked at this:

> We've never done voter registration. And if you really believe totally in democracy, one of the things you ought to do is to have more people participating in the system. But that's been too controversial for our management to buy into. If they tend to be conservative Republicans, . . . their assumption is that the registrants would be liberal Democrats seeking more public goals. And we've got enough problems. And that's tough to accept.

If political limits on corporate philanthropy can be identified in the post-Reagan years, during which big business has felt relatively secure politically, they were more obvious in the 1970s, when big business felt more embattled. Although support for higher education had become a staple of corporate philanthropy by that time, the considerable radical protest on campus, often aimed at corporations in particular, gave corporate leaders considerable pause about being too free with that support.[6]

Coming into the 1970s, the Committee for Corporate Support of American Universities and other organizations had encouraged corporations to give *unrestricted* grants to a select set of major research universities as a way of encouraging advanced research, producing Ph.D.s, and creating a new generation of college professors. Corporate leader David Packard had been active in this organization since the late 1950s and had strongly encouraged such grants. In 1973, in the face of campus protest, he made a u-turn. Speaking at a meeting of the committee, he pointed out that

> hostile groups of scholars are, to a large degree, responsible for the antibusiness bias of many of our young people today. And I do not believe it is in the corporate interest to support them—which is what we do to a greater or a lesser degree with unrestricted funds.[7]

Packard ticked off a list of offenses occurring on university campuses at the time: kicking ROTC (the Reserve Officer Training Corps) off campus, pre-

◈

venting corporations from recruiting on campus, teaching that American corporations are evil, and so on. In light of all this, a different giving strategy was called for:

> In the future, let's focus our money and our energy on those schools and departments which are strong and which also contribute in some specific way to our individual companies, or to the general welfare of our free enterprise system.[8]

Packard captured a developing sense of embattlement in the corporate world, which generally made companies receptive to the clarion calls of conservatives such as William Simon later in the decade and encouraged the conservative corporate mobilization that helped push American politics to the right in the early 1980s (about which we shall say more later in the chapter). Summarizing this attitude with regard to corporate philanthropy at the end of the 1970s, Frank Koch, one-time head of corporate giving at Syntex, laid out a straightforward rule in his influential book, *The New Corporate Philanthropy:*

> Corporations have no obligation to provide funds to organizations or individuals that are devoted to the replacement of our economic, political, and social system by some other system. This would be foolhardy.[9]

This sounds remarkably like the voice of the Capital Research Center, though Koch undoubtedly would have drawn the proscriptive line in a different place.

The point here is that despite the impression left by the conflict between the Capital Research Center and corporate philanthropy, the Conservative Vision has a significant place in corporate philanthropy. Nor are the Conservative and the Pragmatic visions mutually exclusive. Although they can come into conflict, they also can complement each other. Their complicated relationship can be illuminated further by looking at another area of corporate political activity—contributions to political candidates.

Pragmatism and Conservatism in Corporate PACs

Corporate campaign contributions, of course, are quite different from corporate philanthropy. If a corporate donation to a nonprofit might be reasonably seen as a gift, with nothing expected immediately in exchange, a corporate donation to a political candidate certainly seems more imme-

◆

diately self-interested. Members of Congress and other politicians, after all, have something tangible to provide in return: their vote and support on issues important to the corporation.

Yet, they are more similar than they seem. The strategies of corporate political action committees (or PACs), through which political contributions are funneled, fall into two categories very similar to the pragmatic/conservative distinction we have made regarding corporate philanthropy. Furthermore, the notion of a gift is surprisingly relevant to the pragmatic kind of campaign contributions.

Since the early 1980s, students of American politics have noted that PAC funding of political candidates has taken two different forms. Political scientists Edward Handler and John R. Mulkern named this difference for subsequent researchers by distinguishing "ideological" from "pragmatic" PACs.[10] (I have used "conservative" in place of "ideological" in the discussion so far.)

Ideological PACs seek to alter the composition of Congress by electing more conservatives, mainly Republicans; they judge candidates on a range of issues related to the overall functioning of capitalism; and they believe that "the needs and interests of the parent corporation are best served by contributing to the support of candidates that show some overall commitment to [free] enterprise and to the market as an alternative to [government] regulation."[11] Ideological PACs give a disproportionate amount of money to ideological conservatives in close races with more liberal opponents, to Republicans, and to challengers and open-seat contestants. Their strategy reflects an assessment of American politics very similar to that embodied in the Conservative Vision of the Capital Research Center: Ideological PACs perceive a "Manichean" political reality in which big business "is locked in a long-term struggle with enemies such as the media, academia, Common Cause, Congress Watch, organized labor, and the liberal wing of the Democratic party."[12] In such a world, the only reasonable political strategy is to try to unseat the representatives of these enemies by electing a more pro-business Congress.

Pragmatic PACs, in contrast, seek to accommodate to the existing composition of Congress and to secure "a high degree of access" to incumbents of either party; they seek candidates who are "accessible and supportive of the corporation on some special issue or issues that impact directly and immediately on the well-being or the viability of the firm."[13] They support incumbents, regardless of party or ideology, who have particular influence on matters of importance to their corporations and who seem likely to be re-elected.

◈

Money does not simply buy access, nor does access necessarily get the corporation a favorable vote, especially on a big issue. Things are more complicated than that, as Dan Clawson and his colleagues make clear in *Money Talks: Corporate PACs and Political Influence.* To be sure, money certainly makes access easier. As one corporate PAC director told Clawson:

> the PAC gives you access, puts you in the game. You know, some congressman has got X number of ergs of energy, and here's a person or a company who wants to come see him and give him a thousand dollars, and here's another one who wants to just stop by and say hello. And he only has time to see one. Which one? So the PAC's an attention getter.[14]

A contribution rarely stands as an isolated act, however. It is part of a broader relationship the corporation cultivates with a Member of Congress and serves to sustain that relationship. Corporate PAC directors rarely just drop a check in the mail; they or other representatives of the corporation usually deliver the donation personally at a fundraiser or at the Member's office. Furthermore, corporate government affairs managers and congressional staffers spend considerable time together both on and off the job.[15]

It is this longer-term relationship fueled by contributions, rather than the money alone, that incurs an obligation on the part of the Member of Congress. This obligation usually involves not an immediate payback, but rather a general willingness to devote the time to listening to the corporation's position on important issues. What a corporation expects from this kind of conversation is not necessarily to sway the Member's vote on a big piece of legislation, but rather to persuade him or her to propose amendments to that legislation that would make it more favorable to the corporation. Corporations do not expect their few thousand dollars to outweigh constituent pressures, party obligations, and ideological commitments on big issues; but they do expect those dollars to buy the Member's sympathetic attention to obscure amendments to major legislation that may change the impact of the legislation on the corporation.[16] Thus, the corporation expects $2,000 to buy not a vote against progressive tax reform or stronger environmental legislation, but careful attention to proposed amendments exempting it from certain provisions of that legislation.

Because pragmatic PAC contributions are embedded in longer-term relationships (rather than being one-shot transactions) and because they create general, rather than specific, obligations on the part of the Member of Congress, Clawson and his colleagues have characterized them as gifts. Although PAC contributions differ from philanthropic donations in impor-

◆

tant ways, designating both as gifts in this sense captures something important about each.

The strategy of pragmatic PACs assumes a picture of American politics similar to that of the Pragmatic Vision in corporate philanthropy. In contrast to ideological PACs, pragmatic PACs spread their contributions broadly, ignoring differences of party and ideology, because they believe nearly all Members of Congress, Democrats as well as Republicans, liberals as well as conservatives, are amenable to the quiet kind of access they seek. Most Members of Congress believe that corporations have legitimate interests and that otherwise valid legislation may unfairly impinge on some of those interests. They are thus open to carefully crafted, well-argued proposals from businesses seeking to mitigate some of those putatively unfair specific effects.

Pragmatic PACs, in other words, assume a benign pluralism, just as corporate philanthropists do. Clawson and his colleagues began their research with the assumption that corporate PACs "would have many enemies in Congress," but at least for pragmatic PACs, they soon found out this was not so:

> We . . . were surprised to learn that corporations didn't really feel they had enemies in Congress. Yes, there were lots of members who opposed them on any given issue, but no, there weren't any members they considered unreasonable. Essentially all members of Congress are at least potentially willing to help them out, to give them access, to let them make a case.[17]

As a result of their quite different political assumptions and strategies, pragmatic and ideological PACs have often viewed each other with suspicion. Many heads of pragmatic PACs, for example, have little use for their ideological counterparts, viewing them as extremists who risk rocking, indeed sinking, a very seaworthy boat. Why risk a combative strategy that creates enemies when one has none? In return, heads of ideological PACs find their pragmatic brethren short-sighted and unprincipled in their willingness to buy short-term favors for their corporation from politicians who are fundamentally anti-business. Why feed the mouth that might well bite everyone in the future?

Despite the clear differences between the two strategies, many corporations are not irretrievably committed to either. While the pragmatic strategy has usually dominated PAC contributions, the actual mix of the two has varied over time with political conditions. In the mid-1970s, as many corporations formed PACs for the first time, the general bent of contributions was pragmatic, with PACs distributing their money widely among Democratic as well as Republican incumbents, while supporting Republican nonincumbents only for open seats. This brought an angry response from Republicans, who had encouraged corporations to form PACs in the first place, as well as from conservatives and some important corporate leaders.[18] In response to this pressure and to the perceived possibility of building a Republican majority in both Houses of Congress, corporate PACs moved substantially in an ideological direction in the early 1980s. In the 1980 elections, Republican nonincumbents received a high of 29 percent of all corporate PAC money in the House of Representatives races and 58 percent in Senate races. Democratic incumbents in the House, who got four times as much corporate money as their opponents in 1972, actually got less than their opponents in 1980. Support for all Republicans in House races peaked at 63 percent in 1982.[19]

The recession of the early 1980s as well as strong Democratic counter-pressure on big business undercut any further rush of money to Republican nonincumbents, however.[20] By the late 1980s and early 1990s, indeed, corporate money was more pragmatic and Democratic than ever before: In the 1988 House elections, corporate PAC money had all but deserted Republican nonincumbents (6 percent) and was going in greater amounts to Democrats (52 percent) than ever before.[21] Faced with an energetic Republican campaign led by Newt Gingrich in 1994 and another palpable opportunity to elect a Republican Congress, corporate PAC money swung again in the summer and fall of that year behind Republican challengers and open-seat candidates.[22]

In addition, ideological and pragmatic strategies, though apparently at loggerheads, usually complement each other in practice rather than coming into conflict. To begin, although ideological and pragmatic PACs disagree over whom to fund, they agree on whom not to fund. While the pattern of contributions to Republican and Democratic incumbents and Republican nonincumbents varies from corporation to corporation and from election year to election year, one constant is that Democratic nonincumbents get only a tiny proportion of corporate money, ranging from 2 to 4 percent in House races.[23] In the world of campaign finance, pragmatic and ideological strategies thus work together to limit the range of the political universe.

More important, despite different funding strategies and idiosyncratic agendas, corporate PACs rarely find themselves on opposite sides in actual races. In the pivotal 1980 elections, for example, in nearly three-quarters of congressional races more than 90 percent of corporate money went to one candidate rather than the other. The distribution of corporate money

◈

was thus considerably more skewed than the distribution of popular vote.[24] More pointedly in the 1978 and 1980 congressional elections, ideological PACs directed about one-third of their money to Republican challengers who successfully unseated Democratic incumbents, and pragmatic PACs spent virtually nothing to defend those incumbents.[25]

This effective cooperation partly reflects the fact that ideological and pragmatic PACs simply target quite different races with the former focusing on those races with viable Republican challengers and the latter focusing on those with safe incumbents of either party. Partly too, it reflects the fact that individual corporate PACs do not make decisions in isolation. Like other kinds of PACs, they share common sources of information, follow the lead of a small number of coordinating organizations and bellwether PACs, and actively network with each other. There is a culture of corporate PACs much like there is a culture of corporate philanthropy. Pragmatic and ideological PACs thus have approached politics in quite divergent ways without coming into major, wasteful conflict. They work together to serve corporate interests.[26]

The Distinctive Nature of Business Power

In different ways, Conservative and Pragmatic visions fit together in both corporate philanthropy and corporate PAC contributions. Their combination may hold a key to the distinctive nature of corporate political power in general. The power of big business in everyday American politics has two faces, what I shall now call Corporate Conservatism and Corporate Pragmatism. The first seeks to push the political universe in a conservative, pro-business direction; the second, to establish relationships, gain access, and seek influence broadly across the existing political spectrum.[27]

The recent history of corporate politics is in part the story of the changing mix of these two strategies. When big business faces a common threat or an extraordinary political opportunity, it broadly embraces Corporate Conservatism. Such times are also characterized by high degrees of unity, with corporations working together, sometimes under the aegis of broad-based organizations, to pursue collective political goals. At other times, when the status quo is acceptable and the opportunities to "improve" it are few, Corporate Pragmatism tends to dominate. This coincides with more individualized political action, with particular corporations and industries pursuing their specific interests. At all times, neither strategy is wholly absent.

◆

In the late 1970s and early 1980s, big business mobilized to push American politics to the right.[28] It did so partly because corporate leaders perceived a growing set of interrelated economic, political, and ideological crises. Increasing international competition and a weakening domestic economy had led to declining profits. The development of a public-interest movement, the decentralization of power in Congress, and the growing political role of both courts and media all had made politics more complicated and rendered inadequate existing routine modes of corporate influence.[29] Most important, public opinion of corporations and of big business generally had become increasingly negative. In this context, corporate leaders voiced increasing concern over the growth of government regulation, a rising tide of entitlement, and the general failure of both the media and big business itself to communicate the virtues of capitalism.

Corporate Conservatism also came to the fore because of the political opportunities facing big business. Other political actors seemed poised to push American politics to the right. The Republican party had recovered from the debacle of Watergate and was developing well-funded, high-tech national organizations. The conservative movement had grown into a dense network of lobbying, organizing, and policy-formation groups. Fundamentalist and evangelical Christians were mobilizing under the aegis of the New Religious Right.[30]

Three elements of the ensuing corporate conservative mobilization stand out. First, as we have just discussed, corporate PACs shifted some of their donations from incumbents of both parties to conservative Republican challengers in congressional races.

Second, broad-based business organizations, which transcend the interests of particular companies and industries, took the lead in lobbying Congress and federal agencies. The Business Roundtable, whose membership includes the heads of most of the largest corporations, and similar organizations led successful fights against a consumer protection agency and labor law reform in the late 1970s and for the Reagan tax cuts in 1981.

Third, corporate money flowed to conservative research organizations that previously had been a distinctly peripheral part of the policy-planning network, the think tanks that often play a central role in framing the debate of public policy issues. Among the major beneficiaries were the American Enterprise Institute, the Hoover Institution, and the Heritage Foundation, but a host of smaller conservative think tanks benefited as well. These organizations were not mere talking shops; they became conduits for channeling conservative personnel and ideas into the Reagan Administra-

◧

tion and into the political culture generally. They continue to provide a home for conservative polity elites and have helped frame political discussion.

The dominance of Corporate Conservatism and the concomitant unity of big business declined by the beginning of Reagan's second term. This was partly because big business had achieved much of its immediate agenda and because emerging issues such as trade legislation and budget deficits divided the business world. It was also because political opportunities seemed to wane: The deep 1982 recession undercut the possibility of further Republican gains in Congress, while Democrats made a concerted effort to win back corporate support. As we have seen, corporate PACs largely abandoned an ideological contribution strategy and returned to a pragmatic one.

The elections of 1994 coincided with another surge of Corporate Conservatism. This time the cause was less crisis than opportunity. As noted earlier, faced with the real prospect of a Republican takeover of Congress, corporate PACs shifted their contributions to Republican challengers and open-seat candidates late in the campaign. After the elections, through an organization called the Thursday Group, corporate lobbyists, who often pursue the more parochial interests of their firms and industries, united to work closely with the new Republican majorities in Congress to build support for the conservative Contract with America, with its provisions for cutting corporate taxes, scaling back regulation, and limiting the scope of civil law suits.

The day-to-day clout of corporate lobbyists, always significant, became especially visible in Congress, as Republican-controlled congressional committees farmed out the job of drafting key legislation directly to law firms representing the interests of major industries.[31] Summarizing the scene, one observer noted the high degree of corporate unity around the conservative agenda:

> Washington's corporate and business lobbyists represent a myriad of often clashing interests. But there is striking unanimity about the first 100 days of the new Congress: things, they say, could hardly have gone better.[32]

Despite this surge of Corporate Conservatism, the relationship between big business and the Right remained ambivalent. Large corporations may have lined up behind the conservative agenda, but conservatives still weren't totally comfortable with them. As the *New York Times* explained in mid-1995, conservative Republicans "complain that major corporate ex-

◧

ecutives have not been particularly loyal to them, and had been too quick to donate to Democratic incumbents." One corporate lobbyist noted that "there is a resentment against American business for favoring a significant portion of the Democratic agenda that Republicans opposed." As usual, House Majority Leader Dick Armey was particularly pungent. He derided corporate executives as "prags"—"ag" words apparently are favorites with him. "When you're a prag," he said, "you're going to have your finger in the wind and you're going to go where the wind blows you."[33]

This hostility has led some observers to talk about a "seismic shift" in American politics, a new "fault line running through Washington." The "new Republican revolution . . . belongs to small business," argues reporter David Sanger, while "big business now looks like a constituency in search of a party."[34] More accurately, what was happening in the aftermath of the Republican takeover of Congress in the 1994 elections was merely one more chapter in the always complicated relationship between large corporations and the Right, which reflects in turn the mix of Corporate Conservatism and Corporate Pragmatism that big business has pursued for decades.

Together these two strategies give big business a distinctive kind of power matched by no other organized interest in America. This claim may seem strange in one sense. To be sure, the mobilized power of Corporate Conservatism, fighting to elect more conservative leaders and enact more conservative policies, is clear enough. Corporate Pragmatism, however, seems more acquiescence than influence, accepting the status quo rather than putting an imprint on it, going "where the wind blows you." It hardly seems a form of collective power at all, which is probably why conservatives deride it and sociologists usually ignore it.

Certainly, Corporate Pragmatism doesn't fit most conventional ways of conceptualizing the power of big business specifically or for that matter power in general.[35] Roughly speaking we can distinguish three such concepts. First, big business may exert influence as a set of organized interest groups, ranging from single companies to transcorporate groups like the Business Roundtable, capable of procuring government policies in their interests despite the opposition of other groups in society. Here power is the ability to prevail in situations of overt conflict. Second, big business may exert influence through think tanks and other policy discussion groups that help define what issues are important and what options are viable. Here power is the ability to set the political agenda in a way that avoids conflict by limiting the range of legitimate discussion. Third, big business may have its interests served without actually exerting influence, by virtue

◆

of its structural position in society, in particular its control of investment. The state on its own pursues policies conducive to business interests, because it wants to sustain business confidence and investment levels to promote economic growth and hence adequate levels of tax revenues and public trust in government. In this sense, power is rooted in structural indispensability.

These different ways of understanding power vary substantially in the relative importance they give to agency and structure, but none quite covers Corporate Pragmatism. Nonetheless, Corporate Pragmatism does represent a distinct kind of potentially important influence.

To return to the case of corporate PACs: The net effect of many individual PACs supporting specific incumbents with influence over policies of interest to their corporations is to give big business broad access to politicians of various orientations and establish an extensive set of ties with Members of Congress. This gives big business a *pervasiveness* in American politics that no other group has. Not only do corporate and trade association PACs contribute more money to candidates than other kinds of PACs, they also do so in a different way. Other PACs certainly support a mix of incumbents and nonincumbents, depending on their assessment of political conditions, but they rarely cross party and ideological lines the way big business does. Year in and year out, labor PACs give their money overwhelmingly to Democrats; conservative PACs support conservatives; progressive PACs back progressives. Corporate politics too has its partisan aspect, which is what Corporate Conservatism is all about; but it also has the second element of Corporate Pragmatism.

Sociologist Clawson and his colleagues put it this way:

> The pragmatic approach can be viewed as a narrow and short-sighted perspective. But it could also be argued that it is a sophisticated attempt to be sure that both parties and all candidates are pressured to be "pro-business." . . . If both parties are in bed with, and in debt to, business, then corporations face a "heads I win, tails you lose" situation.[36]

In short, while directly aimed at winning access for an individual corporation to Members of Congress, pragmatic PAC contributions may also serve the broader interests of big business generally by getting corporate voices heard by virtually all of Congress. In a similar sense, corporate philanthropy also contributes to the pervasiveness of big business in American society. Together with pragmatic PAC contributions and other activities, it establishes a wide set of ties between corporations and other important individuals and institutions. In other words, Corporate Pragmatism has its own classwide rationality.

◆

This pervasiveness represents a distinct kind of power. It is not power in the sense of prevailing in overt conflict, or being able to set the political agenda, or possessing structural indispensability. Instead it involves a more subtle and perhaps smaller-scale kind of power than any of these—a presence at multiple levels in society and a place in multiple conversations, which allows a set of voices to be heard and a set of interests to be taken seriously almost everywhere. This is power as a discursive presence.

Regarding pervasiveness as an important kind of power is consistent with at least two significant recent analyses of American politics. In *Who Will Tell the People: The Betrayal of American Democracy,* William Greider argues that one key to political power in the United States is establishing long-term relationships with government leaders in both Congress and the executive branch. These relationships, along with money and the ability to marshal appropriate expertise, allow one to maintain a persistent presence in the nonstop process of policymaking, which goes on long before and long after the actual moment at which legislation is publicly debated. Greider credits large corporations with a unique ability to maintain such a presence. In *Protecting Soldiers and Mothers: The Political Origins of Social Policy in the United States,* Theda Skocpol argues that the most successful actors in American politics are those who can bring influence to bear in multiple places in a decentralized, fragmented political system. Although she has in mind the success of women's and veteran's groups in procuring social welfare legislation in the late nineteenth and early twentieth centuries, the wide network of relationships cultivated by Corporate Pragmatism may give large corporations a similar advantage in the present day.[37]

Corporate pragmatism, then, plausibly adds an important dimension to the collective power of big business in American society. Certainly no other group combines the capacity to mobilize immense resources to collective ends with the ability to establish a broad network of relationships. It is this mix, again, that makes the power of big business in American society distinctive.

8

Conclusion

An Economic Act with Social and Political Dimensions

◆

At the beginning of this book, I argued that corporate philanthropy is an economic act with social and political dimensions. It certainly seeks to serve corporate interests and corporate profit, but we cannot understand it fully simply by looking at its economic purposes. The ensuing chapters have developed this argument along three lines.

First, although corporate philanthropy serves corporate interests, giving program and company have a complicated relationship to each other. This is not for the most obvious reason, that giving a little money away is necessarily antithetical to making a lot. Rather it has to do with the conflicting needs of corporate philanthropy itself to maintain close ties to its company's strategic interests and to top management without losing the distinctiveness that justifies its existence as an independent, serious corporate function. We have seen that these contradictory imperatives play out in how corporate philanthropists talk about their work (chapter 4) and in how they handled the Planned Parenthood controversy (chapter 5).

Second, corporate philanthropy programs are embedded in a culture of corporate philanthropy and in a transcorporate network of relationships with each other. Corporate philanthropy is thus a collective enterprise in significant ways. Corporate leaders and important transcorporate organizations have influenced the development of corporate giving programs since the mid twentieth century, as we saw in chapter 2. The corporate world has a powerful set of shared understandings, embodied in a substantial body of books, articles, and papers, about why philanthropy is important, to what organizations donations should be made, and how giving should be organized. Individual corporate giving programs would be hard to sustain without the direction and information this shared culture supplies. We have reviewed the central themes of the written culture and presented evidence for the importance of the transcorporate network (chapter 2). We have also heard the cultural themes echoed in the voices of individual corporate philanthropists and have seen the everyday relevance of network ties. Yet, corporate giving officers are not simple reflections of this culture; they may be social beings, but they are not wholly socialized ones. Their workaday worldviews, as displayed in chapters 3 and 4, are at once more limited and more complex than the official culture. In the face of a crisis like the Planned Parenthood controversy, corporate philanthropists draw upon their shared culture and network of relationships, but each stands largely alone in deciding how to respond.

Third, as chapters 6 and 7 argue, corporate philanthropy has a broader political meaning as well, even though corporate philanthropists insist their work is apolitical and nonideological. It embodies a Pragmatic Vision, a distinct set of assumptions, rarely made explicit, about how big business can secure its place in American society. In the aggregate, it is part of Corporate Pragmatism, a strategy by which large corporations build and maintain relationships with other important political actors in American society. These relationships help give big business a pervasiveness in American political life. They make sure corporate voices are part of nearly every political conversation and thus give large corporations a subtle kind of power in American life. Corporate Pragmatism complements a Corporate Conservatism that is also part of corporate politics, even though the assumptions of the two strategies about the place of big business in American society clash with each other. The mix of the two explains the love-hate relationship between the Right and big business and more important, helps account for what is distinctive about corporate power.

The Paradox of Corporate Philanthropy

The picture of corporate philanthropy that emerges from this analysis is paradoxical. It seems at once insignificant and significant, weak and strong. On the one hand, corporate donations loom small in the larger social landscape. At about $7 billion a year they are but a few percent both of all dollars contributed in the United States and of all corporate before-tax profits. Corporate philanthropy programs, furthermore, have a tenuous, contradictory place in the corporation and are often called on to show that they are more than a frivolity. Demonstrating that corporate philanthropy serves the corporation in immediate, palpable ways often requires obscuring what is distinctive about the enterprise and making it more like an adjunct of public relations, marketing, or human resources.

◆

On the other hand, the corporate leaders who have nurtured corporate philanthropy over the last half century have always had grand dreams for it, giving it an important place in the survival strategy of big business. This book in effect agrees with them, arguing that corporate philanthropy is one example of an important kind of power that big business exercises within and over American society and an important contributor to that power.

Corporate philanthropy may well indeed be of dubious value to the individual corporation (in the short term) and an asset for big business as a whole (in the long term), precisely because it is a gift, in the sense we used the term in chapter 7. A gift implies that there is no quid pro quo, no immediate payoff to the donor corporation. A donation is not a market exchange that nets the corporation an immediate, tangible return. At the same time, a gift also implies the building of a longer-term relationship between donor and recipient with a certain level of understanding and respect. In the aggregate, corporate philanthropy programs insert corporations into a web of relationships in which they are owed not tangible returns but a diffuse regard and understanding, and this helps give big business a subtle but distinct edge in political life.

Corporate Philanthropy, the Nonprofit Sector, and the Right

Our analysis of the social and political dimensions of corporate philanthropy may also help us understand its likely place in the renewed conservative climate that emerged after the 1994 elections. As I write these words in early 1996, the conservative agenda has driven American politics for nearly a year and a half. While substantial Democratic victories in the 1996 elections may reduce the influence of this agenda, they will not make it go away.

This agenda calls in part for a new relationship between government and the nonprofit sector.[1] The nonprofit sector, conservatives argue, should take over providing many of the services for the needy now provided by government, making up for the cuts in federal spending that they plan to make. At the same time, the nonprofit sector should break its dependency on government support and become the "independent" sector it has always claimed to be.

Conservatives argue that their policies will help the nonprofit sector take on its new responsibilities and remake itself. Cuts in tax rates and regulation will spur economic growth and increase incomes. Expanded tax credits for donations, especially to organizations serving the needy, will increase incentives for directing some of this increased income to charitable giving. Citing the precedent of the Reagan years, during which charitable giving doubled from $48.6 billion in 1980 to $98.4 billion in 1988 in current dollars (an increase of 25 percent in real terms), conservatives argue, in the words of Leslie Lenkowsky, president of the Hudson Institute, that "a positive attitude towards the importance of charities, a supportive tax policy, and an outlook that instill[s] confidence in the future" can work wonders for the nonprofit sector.[2]

As critics have pointed out, the conservative analysis obscures or misses several important points. First, government funds are much more than a small supplement to nonprofit sector income. Government currently provides about 30 percent of all money the nonprofit sector spends. More important, it provides 40 percent of funds for health services and half of all funds for social services, the areas targeted for the biggest cuts in federal spending and the ones where the needy are most likely to be served. Re-orienting the nonprofit sector requires more than modest changes in sources of funding.[3]

Second, little of what Americans currently give goes to services for the needy. In 1994, less than 20 percent of the $130 billion in donations went for health and human services, while nearly 50 percent went to religious organizations, 13 percent to education, and 8 percent to the arts and humanities. Relatively few donations to the latter three categories filter down to the poor.[4] In general, as Julian Wolpert has argued, "donors tend to give to charities for services the donors themselves use, and not to sustain safety nets."[5]

Third, how much and to what people give are not a simple function of financial incentives, including tax breaks. Existing patterns of giving are often reinforced by powerful, durable cultural norms. For example, based on interviews with wealthy philanthropists, sociologist Francie Ostrower argues that "affluent donors have their own philanthropic agendas and personal interests and priorities" that do not include "programs that serve poor and disadvantaged people." They are unlikely to alter their giving to "take up tasks that were previously carried out by government," partly because their priorities are shaped by a strong culture of philanthropy among the social elite. This culture places a high value on giving to certain kinds of prominent educational and cultural institutions but not to services for the needy. Supporting the right kinds of organizations is reinforced by family, friends, and business associates and helps the donor establish and maintain valued relationships with other members of the elite.[6]

Fourth, charity generally starts at home and stays there. Most money raised by charity organizations, even that portion that helps the needy, supports services and projects in the local community. It does not flow across community lines, especially from more affluent ones to needier ones. In essence this means that those that have get. Affluent communities that have the smallest proportion of needy raise the most money.[7]

In short, the conservative project, "where government was, there shall the nonprofit sector be," runs afoul not only of the very reliance of nonprofit organizations on government that the Right decries but also (and more important) of established and durable patterns of private giving. These patterns are not simply a function of financial incentives and are not likely to alter dramatically in response to changing incentives. This is not to say that the massive change in the relationship between government and the nonprofit sector envisioned by conservatives is impossible, but merely that they do not have a plausible theory of how it might be done.

What applies to giving in the United States generally applies as well to corporate giving. Corporate giving grew dramatically in the Reagan years, as we discussed in chapter 2, but has stagnated since then. Increased tax incentives for giving is unlikely to turn this around, since hardly any companies respond to the incentives now on the books: Corporations can deduct up to 10 percent of pretax income for federal tax purposes, but corporate giving has stayed consistently below 2 percent.

If conservative policies were to succeed in stimulating economic growth, companies may make higher profits and thus have more money to give away. The picture of corporate philanthropy we have painted in this book, however, implies that this will not necessarily lead to more giving and that additional giving would likely not go to the needy.

Consider again the place of philanthropy within the corporation. Companies favor functions that add immediate value in palpable ways. They are thus unlikely to give philanthropy high priority for receiving additional money. If they did invest more in philanthropy, that money is likely to go to projects that provide short-term, visible returns. Corporations are likely to support highly visible educational and cultural projects that clearly boost the company image. If they fund health and human services, the money is likely to target the company's employees and their communities. Neither kind of philanthropy is likely to go primarily to the needy. Corporate philanthropists themselves may favor more donations to organizations that make palpable differences in the lives of the America's neediest, but they also recognize the reality of their place in the corporation. As one remarked in chapter 4, the best a corporate giving officer can hope for is to mix a little doing good with a lot of making the corporation look good.

◆

The existing culture of corporate philanthropy is likely to reinforce these kinds of giving priorities in the future. Although it sanctions a range of giving, its top priority has always been education, and it has never placed disproportionate emphasis on helping the disadvantaged. There are, after all, organizations dedicated to facilitating corporate support for education and the arts, but not for the needy. Furthermore, in recent years, the culture of corporate philanthropy has urged corporate giving programs to tend carefully to their relations to their companies by linking their donations closely to the needs of public relations, human resources, or marketing. This too is not a promising ground for new departures in corporate giving.

Finally, in the aggregate, corporate philanthropy contributes to the political project of establishing and maintaining relationships with important organizations in the nonprofit sector. Most of these organizations do not primarily serve the needy and are unlikely to start doing so in the near future.

In short, corporate philanthropy is unlikely to play a significant role in the Right's plan to re-create the nonprofit sector. This is not because it is too "liberal," but because of its social and political place in the corporate world.

NOTES

1. Introduction

1. The ads ran in major newspapers beginning April 5, 1990, shortly after a decision by the AT&T Foundation to stop funding Planned Parenthood. Kara Swisher, "Backing Away from Controversy," *Washington Post,* April 5, 1990, p. E1. For an example of the more positive press that AT&T usually gets from its donations, especially to the arts, see William Harris, "How AT&T Tosses a Lifeline to the Arts," *New York Times,* May 27, 1990, p. H5.

2. In 1994, corporate philanthropy amounted to $6.11 billion. Education received 35 percent of that (half of which went to colleges and universities); health and human services, 25 percent (half of which went to the United Way and other federated campaigns); culture and the arts, 11 percent; and civic and community affairs, 12 percent. Corporate donations constitute about 5 percent of all giving in the United States and about 1 percent of corporate pretax income. *Chronicle of Philanthropy,* June 1, 1995, p. 21; ibid., September 25, 1995, p. 12.

3. Chapter 5 discusses the Planned Parenthood controversy in detail.

4. Chapter 6 discusses the conflict between the Capital Research Center and corporate philanthropy.

5. Examples of this practical literature include the following: Council on Foundations, *Corporate Philanthropy: Philosophy, Management, Trends, Future, Background* (Washington, D.C., 1982); idem, *Corporate Giving in the 1990s—The Next Generation* (Washington, D.C., 1987); idem, *Corporations and Communities* (Washington, D.C., 1988); idem, *Administering Corporate Giving* (Washington, D.C., 1991); idem, *How to Position the Corporate Grantmaking Program: Strategies That Work* (Washington, D.C., 1991); Frank Koch, *The New Corporate Philanthropy: How Society and Business Can Profit* (New York: Plenum, 1979); Vic Murray, *Improving Corporate Donations* (San Francisco: Jossey-Bass, 1991); James Shannon, ed., *The Corporate Contributions Handbook* (San Francisco: Jossey-Bass, 1991); Arthur H. White and John S. Bartolomeo, *Corporate Giving: The View of Chief Executive Officers of Major American Corporations* (Washington, D.C.: Council on Foundations, 1982).

6. Ronald Burt, "Corporate Philanthropy as a Cooptive Relation," *Social Forces* 62 (1983): 419–49; Joseph Galaskiewicz, "Corporate Contributions to Charity: Nothing More Than a Marketing Strategy?" in *Philanthropic Giving: Studies in Varieties and Goals,* ed. Richard Magat (New York: Oxford University Press, 1989), pp. 246–60; Galaskiewicz, "An Urban Grants Economy Revisited: Company Contributions in the Twin Cities, 1979–1989," unpublished manuscript,

◈

1983; Katherine E. Maddox and John J. Siegfried, "The Effect of Economic Structure on Corporate Philanthropy," in *The Economics of Firm Size, Market Structure, and Social Performance,* ed. John J. Siegfried (Washington, D.C.: Federal Trade Commission, n.d.); Katherine Maddox McElroy and John J. Siegfried, "The Effects of Firm Size and Mergers on Corporate Philanthropy," in *The Impact of the Modern Corporation,* ed. Betty Bock, Harvey J. Goldschmid, Ira M. Millstein, and F. M. Scherer (New York: Columbia University Press, 1984), pp. 95–157; Peter Navarro, "Why Do Corporations Give to Charity?" *Journal of Business* 61 (1988): 65–93; John J. Siegfried, Katherine Maddox McElroy, and Diane Biernot-Fawkes, "The Management of Corporate Contributions," *Research in Corporate Social Performance and Policy* 5 (1983): 87–102; Michael Useem, "Corporate Philanthropy," in *The Nonprofit Sector: A Research Handbook,* ed. Walter W. Powell (New Haven: Yale University Press, 1987), pp. 340–59; Michael Useem and Stephen I. Kutner, "Corporate Contributions to Culture and the Arts," in *Nonprofit Enterprise in the Arts: Studies in Mission and Constraint,* ed. Paul J. DiMaggio (New York: Oxford University Press, 1986), pp. 93–112.

7. Michael Useem, "Organizational and Managerial Factors in the Shaping of Corporate Social and Political Action," *Research in Corporate Social Performance and Policy* 12 (1991): 63–92, 85. For a general discussion of "embeddedness," see Mark Granovetter, "Economic Action and Social Structure: The Problem of Embeddedness," *American Journal of Sociology* 91 (1985): 481–510.

8. For references and a fuller discussion of this point, see chapter 2.

9. For examples of this work, see Dan Clawson, Alan Neustadtl, and Denise Scott, *Money Talks: Corporate PACs and Political Influence* (New York: Basic, 1992); Mark S. Mizruchi, *The Structure of Corporate Political Action: Interfirm Relations and Their Consequences* (Cambridge: Harvard University Press, 1992); Mark S. Mizruchi and Michael Schwartz, eds., *Intercorporate Relations: The Structural Analysis of Business* (New York: Cambridge University Press, 1987); Michael Schwartz, ed., *The Structure of Power in America* (New York: Holmes and Meier, 1987); Michael Useem, *The Inner Circle: Large Corporations and the Rise of Business Political Activity in the U.S. and U.K.* (New York: Oxford University Press, 1984).

10. See especially Useem, *Inner Circle.*

11. Taft Group, *1991 Annual Review,* pp. 87–97. Data faxed by David Kroeger, August 16, 1992. To replace Kraft General Foods, I added number fifty-one, ALCOA, to the top fifty.

12. Clawson et al., *Money Talks;* Denise Scott, "The Power of Women's Ties in the Workplace, Community, and Family: A Study of Women in Corporate-Government Affairs," Ph.D. dissertation, sociology, University of Massachusetts, Amherst, 1996.

2. The Making of Corporate Philanthropy

1. F. Emerson Andrews, *Corporation Giving* (New York: Russell Sage, 1952), p. 90.

2. Ibid., pp. 72–73.

◆

3. Peter Dobkin Hall, *The Organization of American Culture, 1700–1900: Private Institutions, Elites, and the Origins of American Nationality* (New York: New York University Press, 1982); idem, *Inventing the Nonprofit Sector and Other Essays on Philanthropy, Voluntarism, and Nonprofit Organizations* (Baltimore: Johns Hopkins University Press, 1992). See also Robert Bremner, *American Philanthropy,* 2nd rev. ed. (Chicago: University of Chicago Press, 1988); Merle Curti and Roderick Nash, *Philanthropy in the Shaping of American Higher Education* (New Brunswick, N.J.: Rutgers University Press, 1965); Kathleen D. McCarthy, *Noblesse Oblige: Charity and Cultural Philanthropy in Chicago, 1849–1929* (Chicago: University of Chicago Press, 1982); Waldemar A. Nielsen, *The Golden Donors: A New Anatomy of the Great Foundations* (New York: Dutton, 1985); Ben Whitaker, *The Philanthropoids: Foundations and Society* (New York: Morrow, 1974).

4. Peter Dobkin Hall, "Business Giving and Social Investment in the United States," in *Philanthropic Giving: Studies in Varieties and Goals,* ed. Richard Magat (New York: Oxford University Press, 1989), pp. 221–45.

5. The following historical summary draws from Andrews, *Corporation Giving,* unless otherwise noted.

6. Information on IBM's early philanthropy was provided by Neil S. Callaghan, Program Manager, Cultural and Human Services Program, IBM, May 18, 1993.

7. The following historical summary of laws relating to corporate philanthropy draws on Phillip I. Blumberg, "Corporate Social Responsibility and the Social Crisis," *Boston University Law Review* 50 (1970): 157–210; Shelby D. Green, "Corporate Philanthropy and the Business Benefit: The Need for Clarity," *Golden Gate University Law Review* 20 (1990): 239–60; Daniel J. Morrissey, "Toward a New/Old Theory of Corporate Social Responsibility," *Syracuse Law Review* 40 (1989): 1005–39.

8. Morrissey, "Corporate Social Responsibility," p. 1015.

9. Ibid., p. 1010.

10. Green, "Corporate Philanthropy," pp. 247–48.

11. I follow here the historical picture drawn by Curti and Nash, *Philanthropy in the Shaping of American Higher Education.*

12. For Conference Board data, see Marion R. Fremont-Smith, *Philanthropy and the Business Corporation* (New York: Russell Sage, 1972).

13. Andrews, *Corporation Giving,* p. 199; Curti and Nash, *Philanthropy in the Shaping of American Higher Education,* p. 251.

14. Curti and Nash, *Philanthropy in the Shaping of American Higher Education,* p. 251.

15. Ibid., p. 242.

16. Blumberg, "Corporate Social Responsibility," p. 185.

17. Richard Eells, *Corporation Giving in a Free Society* (New York: Harper and Row, 1956), p. 136.

18. Ibid., p. 104.

19. Blumberg, "Corporate Social Responsibility," p. 176.

20. Green, "Corporate Philanthropy," p. 252.

21. Ibid., p. 254.

◆

22. The Conference Board, *Survey of Corporate Contributions, 1990 edition* (New York, 1990), p. 11; John Murawski, "A Modest Rise in Donations," *Chronicle of Philanthropy*, June 1, 1995, pp. 19–22.

23. Fremont-Smith, *Philanthropy and the Business Corporation*; *Chronicle of Philanthropy*, September 21, 1995, p. 12.

24. Michael Useem, Introduction to F. Emerson Andrews, *Corporation Giving*, 2nd ed. (New Brunswick, N.J.: Transaction, 1993), pp. 3–14.

25. David Rockefeller, "Culture and the Corporation," Founding Address, Business Committee for the Arts, September 20, 1966, pp. 2, 3.

26. Ibid., p. 11.

27. Ibid., p. 11.

28. The Business Committee for the Arts has put out a basic information booklet, "Why Business Should Support the Arts" (2nd ed., New York, September 1992), as well as a series of more specific pamphlets on "involving the arts" in corporate public relations, marketing, and advertising. They also publish a long list of "executive viewpoints" on corporate support for the arts. Finally, they give yearly BCA Founders Awards and Business in the Arts awards to exemplary corporate giving programs. The Founders Awards were first given in 1992 on the occasion of the BCA's twenty-fifth anniversary; they are meant as "a hall of fame designation—to recognize those companies that have exhibited leadership, vision and innovation in developing alliances with the arts." The first winners were American Express, AT&T, Dayton Hudson, Philip Morris, and Texaco. See Business Committee for the Arts, "The BCA Founders Award and Business in the Arts Awards" (New York, 1992).

29. Quoted in Louis B. Lundborg, *Future without Shock* (New York: Norton, 1972), p. 93.

30. Ibid., p. 94.

31. Ibid., p. 84.

32. Council on Foundations, *Corporations and Communities* (Washington, D.C., 1988), pp. 4–5.

33. Kenneth A. Bertsch, *Corporate Philanthropy* (Washington, D.C.: Investor Responsibility Research Center, 1982).

34. Brian O'Connell, ed., *America's Voluntary Spirit: A Book of Readings* (New York: Foundation Center, 1983), p. 391.

35. Jerome L. Himmelstein, *To the Right: The Transformation of American Conservatism* (Berkeley: University of California Press, 1990), pp. 129–64.

36. Council on Foundations, *Corporate Philanthropy: Philosophy, Management, Trends, Future, Background* (Washington, D.C., 1982), pp. 14–34.

37. Business Roundtable, "Corporate Philanthropy—An Integral Part of Corporate Social Responsibility," in O'Connell, ed., *America's Voluntary Spirit*, pp. 385–87.

38. Ibid., p. 385.

39. Ibid., pp. 386–87.

40. Murawski, "Modest Rise in Donations," p. 21. In constant 1994 dollars, corporate giving increased from $4.01 billion in 1978 to $7.49 billion in 1987.

◈

41. Eric Wentworth, *Agents of Change: Exemplary Corporate Policies and Practices to Improve Education* (Washington, D.C.: Business Roundtable, 1992).

42. Figures computed from data available in Conference Board, *Survey of Corporate Contributions, 1990 edition* and *Chronicle of Philanthropy,* September 21, 1995, p. 12.

43. Michael Useem, *The Inner Circle: Large Corporations and the Rise of Business Political Activity in the U.S. and the U.K.* (New York: Oxford University Press, 1984); idem, "Company vs. Classwide Rationality in Corporate Decisionmaking," *Administrative Science Quarterly* 27 (1982): 199–226.

44. Eells, *Corporation Giving in a Free Society,* pp. ix, 5.

45. Ibid., pp. 7, 135.

46. Stanley G. Karson, "The Controversy about Corporations," *Response* (February 1991): 2.

47. James Shannon, ed., *The Corporate Contributions Handbook* (San Francisco: Jossey-Bass, 1991), p. 122.

48. Walter V. Shipley, Lawrence A. Wien Prize Lecture in Corporate Social Responsibility, Columbia University, April 29, 1991, p. 4.

49. Shannon, *Corporate Contributions Handbook,* p. 48.

50. John H. Bryan, Jr., "The Corporation and the Executive in the Community," *Columbia Business Law Review* (1987): 695–703.

51. Business Committee for the Arts, "Why Business Should Support the Arts," 2nd ed. (New York, 1992).

52. Shannon, *Corporate Contributions Handbook,* p. 56.

53. Ibid., p. 123.

54. Shipley, Wien Prize Lecture, p. 5.

55. Sanford Cloud, Jr., "The Corporate Perspective on Philanthropy," speech to the Coordinating Council on Foundations, June 26, 1992.

56. Shannon, *Corporate Contributions Handbook,* p. 99.

57. Ibid., pp. 109–10.

58. Ibid., p. 124.

59. Ibid., p. 57.

60. For a more detailed discussion, see Alex J. Plinio and Joanne B. Scanlan, "Total Resource Leveraging and Matching: Expanding the Concept of Corporate Community Involvement," in *Corporate Contributions Handbook,* ed. Shannon, pp. 283–98.

61. Shannon, *Corporate Contributions Handbook,* p. 379.

62. Ibid., p. 376.

63. Frank Koch, *The New Corporate Philanthropy: How Society and Business Can Profit* (New York: Plenum, 1979), p. 16.

64. Ibid., p. 12.

65. Ibid., p. 35.

66. Shannon, *Corporate Contributions Handbook,* p. 71.

67. Ibid., p. xiv.

68. E. B. Knauft, "The Management of Corporate Giving Programs," Program on Non-Profit Organizations, Working Paper No. 114, June 1986, p. 7.

◆

69. Joseph Galaskiewicz, *Social Organization of an Urban Grants Economy: A Study of Business Philanthropy and Nonprofit Organizations* (Orlando: Academic, 1985); idem, "An Urban Grants Economy Revisited: Company Contributions in the Twin Cities, 1979–1989," unpublished manuscript, October 1993.

70. Joseph Galaskiewicz, "Professional Networks and the Institutionalization of a Single Mind Set," *American Sociological Review* 50 (1985): 639–58; Joseph Galaskiewicz and Ronald S. Burt, "Interorganization Contagion in Corporate Philanthropy," *Administrative Science Quarterly* 36 (1991): 88–105. Related work includes Galaskiewicz, "Corporate Contributions to Charity: Nothing More Than a Marketing Strategy?" in *Philanthropic Giving: Studies in Varieties and Goals,* ed. Richard Magat (New York: Oxford University Press, 1989), pp. 246–60; Lisa Atkinson and Joseph Galaskiewicz, "Stock Ownership and Company Contributions to Charity," *Administrative Science Quarterly* 33 (1988): 82–100.

71. Michael Useem and Stephen I. Kutner, "Corporate Contributions to Culture and the Arts," in *Nonprofit Enterprise in the Arts: Studies in Mission and Constraint,* ed. Paul J. DiMaggio (New York: Oxford University Press, 1986), pp. 93–112. Michael Useem, "Organizational and Managerial Factors in the Shaping of Corporate Social and Political Action," *Research in Corporate Social Performance and Policy* 12 (1991): 63–92. Related work includes Useem, "Trends and Preferences in Corporate Support for the Arts," in *Guide to Corporate Giving in the Arts 4,* ed. Robert A. Porter (New York: American Council for the Arts, 1987), pp. ix–xv; idem, "Corporate Funding of the Arts in a Turbulent Environment," *Nonprofit Management and Leadership* 1 (1991): 329–43.

72. Galaskiewicz, *Social Organization of an Urban Grants Economy,* p. 219; Useem, "Organizational and Managerial Factors," pp. 67, 86.

73. Useem, "Organizational and Managerial Factors," p. 86.

74. For example, see Council on Foundations, *Corporate Giving in the 1990s;* idem, *Corporations and Communities;* Stanley Karson, "Why Corporate Executives Must Be Civic Leaders," *Chronicle of Philanthropy,* November 2, 1995, pp. 66–67; Michael Useem, introduction to F. Emerson Andrews, *Corporation Giving,* 2nd ed. (New Brunswick, N.J.: Transaction, 1993), pp. 3–14; Pablo Eisenberg, "Today's Corporate Philanthropy: More 'Self-Interest' Than 'Enlightened,'" *Chronicle of Philanthropy,* January 26, 1995, pp. 37–38. Often a contrast is drawn between the civic-minded corporate leaders of earlier years and the solely business-oriented leaders of today.

3. "A Wonderful Job"

1. The portrait of corporate philanthropists based on my interviews is consistent with more systematic data gathered by two other studies, a 1990 survey by the Council on Foundations of 124 corporations (mostly its members) and a 1991 survey by the Indiana University Center on Philanthropy of one hundred companies selected to represent a cross section of industries and geographical locations. See Council on Foundations, *Administering Corporate Giving* (Washington, D.C., 1991); Indiana University Center on Philanthropy, *Managing Corporate Support: Responses to Challenging Times* (Indianapolis, 1992). The Consulting Network did

◆

the latter study. These studies also provide additional information about corporate giving officers, the most interesting of which has to do with gender. Although roughly as many women as men run corporate giving programs, the appearance of equality is deceptive. Women corporate philanthropists follow different career lines and partly as a result occupy less prestigious positions. They are less likely than their male counterparts to have advanced degrees such as an M.B.A. and more likely to have come to their position from outside the corporation. They are also less likely to run the larger giving programs and those with a separate foundation for processing donations. They tend as well to have less prestigious ranks and to report to lower-ranked executives.

2. See chapter 6 for more on this charge.

3. Salary data confirm the "upper middle management" label. Heads of corporate foundations averaged $89,300 in 1994. *Chronicle of Philanthropy,* November 19, 1994, p. 28. I have found no data on managers of corporate contributions programs not organized as foundations.

4. Whenever I discuss a corporate philanthropist at any length, I refer to her/ him by a pseudonym.

5. Joseph Galaskiewicz, "An Urban Grants Economy Revisited: Company Contributions in the Twin Cities, 1979–1989," unpublished manuscript, 1993; Michael Useem, "Organizational and Managerial Factors in the Shaping of Corporate Social and Political Action," *Research in Corporate Social Performance and Policy* 12 (1991): 63–92.

4. "The Struggle between Looking Good and Doing Good"

1. John Murawski, "A Banner Year for Giving," *Chronicle of Philanthropy,* May 30, 1996, pp. 1, 27–30; John Murawski, "A Modest Rise in Donations," *Chronicle of Philanthropy,* June 1, 1995, pp. 19–22; "Corporate Profits Up 84% since '87, Corporate Giving Grows Only 11%," *Responsive Philanthropy* (Fall 1995): 4. The figures on corporate philanthropy as a percentage of pretax profits are from *Responsive Philanthropy,* which seems to be citing data from the American Association of Fundraising Council. Drawing on data from the Conference Board, the *Chronicle of Philanthropy* (September 21, 1995, p. 1) notes a similar trend, but with different numbers: Corporate giving constituted 1.3 percent of pretax profits in 1991, but only 0.7 percent in 1994.

2. Bruce Millar, "Big Cuts at a Leading Corporate Grant Maker," *Chronicle of Philanthropy,* August 9, 1994, pp. 6–7, 10. See also "Philanthropic Earthquake at ARCO," *Responsive Philanthropy* (Fall 1994): 7–9; Waldemar Nielsen, "O.J. and ARCO: 2 Icons Go on Trial in Los Angeles," *Chronicle of Philanthropy,* September 6, 1994, pp. 53–54.

3. Milt Freudenheim, "A Doting Uncle Cuts Back, and a City Feels the Pain," *New York Times,* October 8, 1995, pp. F1, F9.

4. "Corporate Philanthropy: A Time of Challenge and Opportunity," Mandel Center for Nonprofit Organizations, Cleveland, Ohio, April 28–29, 1994.

5. Council on Foundations, *How to Position the Corporate Grantmaking Program: Strategies That Work* (Washington, D.C., 1991), p. iii.

◆

6. Council on Foundations, *Corporation Giving in the 1990s—The Next Generation* (Washington, D.C., 1987). According to this report, between 1950 and 1986, the percentage of CEOs coming from sales/marketing or finance rose from 34 percent to 59 percent, while the percentage coming from production/operations, engineering, design, or general management declined from 54 percent to 23 percent. In 1976, only 19 percent of CEOs had been with their companies less than ten years; by 1986, 38 percent had.

7. Council on Foundations, *How to Position,* p. iii.

8. Timothy S. Mescon and Donn J. Tilson, "Corporate Philanthropy: A Strategic Approach to the Bottom-Line," *California Management Review* 29, 2 (Winter 1987): 49–61. Quoted passages are on pp. 49, 51.

9. Craig Smith, "After the Wall Caves In," *Corporate Philanthropy Report* (November 1991): 1, 10–11.

10. Craig Smith, "Employee Connection," *Corporate Philanthropy Report* (April 1992): 1, 8–11; Craig Smith and Judith Yarrow, "Message to Rio," *Corporate Philanthropy Report* (May 1992): 1, 10–11.

11. Smith, "After the Wall Caves In," p. 1.

12. Conference Board, "Corporate Giving Strategies That Add Business Value." This report is discussed in "Companies Seek to Do Well from Giving," *Chronicle of Philanthropy,* September 7, 1995, p. 13.

13. Sylvia Clark, "It All Adds Up," *Foundation News* (March–April 1994): 47–49.

14. Craig Smith, "Desperately Seeking Data," keynote address, "Corporate Philanthropy: A Time of Challenge and Opportunity," Mandel Center for Nonprofit Organizations, Cleveland, Ohio, April 28, 1994, p. 2. See also idem, "The New Corporate Philanthroy," *Harvard Business Review* 72 (May–June 1994): 105ff.

15. Smith, "Desperately Seeking Data," p. 4.

16. For other discussion of the fiscal squeeze and corporate philanthropy, see Mary Ann Zehr, "Surviving Moves and Mergers," *Foundation News* (January–February 1994): 42–43; Marina Dundjerski and Jennifer Moore, "A Rebound Ahead for Corporate Donations?" *Chronicle of Philanthropy,* September 6, 1994, pp. 1ff.

17. Michael Useem, "Corporate Philanthropy," in *The Nonprofit Sector: A Research Handbook,* ed. Walter W. Powell (New Haven: Yale University Press, 1987), pp. 340–59; idem, introduction to F. Emerson Andrews, *Corporation Giving,* 2nd ed. (New Brunswick, N.J.: Transaction, 1993), pp. 3–14; Hayden Smith, "The Maturity of Corporate Giving," annual meetings of the Association for Research on Nonprofit Organizations and Voluntary Action, New Haven, Connecticut, 1992, p. 24; E. B. Knauft, "The Management of Corporate Giving Programs," Program on Non-Profit Organizations, Working Paper No. 114, June 1986, p. 2; Peter Dobkin Hall, "Business Giving and Social Investment in the United States," in *Philanthropic Giving: Studies in Varieties and Goals,* ed. Richard Magat (New York: Oxford University Press, 1989), pp. 221–45, p. 240.

18. Joseph Galaskiewicz, "Corporate Contributions to Charity: Nothing More Than a Marketing Strategy?" in *Philanthropic Giving: Studies in Varieties and Goals,* ed. Richard Magat (New York: Oxford University Press, 1989), pp. 246–60.

◆

19. Elizabeth Greene, Bruce Millar, and Jennifer Moore, "The Midwest's Charitable Advantage," *Chronicle of Philanthropy,* February 22, 1994, pp. 1, 22–26.

20. Council on Foundations, *The Climate for Giving: The Outlook for Current and Future CEOs* (Washington, D.C., 1988). This study reports the results of interviews with 255 CEOs and one hundred senior executives who might become CEOs. Asked what they think accounts for a CEO's involvement in the corporate giving function, the interviewees were more likely to mention such reasons as personal desire to contribute to a worthy organization (72 percent), personal sense of ethics (67 percent), or personal background in social causes (49 percent). Fewer of them mentioned corporate reasons, such as desire to continue corporate policy/tradition (43 percent), recognition that giving is in company's interest (40 percent), belief that giving enhances business climate (39 percent), or belief that it contributes directly to profits (13 percent).

21. Robert H. Hayes and William J. Abernathy, "Managing Our Way to Economic Decline," *Harvard Business Review* 58 (July–August 1980): 67–77.

22. Robert Jackall, *Moral Mazes: The World of Corporate Managers* (New York: Oxford University Press, 1988), pp. 94, 199.

23. Reviewing the literature on this topic and on the more general issue of competitiveness, economist Bennett Harrison argues that the "counterproductive short-term approach to investing" reflects the whole national system for allocating capital in the United States. See Harrison, "Where Private Investment Fails," *American Prospect* 11 (Fall 1992): 106–14.

5. Corporate Giving under Fire I

1. See chapter 6.

2. *Border Watch* (May 1992): 4.

3. Anne Lowrey Bailey, "Some Foundations and Other Private Grant Makers Now Rethinking Their Stances on Financing Controversial Art," *Chronicle of Philanthropy,* November 28, 1989, pp. 9, 11; Kristin A. Goss, "Boy Scouts: Under Fire—and Firing Back," *Chronicle of Philanthropy,* January 14, 1992, pp. 1, 25–29. When BankAmerica appeared to back off its refusal to support the Boy Scouts, they received a storm of protest from San Francisco's gay community. For general discussions of right-wing criticism of corporate philanthropy, see David Ransom, *Special Report: Rightwing Attacks on Corporate Giving* (Washington, D.C.: National Committee for Responsive Philanthropy, 1990); Anne Lowrey Bailey, "Corporate Giving under Siege," *Chronicle of Philanthropy,* May 1, 1990, pp. 1, 16–18; Deborah L. Jacobs, "Corporation Donations under Attack," *New York Times,* September 30, 1990, p. F23.

4. *Responsive Philanthropy* (Winter 1994): 1. See also virtually any other issue of *Responsive Philanthropy.*

5. Anna Quindlen, "Good Causes, Bad Money," *New York Times,* November 15, 1992, p. E19. Other articles on criticism of philanthropy by Philip Morris and other tobacco companies include Marjorie Williams, "Tobacco's Hold on Women's Groups," *Washington Post,* November 14, 1991, p. A1; Charles R. Babcock, "Philip Morris Donations Target Minority Groups," *Washington Post,* August 15, 1992, p.

◆

A6; Paul W. Valentine, "Philip Morris Draws Protest over Bill of Rights Exhibit," *Washington Post,* December 11, 1990, p. B7.

6. ACT UP called off the boycott after Philip Morris doubled its grants to AIDS groups, though the company denied that it was responding to boycott pressure. Arts groups resisted ACT UP's call to dissociate themselves from Philip Morris, because, as they noted, the company is one of the most generous supporters of experimental art and attaches no strings to its grants. Mervyn Rothstein, "Uneasy Partners: Arts and Philip Morris," *New York Times,* December 18, 1990, p. C15f; Vince Stehle, "Arts Groups Debate Propriety of Accepting Philip Morris Money," *Chronicle of Philanthropy,* September 18, 1990, p. 5f; "Philip Morris to Double Giving to AIDS Groups," *Chronicle of Philanthropy,* June 4, 1991, p. 8.

7. Peter Monaghan, "Many Local United Ways Caught in the Middle of the Debate over Abortion Rights," *Chronicle of Philanthropy,* November 28, 1989, pp. 4, 6.

8. Jennifer Moore, "Planned Parenthood Looks Ahead to Health Reform," *Chronicle of Philanthropy,* November 2, 1993, p. 42.

9. In chapters 3 and 4, I base my analysis on interviews with forty-three giving officers drawn from the fifty largest corporate philanthropy programs. In contrast, in chapters 5 and 6, I use interviews with giving officers from those programs in the top one hundred who had to deal with the particular controversy under discussion.

10. Based on a 1992 boycott list and press accounts, I tentatively identified eighteen of the one hundred largest corporate giving programs as continuing supporters of Planned Parenthood and seven as defunders between 1985 and 1991. As I interviewed corporate giving officers, however, my list needed modification. Two of the eighteen corporations on the boycott list in fact had already stopped funding Planned Parenthood. In addition, two other corporate givers that I had not previously identified had terminated sustained programs of support for Planned Parenthood and one other was a continuing funder. Finally, three corporations on my initial list, one identified by the boycott leaders as a continuing funder and two claimed as defunders, had never really supported Planned Parenthood in a sustained way to begin with. Their support had been one-shot grants, whose renewal was thus never an issue. The boycott list, "Corporate Supporters of Planned Parenthood," was supplied by Life Decisions International and had been revised on April 21, 1992.

11. Frank Koch, *The New Corporate Philanthropy: How Society and Business Can Profit* (New York: Plenum, 1979), pp. 174–75.

12. "Planned Parenthood Didn't Plan on This," *Business Week,* July 3, 1989, p. 34. Except where noted, this history of the Planned Parenthood controversy is based on published sources. The author would like to thank Anne Bailey of the *Chronicle of Philanthropy,* Bob Bothwell and Beth Daley of the National Committee for Responsive Philanthropy, and Lori Vacek of the Council on Foundations for help with collecting materials on the controversy.

13. "Planned Parenthood Didn't Plan on This"; "Planned Parenthood Donors: Target of Right's Footsoldiers," *Special Report: Rightwing Attacks on Corporate Giving,* p. 4; "AT&T Ceases Support of Planned Parenthood, Christian Action Council Announces," Christian Action Council press release, March 23, 1990; Beth Diemert, "Supporting Her Choice When It Isn't Abortion," *Wall Street Journal,*

◈

January 22, 1992, p. A14; Tamar Lewin, "Anti-Abortion Center's Ads Ruled Misleading," *New York Times,* April 22, 1994, p. A15.

14. Interview with Doug Scott, June 19, 1992.

15. "Planned Parenthood Didn't Plan on This."

16. Reynold Levy, "AT&T Statement in Response to Employee Questions Re: Planned Parenthood Funding," March 22, 1990. See also letter from Levy to Faye Wattleton, president of the Planned Parenthood Federation of America, reprinted in the *Chronicle of Philanthropy,* May 1, 1990; Michael Lev, "AT&T Chief Defends Decision on Abortion," *New York Times,* April 19, 1990, p. A14.

17. Bailey, "Corporate Giving under Siege."

18. Bailey, "Corporate Giving under Siege"; news release, Planned Parenthood Federation of America, April 2, 1990; Tamar Lewin, "Protest Focuses on Abortion Issue," *New York Times,* April 5, 1990, p. A19. For more on Planned Parenthood's position, see an interview with Faye Wattleton, "Planned Parenthood Chief Says Many Economic Boycotts Are Backfiring," *NonProfit Times* (October 1990); letter to Robert E. Allen, CEO of AT&T, from Faye Wattleton, reprinted in the *Chronicle of Philanthropy,* May 1, 1990.

19. Bailey, "Corporate Giving under Siege." One corporate philanthropist, who seemed especially well-informed about events, gave this analysis:

> I think what [Planned Parenthood] would say is that what happened with AT&T was first of all, AT&T's decision got to the Christian Action Council and the media before it got to Planned Parenthood and the implication from Planned Parenthood's perspective I think was that they were being accused of using funds improperly. They were accused of using corporate money for abortions when they shouldn't have. That's my sense of why Planned Parenthood got angry.

20. "AT&T Ceases Support of Planned Parenthood," CAC press release.

21. See, for example, Lewin, "Protest Focuses on Abortion Issue": "AT&T's decision was prompted in good part by a letter-writing campaign, and boycott threat, by anti-abortion groups including the Christian Action Council."

22. JoAnn Greco, "Be Prepared: Controversies over Funding Decisions Often Can't Be Avoided—But They Can Be Managed," *Foundation News* (September–October 1993): 39–40.

23. Bailey, "Corporate Giving under Siege." For more on the AT&T controversy, see Jacobs, "Corporate Donations under Attack"; Kara Swisher, "Backing Away from Controversy," *Washington Post,* April 5, 1990, p. E1; John J. Keller, "Abortion Issue Prompts AT&T to End Its Support for Planned Parenthood," *Wall Street Journal,* March 26, 1990, p. A3A; Michael Matza, "Turning Abortion Sentiments into Market Pressure," *Philadelphia Inquirer,* May 20, 1990; Ransom, *Rightwing Attacks on Corporate Giving.*

24. Elizabeth Klein, "Anti-Abortion Group Says Its Campaign Swayed AT&T on Planned Parenthood," *Chronicle of Philanthropy,* May 1, 1990; Tamar Lewin, "Anti-Abortion Group Urges Boycott of Planned Parenthood," *New York Times,* August 8, 1990, p. A13; "Antiabortion Activists to Boycott Companies," *Washington Post,* August 9, 1990.

◆

25. *Pro-Life Advocate,* vol. 2, no. 2 (no date), p. 3; Sharon Gurfield, "Four Firms Quietly Cut from Boycott," *NonProfit Times* (September 1990); Kristin A. Goss, "After Widespread Protests, Dayton Hudson Foundation to Review Decision to End Aid to Planned Parenthood," *Chronicle of Philanthropy,* September 18, 1990.

26. *Chronicle of Philanthropy,* May 29, 1990.

27. "AT&T Ceases Support of Planned Parenthood."

28. *Pro-Life Advocate,* vol. 2, no. 2 (no date), p. 5.

29. The Dayton Hudson events are covered in Tamar Lewin, "Ending Aid to Family Planning, Large Retailer Is Caught in Storm," *New York Times,* September 1, 1990, p. 8; Karen De Witt, "Company Resumes Planned Parenthood Gift," *New York Times,* September 21, 1990, p. A12; Goss, "After Widespread Protests"; Kevin Kelly, "Dayton Hudson Finds There's No Graceful Way to Flip-Flop," *Business Week,* September 24, 1990. For local press coverage, see Cope Moyers, "Dayton's Reverses on Planned Parenthood," *Minneapolis Star and Tribune,* September 21, 1990, p. 1; Doug Grow, "Dayton's Choice: Fire or Frying Plan," *Minneapolis Star and Tribune,* September 21, 1990, p. 1B; Wayne Wangstad, "Dayton Hudson Reverses Action, Gives to Planned Parenthood," *St. Paul Pioneer Press,* September 21, 1990, p. 1.

30. De Witt, "Company Resumes Planned Parenthood Gift."

31. Interview with Doug Scott. See also Richard Gibson, "Boycott Drive against Pioneer Hi-Bred Shows Perils of Corporate Philanthropy," *Wall Street Journal,* June 10, 1992, p. B1f.

32. "Planned Parenthood Didn't Plan on This."

33. See *Business and Society Review* (March–May 1992); Robert Levering and Milton Moskowitz, *The 100 Best Companies to Work for in America* (Garden City, N.Y.: Doubleday).

34. A "strong reputation for social responsibility" was defined as receiving at least two of the kinds of recognition mentioned in the text. For a good discussion of the difficulties in defining social responsibility, see Ronald Litke, "Shifting Standards," *Foundation News and Commentary* (July–August 1994): 36–37.

35. No other factors seemed to distinguish Stalwarts from Deliberators or both from those corporations that stopped funding Planned Parenthood. How directly the corporate philanthropist reports to top managers, how strong her/his relationship with employees generally, how deep her/his involvement with transcorporate networks, and where she/he worked before taking the current job had no impact on the response to the controversy.

36. For a sense of the general discussion of how to handle controversy in corporate philanthropy, see Greco, "Be Prepared."

6. Corporate Giving under Fire II

1. For general information on the Capital Research Center, see Capital Research Center, *Annual Reports;* William Montague, "A Conservative Study

◆

Center Stirs Heated Controversy by Attacking Corporate Grant Makers' 'Liberal Bias,'" *Chronicle of Philanthropy,* May 15, 1990, p. 1f; John Murawski, "An Influential Plea to End the 'Tragedy' of Compassion," *Chronicle of Philanthropy,* June 15, 1995, pp. 8–11; Vince Stehle, "Center Helps Conservative Lawmakers Battle Liberal Non-Profit Groups," *Chronicle of Philanthropy,* September 21, 1995, p. 34. Willa Johnson, head of the CRC at the time of my research, declined two requests for an interview, once in November 1992 and again in March 1993. For a representative critique of the CRC from the Council on Foundations, see Peter Fromkin, "A Distorted Portrait of Corporate Philanthropy," *Foundation News and Commentary* (March–April 1996): 22–25.

2. "Head of Watchdog Group Steps Down," *Chronicle of Philanthropy,* May 3, 1994, p. 14.

3. For the general role of conservative foundations in recent policy discussion, see Stephen G. Greene and Jennifer Moore, "Conservative Foundations on the Move," *Chronicle of Philanthropy,* February 23, 1995, pp. 1, 10–16.

4. Capital Research Center, *Annual Report,* 1991, p. 3.

5. Capital Research Center, *Annual Report,* 1991, p. 4.

6. Marvin Olasky, *Patterns of Corporate Philanthropy: The Progressive Deception* (Washington, D.C.: Capital Research Center, 1992), p. 5.

7. Capital Research Center, *Annual Report,* 1991, p. 2.

8. Stuart Nolan, *Patterns of Corporate Philanthropy* (Washington, D.C.: Capital Research Center, 1994), p. 4.

9. Anne Lowrey Bailey, "Non-Profits in Politics," *Chronicle of Philanthropy,* July 10, 1990. See also James T. Bennett, "In Health-Care Reform, Where Are the Charities?" *Chronicle of Philanthropy,* February 8, 1994, pp. 42–43; James T. Bennett and Thomas J. DiLorenzo, *Unhealthy Charities: Hazardous to Your Health and Wealth* (New York: Basic, 1994); Montague, "Conservative Study Center Stirs Heated Controversy."

10. Carl O. Helstrom III, "United Way of America: Changing Course?" *Organization Trends* (November 1990).

11. Marvin Olasky, "Philanthropically Correct: The Story of the Council on Foundations" (Washington, D.C.: Capital Research Center, 1993). The passage quoted is found in Jennifer Moore, "Council on Foundations Hobbled by 'Political Correctness,' Report Charges," *Chronicle of Philanthropy,* May 4, 1993, p. 11.

12. In addition to the 1992 Olasky volume and 1994 Nolan volume, see also Roger E. Meiners and David N. Laband, *Patterns of Corporate Philanthropy: Public Affairs Giving and the Forbes 250,* 1988; James T. Bennett, *Patterns of Corporate Philanthropy: Ideas, Advocacy, and the Corporation,* 1989; Thomas J. DiLorenzo, Daniel T. Oliver, and Robert E. Winters, *Patterns of Corporate Philanthropy: The "Suicidal Impulse,"* 1990.

13. DiLorenzo et al., 1990 report, p. 3.

14. Meiners and Laband, 1988 report, p. 2.

15. DiLorenzo et al., 1990 report, p. 2.

16. Nolan, 1994 report, pp. 3–13.

17. Ibid., pp. 7–9.

◆

18. Meiners and Laband, 1988 report, p. v.

19. Olasky, 1992 report, p. 14.

20. Ibid., p. 1. The November 1992 issue of the CRC's publication *Organization Trends* discusses the ideology of corporate giving officers at length:

> What is even more disturbing, . . . this trend is not merely the result of naivete on the part of publicity-conscious corporate executives. Rather, at least in part, it is the product of a concerted effort to recruit corporate charitable giving to the cause of so-called "progressive" philanthropy. . . . A well-informed and determined class of professional contributions managers—whose actions are motivated more by ideology than by concern for their company's or the public's interests—have become the vehicle for this transformation.
>
> Contributions officers who come from government or nonprofit groups with their seals of approval may have impressive resumes but also are likely to support activities simply because they are approved by old friends and ideological allies. (p. 1)

21. Murawski, "Influential Plea," p. 10.

22. Murawski, "Influential Plea"; "War on Nonprofits Continues Unabated," *Responsive Philanthropy* (Fall 1995): 1–3.

23. Vince Stehle, "Conservative Centers Set Agenda on Charities," *Chronicle of Philanthropy,* September 21, 1995, pp. 32–37.

24. Stephen Moore, ed., *Restoring the Dream: The Bold New Plan by House Republicans* (New York: Times Books, 1995), p. 222.

25. Elizabeth Greene, John Murawski, and Grant Williams, "Charities and the Republican Upheaval," *Chronicle of Philanthropy,* January 26, 1995, pp. 1, 22–26.

26. Leslie Lenkowsky, "The New Majority: Non-Profit Leaders Protest Too Much," *Chronicle of Philanthropy,* January 12, 1995, pp. 37, 40. Kimberly O. Dennis, executive director of the conservative Philanthropy Roundtable, makes a similar point: "We worry about the influence that government can have on nonprofit institutions, making them dependent and distorting their missions." See Vince Stehle, "Charities Criticized for Being Too Dependent on Government," *Chronicle of Philanthropy,* March 9, 1995, p. 28.

27. Quoted in Vince Stehle, "Federal Cuts 'Terrifying' for Charities," *Chronicle of Philanthropy,* June 29, 1995, pp. 25–27. As Stehle's piece attests, the nonprofit sector has responded with a mix of anger, fear, and disbelief at the prospect of having to make up for discontinued government grants while taking on an expanded role in providing social services. See also Greene et al., "Charities and the Republican Upheaval"; Karen W. Arenson, "Gingrich's Vision of Welfare Ignores Reality, Charities Say," *New York Times,* June 4, 1995, p. A1f; Milt Freudenheim, "Charities Say Government Cuts Would Jeopardize Their Ability to Help the Needy," *New York Times,* February 5, 1996, p. B8. Nonprofits have been especially upset by efforts to end political lobbying, broadly defined, by groups receiving government grants. The Lobby Disclosure Act finally passed by Congress in 1995 did not include such provisions on lobbying. Marina Dundjerski, "Lobbying-Disclosure Act Omits Provisions That Had Troubled Charities," *Chronicle of Philanthropy,* December 14, 1995,

◆

p. 39. In 1996, Congress again rejected limits on lobbying. See "Charities Deal Major Defeat to Latest Istook Amendment," *Responsive Philanthropy* (Spring 1996): 4–5. For more on the lobbying issue, see John Murawski, "House Votes to Place New Limits on Lobbying by Non-Profit Groups," *Chronicle of Philanthropy,* September 7, 1995, p. 47; Vince Stehle, "'Accusatory' Questions," *Chronicle of Philanthropy,* October 5, 1995, pp. 43–44; "War on Nonprofits Continues Unabated," *Responsive Philanthropy* (Fall 1995): 1–3; Anthony Lewis, "A Menacing Vendetta," *New York Times,* October 2, 1995, p. A17; Frank Rich, "The Big Chill," *New York Times,* November 1, 1995, p. A23. For a conservative reply saying in effect that nonprofits should be upset over the advocacy legislation but not over federal cuts, see Leslie Lenkowsky, "Charities Could Benefit from the Return of 'Greed,'" *Chronicle of Philanthropy,* November 1, 1994, pp. 60–61; idem, "The New Majority: Non-Profit Leaders Protest Too Much"; idem, "Advocacy Debate: An Unrewarding Summer Sequel," *Chronicle of Philanthropy,* July 27, 1995, pp. 43, 45; idem, "Charities' Angst over Federal Cuts Is Misplaced," *Chronicle of Philanthropy,* October 5, 1995, pp. 51, 53.

28. William E. Simon, *A Time for Truth* (New York: Berkley, 1978), especially pp. 208–57.

29. For a representative sampling of conservative writing on the New Class, see Seymour Martin Lipset, ed., *The Third Century* (Stanford: Hoover Institution Press, 1979) and B. Bruce-Briggs, ed., *The New Class?* (New York: McGraw-Hill, 1979). For a thoughtful analysis, see Peter Steinfels, *The Neoconservatives: The Men Who Are Changing America's Politics* (New York: Simon and Schuster, 1979), especially pp. 188–213.

30. Simon, *Time for Truth,* p. 245.

31. Ibid., pp. 248, 249.

32. For a more detailed discussion of these themes in conservative thought, see Jerome L. Himmelstein and Mayer N. Zald, "American Conservatism and Government Support for the Arts and Sciences," *Sociological Inquiry* 54 (1984): 171–87.

33. James Davison Hunter, *Culture Wars: The Struggle to Define America* (New York: Basic, 1991).

34. William J. Bennett, *The De-Valuing of America: The Fight against Our Culture and Our Children* (New York: Simon and Schuster, 1992), p. 26.

35. *Conservative Digest* (June 1981): 40. See also the April 1982 issue of the same journal, which is devoted to "How Washington Funds the Left."

36. See, for example, any of the CRC's annual reports.

37. Olasky, 1992 volume, pp. 8, iii.

38. Nolan, 1994 volume, p. 2.

39. J. Richard Munro, "When Corporate Grantmaking Is Attacked as Too Liberal or Conservative," *Corporate Philanthropy: A Special Report* (Washington, D.C.: Independent Sector, 1991), p. 1.

40. *Corporate Philanthropy Report* argues that corporations can also use their philanthropy to reframe the environmental debate:

> Companies no longer fight rising costs of environmental compliance
> by doing battle with environmentalists in the regulatory process.

◆

Increasingly they use their philanthropy (as well as other forms of investment) to reshape the growth vs. environmentalism debate and to research cost-saving solutions. . . .

See Craig Smith and Judith Yarrow, "Message to Rio," *Corporate Philanthropy Report* (May 1992): 1, 10–11.

41. Michael Useem, "Organizational and Managerial Factors in the Shaping of Corporate Social and Political Action," *Research in Corporate Social Performance and Policy* 12 (1991): 63–92.

7. Corporate Philanthropy and Corporate Politics

1. Reynold Levy and Frank Oviatt, Jr., "Corporate Philanthropy," in *Experts in Action: Inside Public Relations,* ed. Bill Cantor (New York: Longman, 1989), pp. 126–38, p. 133.

2. Ibid., p. 131.

3. Ibid.

4. The argument here follows Barbara Lombardo, "Corporate Philanthropy: Gift or Business Transaction," *Nonprofit Management and Leadership* 5 (1995): 291–301, and Dan Clawson, Alan Neustadtl, and Denise Scott, *Money Talks: Corporate PACs and Political Influence* (New York: Basic, 1992), pp. 53–87. See also Marcel Mauss, *The Gift: Forms and Functions of Exchange in Archaic Societies* (New York: Norton, 1967), and Kenneth Boulding, *A Preface to Grants Economics: The Economy of Love and Fear* (New York: Praeger, 1981).

5. Henry Goldstein, "Philip Morris and the Reality of Corporate Giving," *Chronicle of Philanthropy,* November 1, 1994, p. 61; Irving Warner, "The Real Reason for the Arts' Tobacco Habit," *Chronicle of Philanthropy,* November 1, 1994, pp. 61, 63.

6. The next few paragraphs draw on Frank Koch, *The New Corporate Philanthropy: How Society and Business Can Profit* (New York: Plenum, 1979).

7. Ibid., p. 124.

8. Ibid., p. 126.

9. Ibid., p. 131.

10. Edward Handler and John R. Mulkern, *Business in Politics: Campaign Strategies of Political Action Committees* (Lexington, Mass.: Heath, 1982). The discussion in this section draws upon Jerome L. Himmelstein, "Two Faces of Business Power," *Business and the Contemporary World* 4 (Autumn 1992): 88–94.

11. Handler and Mulkern, *Business in Politics*, p. 14.

12. Ibid., p. 118.

13. Ibid., p. 15.

14. Clawson et al., *Money Talks,* p. 1. The discussion of corporate PACs that follows is indebted to the work of Clawson and his colleagues.

15. For a detailed look at corporate government affairs managers and their relationships with Members of Congress and their aides, see Denise Scott, "The Power of Women's Ties in the Workplace, Community, and Family: A Study in

◈

Corporate-Government Affairs," Ph.D. dissertation, University of Massachusetts, Amherst, 1996.

16. See also Elizabeth Drew, *Money and Politics* (New York: Macmillan, 1983); Larry J. Sabato, *PAC Power: Inside the World of Political Action Committees* (New York: Norton, 1984).

17. Clawson et al., *Money Talks,* p. 114.

18. Brooks Jackson, *Honest Graft: Big Money and the American Political Process* (New York: Knopf, 1988), pp. 70–78; Handler and Mulkern, *Business in Politics.*

19. Norman J. Ornstein, Thomas E. Mann, and Michael J. Malbin, *Vital Statistics on Congress 1989–1990* (Washington, D.C.: Congressional Quarterly, 1990), pp. 104–109; Jerome L. Himmelstein, *To the Right: The Transformation of American Conservatism* (Berkeley: University of California Press, 1990), pp. 141–42, 205.

20. Jackson, *Honest Graft,* pp. 70–78.

21. Ornstein, Mann, and Malbin, *Vital Statistics on Congress,* pp. 104–109.

22. Thomas Ferguson, "G.O.P. $$$ Talked; Did Voters Listen?" *Nation,* December 26, 1994, pp. 792–98.

23. Ornstein, Mann, and Malbin, *Vital Statistics on Congress,* pp. 104–109. See also Allen M. Kaufman, Marvin J. Karson, and Jeffrey Sohl, "Business Fragmentation and Solidarity: An Analysis of PAC Donations in the 1980 and 1982 Elections," pp. 119–35 in Alfred A. Marcus et al., eds., *Business Strategy and Public Policy* (New York: Quorum, 1987), and Theodore J. Eismeier and Philip H. Pollock III, *Business, Money, and the Rise of Corporate PACs in American Elections* (New York: Quorum, 1988).

24. Dan Clawson, Alan Neustadtl, and James Bearden, "The Logic of Business Unity: Corporate Contributions to the 1980 Congressional Elections," *American Sociological Review* 51 (1986): 797–811.

25. Handler and Mulkern, *Business in Politics,* p. 33.

26. Himmelstein, *To the Right,* pp. 143–44.

27. The idea that corporate politics is a mix of Corporate Conservatism and Corporate Pragmatism deliberately leaves little room for what has sometimes been called Corporate Liberalism. The term refers to a political orientation central to a theory of corporate politics developed by G. William Domhoff and others that argues as follows: Through much of the twentieth century, a moderate business elite, representing a significant part of the business community, decisively encouraged the growth of liberal domestic policies (social welfare legislation, government regulation, and collective bargaining). This elite is rooted in the more centrally located and economically dominant parts of the corporate world and the capitalist class. In one variant of the argument, it represents the economically dominant sector of business, larger, more capital-intensive, internationally oriented firms, who have an interest in the social and economic stability that government programs presumably provide and which can afford the costs of these programs. In another variant, the moderate elite is an inner circle of executives well-rooted in intercorporate networks and upper-class social circles, whose

◆

position gives them a broader vision of the interests of business as a whole and hence a commitment to classwide rationality. On the basis of their classwide vision, the moderate elite actively shapes policy, creating the political agenda rather than merely operating within an agenda created elsewhere.

Although this theory has been applied primarily to what Domhoff calls the policy formation process, which takes place in a world of think tanks and other policy discussion groups that provide a conduit from the corporate world to the state, it has implications for the rest of politics as well. Useem, for example, argues that corporations run by executives who are members of the inner circle (in effect, those who sit on the boards of directors of several corporations) tend to embody a classwide rationality (and a Corporate Liberalism) in all their political activities.

If Corporate Liberalism is obviously different from Corporate Conservatism, its differences from Corporate Pragmatism are no less striking. First, pragmatic PACs tend to support well-entrenched incumbents; they do not seek to promote a moderate or liberal political vision by supporting ideologically suitable incumbents or other candidates in close races. Second, while Corporate Liberalism is proactive in its efforts to set a political agenda, Corporate Pragmatism is largely reactive. The access sought by pragmatic PACs is not aimed at broadly shaping the political agenda but at fine-tuning legislation to meet individual corporate needs. Third, Corporate Pragmatism is not rooted at all in the economically dominant corporations or centrally located elements of the corporate elite. Most studies of corporate campaign contributions find little or no relationship between most measures of economic dominance or centrality and measures of Corporate Pragmatism or Corporate Conservatism. Instead, the most pragmatically oriented corporations are those with long-standing relationships to industry-specific regulatory agencies or with large government contracts. In short, the closer one looks, the more striking is the absence of a corporate liberal impulse.

For general statements of a theory of Corporate Liberalism, see G. William Domhoff, *The Higher Circles: The Governing Class in America* (New York: Random House, 1970) and James Weinstein, *The Corporate Ideal in the Liberal State, 1900–1918* (Boston: Beacon, 1968). For the impact of inner-circle executives on corporate political behavior, see Useem, *The Inner Circle*. For studies documenting the lack of a Corporate Liberal impulse in corporate PAC contributions, see Val Burris, "The Political Partisanship of American Business: A Study of Corporate Political Action Committees," *American Sociological Review* 52 (1987): 732–44; Val Burris and James Salt, "The Politics of Capitalist Class Segments: A Test of Corporate Liberal Theory," *Social Problems* 37 (1990): 341–59; Dan Clawson and Alan Neustadtl, "Interlocks, PACs, and Corporate Conservatism," *American Journal of Sociology* 94 (1989): 749–73; Mark S. Mizruchi, "Determinants of Political Opposition among Large American Corporations," *Social Forces* 68 (1990): 1065–88.

28. For a more detailed discussion of the Corporate Conservative mobilization of the late 1970s and early 1980s, see Himmelstein, *To the Right,* pp. 129–64; Patrick J. Akard, "Corporate Mobilization and Political Power: The Transformation of U.S. Economic Policy in the 1970s," *American Sociological Review* 57 (1992): 597–615; Sidney Blumenthal, *The Rise of the Counter-Establishment: From Conservative Ideology to Political Power* (New York: Times Books, 1987); Thomas

◆

Byrne Edsall, *The New Politics of Inequality* (New York: Norton, 1984); Michael Useem, *The Inner Circle: Large Corporations and the Rise of Business Political Activity in the U.S. and the U.K.* (New York: Oxford University Press, 1984).

29. For more detailed discussion of how changes in American politics in the 1960s and early 1970s rendered existing modes of corporate influence inadequate, see David Vogel, *Fluctuating Fortunes: The Political Power of Business in America* (New York: Basic, 1989).

30. For an overview of the political context of the Corporate Conservative mobilization, see Himmelstein, *To the Right.*

31. Stephen Engelberg, "100 Days of Dreams Come True for Lobbyists in Congress," *New York Times,* April 14, 1995, p. A12; idem, "Business Leaves the Lobby and Sits at Congress's Table," *New York Times,* March 31, 1995, p. A1.

32. Engelberg, "100 Days of Dreams Come True."

33. Richard L. Berke, "Republicans Spurning the Big-Business Label," *New York Times,* May 11, 1995, p. B11.

34. David E. Sanger, "Seismic Shift in the Parties Reflects View on Business," *New York Times,* September 24, 1995, pp. E1, E14.

35. For more detailed discussion of different approaches to corporate power, see Himmelstein, *To the Right,* pp. 152–61; Fred Block, "Beyond Corporate Liberalism," *Social Problems* 24 (1977): 352–61; idem, "The Ruling Class Does Not Rule: Notes on the Marxist Theory of the State," *Socialist Revolution* 7 (1977): 6–28; Gosta Esping-Andersen, Rodger Friedland, and Erik Olin Wright, "Modes of Class Struggle and the Capitalist State," *Kapitalistate* 4–5 (1976): 186–220; David Gold, Clarence Y. H. Lo, and Erik Olin Wright, "Some Recent Developments in Marxist Theories of the Capitalist State," *Monthly Review* 27 (October 1975): 29–43; and 27 (November 1975): 36–51. For more detailed discussion of different approaches to power in general, see Steven Lukes, *Power: A Radical View* (London: Macmillan, 1974); idem, ed., *Power* (Oxford: Blackwell, 1986); Thomas E. Wartenberg, ed., *Rethinking Power* (Albany: State University of New York Press, 1992).

36. Clawson et al., *Money Talks,* p. 156.

37. William Greider, *Who Will Tell the People: The Betrayal of American Democracy* (New York: Simon and Schuster, 1992); Theda Skocpol, *Protecting Soldiers and Mothers: The Political Origins of Social Policy in the United States* (Cambridge: Harvard University Press, 1992).

8. Conclusion

1. See chapter 6 for a more detailed discussion of the Right's critique of the nonprofit sector and their proposals for changing it.

2. Leslie Lenkowsky, "Charities Could Benefit from the Return of 'Greed,'" *Chronicle of Philanthropy,* November 1, 1994, pp. 60–61. Lenkowsky generally provides a moderate version of the conservative analysis. See also idem, "The New Majority: Non-Profit Leaders Protest Too Much," *Chronicle of Philanthropy,* January 12, 1995, pp. 37, 40; idem, "Advocacy Debate: An Unrewarding Summer Sequel," *Chronicle of Philanthropy,* July 27, 1995, pp. 43, 45; idem, "Charities'

◆

Angst over Federal Cuts Is Misplaced," *Chronicle of Philanthropy,* October 5, 1995, pp. 51, 53. For the response of nonprofits to proposals in 1996 to offer tax credits for antipoverty donations, see Jennifer Moore, John Murawski, and Grant Williams, "The Debate over Dole's Tax Credit," *Chronicle of Philanthropy,* June 13, 1996, pp. 9–10, 12.

3. Stephen Greene, "Non-Profit Groups' Expanding World," *Chronicle of Philanthropy,* June 28, 1994, pp. 1, 28–30; Milt Freudenheim, "Charities Say Government Cuts Would Jeopardize Their Ability to Help the Needy," *New York Times,* February 5, 1996, p. B8; Karen W. Arenson, "Gingrich's Vision of Welfare Ignores Reality, Charities Say," *New York Times,* June 4, 1995, pp. 1, 30.

4. John Murawski, "A Modest Rise in Donations," *Chronicle of Philanthropy,* June 1, 1995, pp. 19–22.

5. Julian Wolpert, "Charities Won't Make Up for Cuts," *Daily Hampshire Gazette,* July 3, 1995, p. 6. Wolpert's conclusions are based on his study of "Patterns of Generosity in America," the results of which he discusses in part in "Fragmentation in America's Nonprofit Sector," a paper delivered to the Spring Research Forum of the Independent Sector, San Antonio, Texas, March 18, 1993.

6. Ostrower is quoted in Stephen G. Greene, "Rich People: No Safety Net," *Chronicle of Philanthropy,* January 25, 1996, pp. 12, 14. Discussion of her research can be found in Francie Ostrower, *Why the Wealthy Give* (Princeton, N.J.: Princeton University Press, 1995).

7. Wolpert, "Charities Won't Make Up for Cuts."

BIBLIOGRAPHY

Akard, Patrick J. "Corporate Mobilization and Political Power: The Transformation of U.S. Economic Policy in the 1970s." *American Sociological Review* 57 (1992): 597–615.

Andrews, F. Emerson. *Corporation Giving.* New York: Russell Sage, 1952.

"Antiabortion Activists to Boycott Companies." *Washington Post,* August 9, 1990.

Arenson, Karen W. "Gingrich's Vision of Welfare Ignores Reality, Charities Say." *New York Times,* June 4, 1995, p. A1f.

Atkinson, Lisa, and Joseph Galaskiewicz. "Stock Ownership and Company Contributions to Charity." *Administrative Science Quarterly* 33 (1988): 82–100.

Babcock, Charles R. "Philip Morris Donations Target Minority Groups." *Washington Post,* August 15, 1992, p. A6.

Bailey, Anne Lowrey. "Corporate Giving under Siege." *Chronicle of Philanthropy,* May 1, 1990, pp. 1, 16–18.

———. "Non-Profits in Politics." *Chronicle of Philanthropy,* July 10, 1990.

———. "Some Foundations and Other Private Grant Makers Now Rethinking Their Stances on Financing Controversial Art." *Chronicle of Philanthropy,* November 28, 1989, pp. 9, 11.

Bennett, James T. "In Health-Care Reform, Where Are the Charities?" *Chronicle of Philanthropy,* February 8, 1994, pp. 42–43.

———. *Patterns of Corporate Philanthropy: Ideas, Advocacy, and the Corporation.* Washington, D.C.: Capital Research Center, 1989.

Bennett, James T., and Thomas J. DiLorenzo, *Unhealthy Charities: Hazardous to Your Health and Wealth.* New York: Basic, 1994.

Bennett, William J. *The De-Valuing of America: The Fight against Our Culture and Our Children.* New York: Simon and Schuster, 1992.

Berke, Richard L. "Republicans Spurning the Big-Business Label." *New York Times,* May 11, 1995, p. B11.

Bertsch, Kenneth A. *Corporate Philanthropy.* Washington, D.C.: Investor Responsibility Research Center, 1982.

Block, Fred. "Beyond Corporate Liberalism." *Social Problems* 24 (1977): 352–61.

———. "The Ruling Class Does Not Rule: Notes on the Marxist Theory of the State." *Socialist Revolution* 7 (1977): 6–28.

Blumberg, Phillip I. "Corporate Social Responsibility and the Social Crisis." *Boston University Law Review* 50 (1970): 157–210.

Blumenthal, Sidney. *The Rise of the Counter-Establishment: From Conservative Ideology to Political Power.* New York: Times Books, 1987.

Boulding, Kenneth. *A Preface to Grants Economics: The Economy of Love and Fear.* New York: Praeger, 1981.

Bremner, Robert. *American Philanthropy.* 2nd rev. ed. Chicago: University of Chicago Press, 1988.

Bruce-Briggs, B., ed. *The New Class?* New York: McGraw-Hill, 1979.

Bryan, John H., Jr. "The Corporation and the Executive in the Community." *Columbia Business Law Review* (1987): 695–703.

Burris, Val. "The Political Partisanship of American Business: A Study of Corporate Political Action Committees." *American Sociological Review* 52 (1987): 732–44.

Burris, Val, and James Salt. "The Politics of Capitalist Class Segments: A Test of Corporate Liberal Theory." *Social Problems* 37 (1990): 341–59.

Burt, Ronald. "Corporate Philanthropy as a Cooptive Relation." *Social Forces* 62 (1983): 419–49.

Business Committee for the Arts. "The BCA Founders Award and Business in the Arts Awards." New York, 1992.

———. "Why Business Should Support the Arts." 2nd ed. New York, September 1992.

Business Roundtable. "Corporate Philanthropy—An Integral Part of Corporate Social Responsibility." In *America's Voluntary Spirit,* ed. Brian O'Connell, pp. 385–87. New York: Foundation Center, 1983.

Clark, Sylvia. "It All Adds Up." *Foundation News* (March–April 1994): 47–49.

Clawson, Dan, and Alan Neustadtl. "Interlocks, PACs, and Corporate Conservatism." *American Journal of Sociology* 94 (1989): 749–73.

Clawson, Dan, Alan Neustadtl, and James Bearden. "The Logic of Business Unity: Corporate Contributions to the 1980 Congressional Elections." *American Sociological Review* 51 (1986): 797–811.

Clawson, Dan, Alan Neustadtl, and Denise Scott. *Money Talks: Corporate PACs and Political Influence.* New York: Basic, 1992.

Conference Board. *Survey of Corporate Contributions, 1990 edition.* New York, 1990.

"Corporate Profits Up 84% since '87, Corporate Giving Grows only 11%." *Responsive Philanthropy* (Fall 1995): 4.

Council on Foundations. *Administering Corporate Giving.* Washington, D.C., 1991.

———. *The Climate for Giving: The Outlook for Current and Future CEOs.* Washington, D.C., 1988.

———. *Corporate Giving in the 1990s—The Next Generation.* Washington, D.C., 1987.

———. *Corporate Philanthropy: Philosophy, Management, Trends, Future, Background.* Washington, D.C., 1982.

———. *Corporations and Communities.* Washington, D.C., 1988.

———. *How to Position the Corporate Grantmaking Program: Strategies That Work.* Washington, D.C., 1991.

Curti, Merle, and Roderick Nash. *Philanthropy in the Shaping of American Higher Education.* New Brunswick, N.J.: Rutgers University Press, 1965.

◆

De Witt, Karen. "Company Resumes Planned Parenthood Gift." *New York Times,* September 21, 1990, p. A12.

Diemert, Beth. "Supporting Her Choice When It Isn't Abortion." *Wall Street Journal,* January 22, 1992, p. A14.

DiLorenzo, Thomas J., Daniel T. Oliver, and Robret E. Winters. *Patterns of Corporate Philanthropy: The "Suicidal Impulse."* Washington, D.C.: Capital Research Center, 1990.

DiMaggio, Paul J., ed. *Nonprofit Enterprise in the Arts: Studies in Mission and Constraint.* New York: Oxford University Press, 1986.

Domhoff, G. William. *The Higher Circles: The Governing Class in America.* New York: Random House, 1970.

Drew, Elizabeth. *Money and Politics.* New York: Macmillan, 1983.

Edsall, Thomas Byrne. *The New Politics of Inequality.* New York: Norton, 1984.

Eells, Richard. *Corporation Giving in a Free Society.* New York: Harper and Row, 1956.

Eisenberg, Pablo. "Today's Corporate Philanthropy: More 'Self-Interest' Than 'Enlightened.'" *Chronicle of Philanthropy,* January 26, 1995, pp. 37–38.

Eismeier, Theodore J., and Philip H. Pollock III. *Business, Money, and the Rise of Corporate PACs in American Elections.* New York: Quorum, 1988.

Engelberg, Stephen. "Business Leaves the Lobby and Sits at Congress's Table." *New York Times,* March 31, 1995, p. A1.

———. "100 Days of Dreams Come True for Lobbyists in Congress." *New York Times,* April 14, 1995, p. A12.

Esping-Andersen, Gosta, Rodger Friedland, and Erik Olin Wright. "Modes of Class Struggle and the Capitalist State." *Kapitalistate* 4–5 (1976): 186–220.

Ferguson, Thomas. "G.O.P. $$$ Talked: Did Voters Listen?" *Nation,* December 26, 1994, pp. 792–98.

Fremont-Smith, Marion R. *Philanthropy and the Business Corporation.* New York: Russell Sage, 1972.

Freudenheim, Milt. "Charities Say Government Cuts Would Jeopardize Their Ability to Help the Needy." *New York Times,* February 5, 1996, p. B8.

———. "A Doting Uncle Cuts Back, and a City Feels the Pain." *New York Times,* October 8, 1995, pp. F1, F9.

Galaskiewicz, Joseph. "Corporate Contributions to Charity: Nothing More Than a Marketing Strategy?" In *Philanthropic Giving: Studies in Varieties and Goals,* ed. Richard Magat, pp. 246–60. New York: Oxford University Press, 1989.

———. "Professional Networks and the Institutionalization of a Single Mind Set." *American Sociological Review* 50 (1985): 639–58.

———. *Social Organization of an Urban Grants Economy: A Study of Business Philanthropy and Nonprofit Organizations.* Orlando: Academic, 1985.

———. "An Urban Grants Economy Revisited: Company Contributions in the Twin Cities, 1979–1989." Unpublished manuscript, 1983.

Galaskiewicz, Joseph, and Ronald S. Burt. "Interorganization Contagion in Corporate Philanthropy." *Administrative Science Quarterly* 36 (1991): 88–105.

Gibson, Richard. "Boycott Drive against Pioneer Hi-Bred Shows Perils of Corporate Philanthropy." *Wall Street Journal,* June 10, 1992, p. B1f.

◨

Gold, David, Clarence Y. H. Lo, and Erik Olin Wright. "Some Recent Developments in Marxist Theories of the Capitalist State." *Monthly Review* 27 (October
1975): 29–43; and 27 (November 1975): 36–51.

Goldstein, Henry. "Philip Morris and the Reality of Corporate Giving." *Chronicle
of Philanthropy,* November 1, 1994, p. 61.

Goss, Kristin A. "After Widespread Protests, Dayton Hudson Foundation to Review
Decision to End Aid to Planned Parenthood." *Chronicle of Philanthropy,*
September 18, 1990.

———. "Boy Scouts: Under Fire—and Firing Back." *Chronicle of Philanthropy,*
January 14, 1992, pp. 1, 25–29.

Granovetter, Mark. "Economic Action and Social Structure: The Problem of
Embeddedness." *American Journal of Sociology* 91 (1985): 481–510.

Greco, JoAnn. "Be Prepared: Controversies over Funding Decisions Often Can't Be
Avoided—But They Can Be Managed." *Foundation News* (September–October 1993): 39–40.

Green, Shelby D. "Corporate Philanthropy and the Business Benefit: The Need for
Clarity." *Golden Gate University Law Review* 20 (1990): 239–60.

Greene, Elizabeth, Bruce Millar, and Jennifer Moore. "The Midwest's Charitable
Advantage." *Chronicle of Philanthropy,* February 22, 1994, pp. 1, 22–26.

Greene, Elizabeth, John Murawski, and Grant Williams. "Charities and the Republican Upheaval." *Chronicle of Philanthropy,* January 26, 1995, pp. 1, 22–26.

Greene, Stephen G. "Non-Profit Groups' Expanding World." *Chronicle of Philanthropy,* June 28, 1994, pp. 1, 28–30.

———. "Rich People: No Safety Net." *Chronicle of Philanthropy,* January 25,
1996, pp. 12, 14.

Greene, Stephen G., and Jennifer Moore. "Conservative Foundations on the
Move." *Chronicle of Philanthropy,* February 23, 1995, pp. 1, 10–16.

Greider, William. *Who Will Tell the People: The Betrayal of American Democracy.*
New York: Simon and Schuster, 1992.

Gurfield, Sharon. "Four Firms Quietly Cut from Boycott." *NonProfit Times* (September 1990).

Hall, Peter Dobkin. "Business Giving and Social Investment in the United States."
In *Philanthropic Giving: Studies in Varieties and Goals,* ed. Richard Magat, pp.
221–45. New York: Oxford University Press, 1989.

———. *Inventing the Nonprofit Sector and Other Essays on Philanthropy, Voluntarism, and Nonprofit Organizations.* Baltimore: Johns Hopkins University
Press, 1992.

———. *The Organization of American Culture, 1700–1900: Private Institutions,
Elites, and the Origins of American Nationality.* New York: New York University Press, 1982.

Handler, Edward, and John R. Mulkern. *Business in Politics: Campaign Strategies
of Political Action Committees.* Lexington, Mass.: Heath, 1982.

Harris, William. "How AT&T Tosses a Lifeline to the Arts." *New York Times,* May
27, 1990, p. H5.

Harrison, Bennett. "Where Private Investment Fails." *American Prospect* 11 (Fall
1992): 106–14.

◨

Hayes, Robert H., and William J. Abernathy. "Managing Our Way to Economic Decline." *Harvard Business Review* 58 (July–August 1980): 67–77.

Helstrom, Carl O., III. "United Way of America: Changing Course?" *Organization Trends* (November 1990).

Himmelstein, Jerome L. "Corporate Philanthropy and Business Power." In *Corporate Philanthropy at the Crossroads,* ed. Dwight Burlingame and Dennis R. Young. Bloomington: Indiana University Press, 1996.

———. *To the Right: The Transformation of American Conservatism.* Berkeley: University of California Press, 1990.

———. "Two Faces of Business Power." *Business and the Contemporary World* 4 (Autumn 1992): 88–94.

Himmelstein, Jerome L., and Mayer N. Zald. "American Conservatism and Government Support for the Arts and Sciences." *Sociological Inquiry* 54 (1984): 171–87.

Hunter, James Davison. *Culture Wars: The Struggle to Define America.* New York: Basic, 1991.

Indiana University Center on Philanthropy. *Managing Corporate Support: Responses to Challenging Times.* Indianapolis, 1992.

Jackall, Robert. *Moral Mazes: The World of Corporate Managers.* New York: Oxford University Press, 1988.

Jackson, Brooks. *Honest Graft: Big Money and the American Political Process.* New York: Knopf, 1988.

Jacobs, Deborah L. "Corporation Donations under Attack." *New York Times,* September 30, 1990, p. F23.

Karson, Stanley G. "The Controversy about Corporations." *Response* (February 1991): 2.

———. "Why Corporate Executives Must Be Civic Leaders." *Chronicle of Philanthropy,* November 2, 1995, pp. 66–67.

Kaufman, Allen M., Marvin J. Karson, and Jeffrey Sohl. "Business Fragmentation and Solidarity: An Analysis of PAC Donations in the 1980 and 1982 Elections." In *Business Strategy and Public Policy,* ed. Alfred A. Marcus et al., pp. 119–35. New York: Quorum, 1987.

Keller, John J. "Abortion Issue Prompts AT&T to End Its Support for Planned Parenthood." *Wall Street Journal,* March 26, 1990, p. A3A.

Kelly, Kevin. "Dayton Hudson Finds There's No Graceful Way to Flip-Flop." *Business Week,* September 24, 1990.

Klein, Elizabeth. "Anti-Abortion Group Says Its Campaign Swayed AT&T on Planned Parenthood." *Chronicle of Philanthropy,* May 1, 1990.

Knauft, E. B. "The Management of Corporate Giving Programs." Program on Non-Profit Organizations, Working Paper No. 114, June 1986.

Koch, Frank. *The New Corporate Philanthropy: How Society and Business Can Profit.* New York: Plenum, 1979.

Lenkowsky, Leslie. "Advocacy Debate: An Unrewarding Summer Sequel." *Chronicle of Philanthropy,* July 27, 1995, pp. 43, 45.

———. "Charities' Angst over Federal Cuts Is Misplaced." *Chronicle of Philanthropy,* October 5, 1995, pp. 51, 53.

⬦

————. "Charities Could Benefit from the Return of 'Greed.'" *Chronicle of Philanthropy,* November 1, 1994, pp. 60–61.

————. "The New Majority: Non-Profit Leaders Protest Too Much." *Chronicle of Philanthropy,* January 12, 1995, pp. 37, 40.

Lev, Michael. "AT&T Chief Defends Decision on Abortion." *New York Times,* April 19, 1990, p. A14.

Levy, Reynold, and Frank Oviatt, Jr. "Corporate Philanthropy." In *Experts in Action: Inside Public Relations,* ed. Bill Cantor, pp. 126–38. New York: Longman, 1989.

Lewin, Tamar. "Anti-Abortion Center's Ads Ruled Misleading." *New York Times,* April 22, 1994, p. A15.

————. "Anti-Abortion Group Urges Boycott of Planned Parenthood." *New York Times,* August 8, 1990, p. A13.

————. "Ending Aid to Family Planning, Large Retailer Is Caught in Storm." *New York Times,* September 1, 1990, p. 8.

————. "Protest Focuses on Abortion Issue." *New York Times,* April 5, 1990, p. A19.

Lipset, Seymour Martin, ed. *The Third Century.* Stanford: Hoover Institution Press, 1979.

Litke, Ronald. "Shifting Standards." *Foundation News and Commentary* (July–August 1994): 36–37.

Lombardo, Barbara. "Corporate Philanthropy: Gift or Business Transaction." *Nonprofit Management and Leadership* 5 (1995): 291–301.

Lukes, Steven. *Power: A Radical View.* London: Macmillan, 1974.

Lukes, Steven, ed. *Power.* Oxford: Blackwell, 1986.

Lundborg, Louis B. *Future without Shock.* New York: Norton, 1972.

Maddox, Katherine E., and John J. Siegfried. "The Effect of Economic Structure on Corporate Philanthropy." In *The Economics of Firm Size, Market Structure, and Social Performance,* ed. John J. Siegfried. Washington, D.C.: Federal Trade Commission, n.d.

Magat, Richard, ed. *Philanthropic Giving: Studies in Varieties and Goals.* New York: Oxford University Press, 1989.

Matza, Michael. "Turning Abortion Sentiments into Market Pressure." *Philadelphia Inquirer,* May 20, 1990.

Mauss, Marcel. *The Gift: Forms and Functions of Exchange in Archaic Societies.* New York: Norton, 1967.

McCarthy, Kathleen D. *Noblesse Oblige: Charity and Cultural Philanthropy in Chicago, 1849–1929.* Chicago: University of Chicago Press, 1982.

McElroy, Katherine Maddox, and John J. Siegfried. "The Effects of Firm Size and Mergers on Corporate Philanthropy." In *The Impact of the Modern Corporation,* ed. Betty Bock, Harvey J. Goldschmid, Ira M. Millstein, and F. M. Scherer, pp. 95–157. New York: Columbia University Press, 1984.

Meiners, Roger E., and David N. Laband. *Patterns of Corporate Philanthropy: Public Affairs Giving and the Forbes 250.* Washington, D.C.: Capital Research Center, 1988.

◆

Mescon, Timothy S., and Donn J. Tilson. "Corporate Philanthropy: A Strategic Approach to the Bottom-Line." *California Management Review* 29 (Winter 1987): 49–61.

Millar, Bruce. "Big Cuts at a Leading Corporate Grant Maker." *Chronicle of Philanthropy,* August 9, 1994, pp. 6–7, 10.

Mizruchi, Mark S. "Determinants of Political Opposition among Large American Corporations." *Social Forces* 68 (1990): 1065–88.

———. *The Structure of Corporate Political Action: Interfirm Relations and Their Consequences.* Cambridge: Harvard University Press, 1992.

Mizruchi, Mark S., and Michael Schwartz, eds. *Intercorporate Relations: The Structural Analysis of Business.* New York: Cambridge University Press, 1987.

Monaghan, Peter. "Many Local United Ways Caught in the Middle of the Debate over Abortion Rights." *Chronicle of Philanthropy,* November 28, 1989, pp. 4, 6.

Montague, William. "A Conservative Study Center Stirs Heated Controversy by Attacking Corporate Grant Makers' 'Liberal Bias.'" *Chronicle of Philanthropy,* May 15, 1990, p. 1f.

Moore, Jennifer. "Council on Foundations Hobbled by 'Political Correctness,' Report Charges." *Chronicle of Philanthropy,* May 4, 1993, p. 11.

———. "Planned Parenthood Looks Ahead to Health Reform." *Chronicle of Philanthropy,* November 2, 1993, p. 42.

Moore, Stephen, ed. *Restoring the Dream: The Bold New Plan by House Republicans.* New York: Times Books, 1995.

Morrissey, Daniel J. "Toward a New/Old Theory of Corporate Social Responsibility." *Syracuse Law Review* 40 (1989): 1005–39.

Munro, J. Richard. "When Corporate Grantmaking Is Attacked as Too Liberal or Conservative." *Corporate Philanthropy: A Special Report.* Washington, D.C.: Independent Sector, 1991.

Murawski, John. "A Banner Year for Giving," *Chronicle of Philanthropy,* May 30, 1996, pp. 1, 27–30.

———. "An Influential Plea to End the 'Tragedy' of Compassion." *Chronicle of Philanthropy,* June 15, 1995, pp. 8–11.

———. "A Modest Rise in Donations." *Chronicle of Philanthropy,* June 1, 1995, pp. 19–22.

Murray, Vic. *Improving Corporate Donations.* San Francisco: Jossey-Bass, 1991.

Navarro, Peter. "Why Do Corporations Give to Charity?" *Journal of Business* 61 (1988): 65–93.

Nielsen, Waldemar A. *The Golden Donors: A New Anatomy of the Great Foundations.* New York: Dutton, 1985.

Nolan, Stuart. *Patterns of Corporate Philanthropy.* Washington, D.C.: Capital Research Center, 1994.

O'Connell, Brian, ed. *America's Voluntary Spirit: A Book of Readings.* New York: Foundation Center, 1983.

Olasky, Marvin. *Patterns of Corporate Philanthropy: The Progressive Deception.* Washington, D.C.: Capital Research Center, 1992.

◻

Ornstein, Norman J., Thomas E. Mann, and Michael J. Malbin. *Vital Statistics on Congress 1989–1990*. Washington, D.C.: Congressional Quarterly, 1990.

Ostrower, Francie. *Why the Wealthy Give*. Princeton, N.J.: Princeton University Press, 1995.

"Philip Morris to Double Giving to AIDS Groups." *Chronicle of Philanthropy,* June 4, 1991, p. 8.

"Planned Parenthood Didn't Plan on This." *Business Week,* July 3, 1989, p. 34.

Powell, Walter W., ed. *The Nonprofit Sector: A Research Handbook*. New Haven: Yale University Press, 1987.

Quindlen, Anna. "Good Causes, Bad Money." *New York Times,* November 15, 1992, p. E19.

Ransom, David. *Special Report: Rightwing Attacks on Corporate Giving*. Washington, D.C.: National Committee for Responsive Philanthropy, 1990.

Rockefeller, David. "Culture and the Corporation." Founding Address, Business Committee for the Arts, September 20, 1966.

Rothstein, Mervyn. "Uneasy Partners: Arts and Philip Morris." *New York Times,* December 18, 1990, p. C15f.

Sabato, Larry J. *PAC Power: Inside the World of Political Action Committees*. New York: Norton, 1984.

Sanger, David E. "Seismic Shift in the Parties Reflects View on Business." *New York Times,* September 24, 1995, pp. E1, E14.

Schwartz, Michael, ed. *The Structure of Power in America*. New York: Holmes and Meier, 1987.

Scott, Denise. "The Power of Women's Ties in the Workplace, Community, and Family: A Study of Women in Corporate-Government Affairs." Ph.D. dissertation, sociology, University of Massachusetts, Amherst, 1996.

Shannon, James, ed. *The Corporate Contributions Handbook*. San Francisco: Jossey-Bass, 1991.

Shipley, Walter V. "Lawrence A. Wien Prize Lecture in Corporate Social Responsibility." Columbia University, April 29, 1991.

Siegfried, John J., Katherine Maddox McElroy, and Diane Biernot-Fawkes. "The Management of Corporate Contributions." *Research in Corporate Social Performance and Policy* 5 (1983): 87–102.

Simon, William E. *A Time for Truth*. New York: Berkley, 1978.

Skocpol, Theda. *Protecting Soldiers and Mothers: The Political Origins of Social Policy in the United States*. Cambridge: Harvard University Press, 1992.

Smith, Craig. "After the Wall Caves In." *Corporate Philanthropy Report* (November 1991): 1, 10–11.

———. "Desperately Seeking Data." Keynote address, "Corporate Philanthropy: A Time of Challenge and Opportunity." Mandel Center for Nonprofit Organizations. Cleveland, Ohio, April 28, 1994.

———. "Employee Connection." *Corporate Philanthropy Report* (April 1992): 1, 8–11.

———. "The New Corporate Philanthropy." *Harvard Business Review* 72 (May–June 1994): 105f.

◆

Smith, Craig, and Judith Yarrow. "Message to Rio." *Corporate Philanthropy Report* (May 1992): 1, 10–11.

Smith, Hayden. "The Maturity of Corporate Giving." Paper delivered at annual meetings of the Association for Research on Nonprofit Organizations and Voluntary Action (ARNOVA). New Haven, Connecticut, 1992.

Stehle, Vince. "Arts Groups Debate Propriety of Accepting Philip Morris Money." *Chronicle of Philanthropy,* September 18, 1990, p. 5f.

———. "Center Helps Conservative Lawmakers Battle Liberal Non-Profit Groups." *Chronicle of Philanthropy,* September 21, 1995, p. 34.

———. "Charities Criticized for Being Too Dependent on Government." *Chronicle of Philanthropy,* March 9, 1995, p. 28.

———. "Conservative Centers Set Agenda on Charities." *Chronicle of Philanthropy,* September 21, 1995, pp. 32–37.

———. "Federal Cuts 'Terrifying' for Charities." *Chronicle of Philanthropy,* June 29, 1995, pp. 25–27.

Steinfels, Peter. *The Neoconservatives: The Men Who Are Changing America's Politics.* New York: Simon and Schuster, 1979.

Swisher, Kara. "Back away from Controversy." *Washington Post,* April 5, 1990, p. E1.

Useem, Michael. "Company vs. Classwide Rationality in Corporate Decision-making." *Administrative Science Quarterly* 27 (1982): 199–226.

———. "Corporate Funding of the Arts in a Turbulent Environment." *Nonprofit Management and Leadership* 1 (1991): 329–43.

———. "Corporate Philanthropy." In *The Nonprofit Sector: A Research Handbook,* ed. Walter W. Powell, pp. 340–59. New Haven: Yale University Press, 1987.

———. Introduction to *Corporation Giving,* by F. Emerson Andrews. 2nd ed., pp. 3–14. New Brunswick, N.J.: Transaction, 1993.

———. *The Inner Circle: Large Corporations and the Rise of Business Political Activity in the U.S. and U.K.* New York: Oxford University Press, 1984.

———. "Organizational and Managerial Factors in the Shaping of Corporate Social and Political Action." *Research in Corporate Social Performance and Policy* 12 (1991): 63–92.

———. "Trends and Preferences in Corporate Support for the Arts." In *Guide to Corporate Giving in the Arts 4,* ed. Robert A. Porter, pp. ix–xv. New York: American Council for the Arts, 1987.

Useem, Michael, and Stephen I. Kutner. "Corporate Contributions to Culture and the Arts." In *Nonprofit Enterprise in the Arts: Studies in Mission and Constraint,* ed. Paul J. DiMaggio, pp. 93–112. New York: Oxford University Press, 1986.

Valentine, Paul W. "Philip Morris Draws Protest over Bill of Rights Exhibit." *Washington Post,* December 11, 1990, p. B7.

Vogel, David. *Fluctuating Fortunes: The Political Power of Business in America.* New York: Basic, 1989.

"War on Nonprofits Continues Unabated." *Responsive Philanthropy* (Fall 1995): 1–3.

Warner, Irving. "The Real Reason for the Arts' Tobacco Habit." *Chronicle of Philanthropy,* November 1, 1994, pp. 61, 63.

◆

Wartenberg, Thomas E., ed. *Rethinking Power.* Albany: State University of New York Press, 1992.

Weinstein, James. *The Corporate Ideal in the Liberal State, 1900–1918.* Boston: Beacon, 1968.

Wentworth, Eric. *Agents of Change: Exemplary Corporate Policies and Practices to Improve Education.* Washington, D.C.: Business Roundtable, 1992.

Whitaker, Ben. *The Philanthropoids: Foundations and Society.* New York: Morrow, 1974.

White, Arthur H., and John S. Bartolomeo. *Corporate Giving: The View of Chief Executive Officers of Major American Corporations.* Washington, D.C.: Council on Foundations, 1982.

Williams, Marjorie. "Tobacco's Hold on Women's Groups." *Washington Post,* November 14, 1991, p. A1.

Wolpert, Julian. "Charities Won't Make Up for Cuts." *Daily Hampshire Gazette,* July 3, 1995, p. 6.

———. "Fragmentation in America's Nonprofit Sector." Paper delivered to the Spring Research Forum of the Independent Sector. San Antonio, Texas, March 18, 1993.

INDEX

◆

◆